A Critical History of Old English Literature

Front Panel of the Franks Casket
(see discussion of *Deor*, Ch. XI)

The left section depicts a scene from Germanic story: Weland the Smith after he has killed King Niðhad's sons and made cups of their skulls (one torso lies behind his feet). He seems to be holding one cup with tongs and proffering the other to Beaduhild, the King's daughter, who is accompanied by an attendant. Weland's brother Egill (?) is catching birds with which to make wings for their escape. The right section represents the Christian subjects of the Adoration of the Magi, runes for *Magi* appearing in the top center of the section.

A runic inscription in alliterative verse runs around the panel. It bears no relation to either Christian or Germanic subject in the compartments, but says in effect: "The ocean cast up the fish on the cliff-bank; the whale became sad [or, the ocean became turbid] where he swam aground on the shingle. Whale's bone."

A CRITICAL HISTORY OF

Old English Literature

by STANLEY B. GREENFIELD

NEW YORK UNIVERSITY PRESS

64378

SECOND PRINTING 1968
THIRD PRINTING 1972
FOURTH PRINTING 1974
© 1965 BY NEW YORK UNIVERSITY
LIBRARY OF CONGRESS CATALOG CARD NUMBER: 65-19516
MANUFACTURED IN THE UNITED STATES OF AMERICA
ISBN 0-8147-2950-9

The maps of England in the tenth century and of the early kingdoms of the southern English are reproduced by permission of Cambridge University Press from P. H. Blair's *An Introduction to Anglo-Saxon England*. The *Beowulf* facsimile is reproduced by permission of The Early English Text Society and the Trustees of the British Museum. The photograph of the Franks Casket (frontispiece) is reproduced by permission of the Trustees of the British Museum.

ACKNOWLEDGMENTS: to Oxford University Press, Inc., for permission to reprint translations from Charles W. Kennedy, *The Earliest English Poetry* © 1943, from Charles W. Kennedy, *Early English Christian Poetry*, © 1952, from Dorothy Whitelock, *English Historical Documents, I,* © 1955; to the University of Nebraska Press for permission to reprint translations from Burton Raffel, *Poems from the Old English,* © 1960, 1964; to the New American Library for permission to reprint selections from Burton Raffel, *Beowulf,* © 1963; to Duke University Press for permission to cite from Paull F. Baum, *Anglo-Saxon Riddles from the Exeter Book,* © 1963; to Princeton University Press for permission to cite from J. J. Campbell, *The Advent Lyrics of the Exeter Book,* © 1959; and to The Macmillan Company for permission to cite from E. S. Duckett, *Anglo-Saxon Saints and Scholars,* © 1947.

To My Wife—
Thelma

IT IS a great pleasure to acknowledge the aid and comfort afforded me by various people in the course of writing this *Critical History*. First, to Kemp Malone and Charles Dunn, for recommending me for the volume to the General Editor, Oscar Cargill, and to Mr. Cargill for his encouragement at various stages of the enterprise. Then, to James E. Cross and Dorothy Bethurum, who carefully read the Introduction and the chapters on the prose, making suggestions both as to fact and style that have proved invaluable. To the staff of the University of Oregon Library for their cooperation, and to Mrs. Roxanne Erb and Sue Hamilton for their kindness and diligence in typing the manuscript. I am indebted most of all to Arthur G. Brodeur, Thelma C. Greenfield, and Jess B. Bessinger, Jr., who painstakingly read the entire manuscript; their tactful suggestions have spared my readers many an unconscious ambiguity of meaning and many a graceless phrasing, as well as spared me many a later blush at factual oversights. Such errors of fact and difficulties of style as remain I must acknowledge as my own.

Eugene, Oregon   STANLEY B. GREENFIELD

ABBREVIATIONS OF BOOK, MANUSCRIPT, AND JOURNAL TITLES

ABR	*American Benedictine Review*
AGB	*Studies in Old English Literature in Honor of Arthur G. Brodeur*, ed. S. B. Greenfield
ASPR	*Anglo-Saxon Poetic Records*, eds. Krapp and Dobbie
BAP	*Bibliothek der angelsächsischen Prosa*, eds. Grein and Wülker
BR	*Benedictine Review*
CCCC	Corpus Christi College, Cambridge
CP	C. W. Kennedy's *The Cædmon Poems*
EECP	C. W. Kennedy's *Early English Christian Poetry*
EEMSF	Early English Manuscripts in Facsimile (Copenhagen, Rosenkilde and Bagger)
EEP	C. W. Kennedy's *The Earliest English Poetry*
EETS	Early English Text Society
EGS	*English and Germanic Studies*
EHD	*English Historical Documents*, I, ed. D. Whitelock
EHR	*English Historical Review*
ELH	*ELH: A Journal of English Literary History*
ES	*English Studies*
E&S	*Essays and Studies* by Members of the English Association

HE	Bede's *Historia Ecclesiastica Gentis Anglorum*
JEGP	*Journal of English and Germanic Philology*
KHVL	*Kungl. Humanistiska Vetenskapssamfundets i Lund*
MÆ	*Medium Ævum*
MHG	*Monumenta Germaniae Historica*
MLN	*Modern Language Notes*
MLQ	*Modern Language Quarterly*
MLR	*Modern Language Review*
MP	*Modern Philology*
MS	*Medieval Studies*
Neophil	*Neophilologus*
NM	*Neuphilologische Mitteilungen*
N&Q	*Notes and Queries*
PBA	*Proceedings of the British Academy*
P. L.	*Patrologiae cursus completus. Series latina*
PMLA	*Publications of the Modern Language Association*
PQ	*Philological Quarterly*
QJS	*Quarterly Journal of Speech*
RES	*Review of English Studies*
SBVS	*Saga Book of the Viking Society*
SN	*Studia Neophilologica*
SOEL	*Studies in Old English Literature*, ed. E. G. Stanley
SP	*Studies in Philology*
TPS	*Transactions of the Philological Society*
TRHS	*Transactions of the Royal Historical Society*
UTQ	*University of Toronto Quarterly*
VSL	*Vetenskaps-Societetens i Lund*

Abbreviations of Old English titles are conventional. References to chapters and footnote numbers in this volume are indicated thus: (I, 4).

CONTENTS

A Critical History of Old English Literature

Introduction

Quid Hinieldus cum Christo? "What has Ingeld to do with Christ?" Alcuin's famous remonstrance to Hygebald, Bishop of Lindisfarne, in a letter of 797, concerning the monks' fondness for listening in the refectory to heroic song rather than to spiritual wisdom, is for several reasons a suitable prolegomenon to a history of Old English literature. For one thing, the context of the statement suggests something of the significance of cultural, political, social, and linguistic forces that are involved with the literature. The fact that Lindisfarne was founded by the Irish bishop Aidan from Iona calls attention to the Celtic force in the complex structure of Anglo-Saxon society, while Alcuin's words themselves attest to the pagan Germanic and Christian Latinic concepts that either dramatically confront each other, as here, or else harmoniously fuse in the culture and literature of this earliest English era. The opposition between *lector* and *citharist* in the passage—*Verba dei legantur in sacerdotali convivio; ibi decet lectorem audiri, non citharistam, sermones patrum, non carmina gentilium*—emphasizes the singer-preacher dichotomy; though the twelfth-century historian William of Malmesbury tells us that the seventh-century Aldhelm was wont to sing songs on the bridge that he might find an audience for his sermons in the church. We may see in the implications about the strong attraction of secular poetry for even those most dedicated to spiritual concerns a reason, perhaps, for the

1

preservation of those few pieces of literature from the period which seem untouched by Christian matter or doctrine; for the clergy was the main preserver of our extant literary documents. In this connection, the incalculable loss of manuscripts and records should be mentioned: the sacking of Lindisfarne by Viking pirates four years prior to Alcuin's letter was but the first of a long series of barbarities extending down to and beyond the dissolution of the monasteries in Henry VIII's reign that have, along with natural disasters, deprived us of part of our literary and cultural heritage.[1]

The place of Old English literature in that heritage is a significant one. In the first instance, there are many Old English works that have intrinsic literary value and are worthy of study in their own right.[2] Second, Old English prose and poetry present a culture which is at times noble and in many respects distinctive. Further, they furnish a sense of depth in English thought, since the basic Christian tradition which underlies most Old English literature is also the foundation for much of the creative writing of later times. Both Renaissance and Anglo-Saxon writers, for example, drank from the same classical and Biblical springs, the former directly and the latter through the Christian Fathers as well. Microcosm and macrocosm, *ubi sunt*, consolation, Trinitarianism—these are but some of the ideas and motifs that Old English literature shares with the works of later writers like Donne, Arnold, Tennyson, and Milton.[3] In contrast to this community of thematic interest, Old English literature presents *stylistically* a unique body of material

1. On the losses in the medieval period, see R. M. Wilson, *The Lost Literature of Medieval England* (London, 1952). On extant documents, see N. R. Ker, *Catalogue of Manuscripts Containing Anglo-Saxon* (Oxford, 1957); rev. by R. Willard, JEGP, LIX (1960), 129–136.

2. For some recent critical studies emphasizing that value, see A. G. Brodeur, *The Art of Beowulf* (Berkeley, 1959); A. Bonjour, *Twelve Beowulf Papers* (Neuchâtel, 1962); *Old English Studies in Honor of Arthur G. Brodeur*, ed. S. B. Greenfield (Eugene, Ore., 1963); *Studies in Old English Literature*, ed. E. G. Stanley (Edinburgh, to be published); *New Approaches to Old English Poetry*, ed. R. P. Creed (Providence, R. I., to be published).

3. See the papers of J. E. Cross cited in this volume.

within the continuum, where oral poetic techniques are fused with literary and rhetorical methods. Its stylistic uniqueness, even so, does not prevent it from revealing a certain continuity in style as well as in subject matter with the literature since the Norman Conquest,[4] and the influence of Old English mood and technique on poets like Hopkins, Pound, and Auden is part of the modern critical canon. Even the portmanteau-isms and stylistic idiosyncrasies of a Stein or Joyce are not so far removed from the Hisperic incomprehensibility in the word-minting and syntactical convolutions of some early Irish and English Latinate literature.

Some of the problems facing the writer of a history of Old English literature have been implied in the foregoing paragraphs: the necessity of filling in historical background; of determining how much culture is "literary" or important for literary understanding; of assessing the role as "Old English" of Latin writings by those of Anglo-Saxon stock; of explaining certain linguistic features; and so on.[5] More properly the domain

4. R. W. Chambers, *On the Continuity of English Prose from Alfred to More and His School* (Oxford, 1957); reprtd. from EETS 186, 1932; C. L. Wrenn, "On the Continuity of English Poetry," *Anglia*, LXXVI (1958), 41–59.

5. For the history and culture of the Old English period, see F. M. Stenton, *Anglo-Saxon England*, 2nd ed. (Oxford, 1947); P. H. Blair, *An Introduction to Anglo-Saxon England* (Cambridge, 1956); D. Whitelock, ed. *English Historical Documents, I: c. 500–1042* (Oxford, 1955)—all have excellent bibliographies, and the last has not only a general Introduction but comments on different sections and on specific works translated therein. For further historical and cultural bibliography, see W. Bonser, *An Anglo-Saxon and Celtic Bibliography (450–1087)* (Oxford, 1957). Of the many grammars, Quirk and Wrenn's *An Old English Grammar*, 2nd ed. (London, 1958), is invaluable for its discussion of syntax. The standard dictionary is that of Bosworth and Toller, *An Anglo-Saxon Dictionary*, with a *Supplement* by Toller (Oxford, 1882, 1920); there is also *A Concise Anglo-Saxon Dictionary* by J. R. Clark Hall, 4th ed. with supplement by H. D. Meritt (Cambridge, 1960). Of previous histories of Old English literature, we may cite K. Malone's in *A Literary History of England*, ed. A. C. Baugh (New York, 1948), and, with reservations, G. K. Anderson, *The Literature of the Anglo-Saxons* (Princeton, 1949); see also D. M. Zesmer, *Guide to English Literature from Beowulf through Chaucer and Medieval Drama*, with annotated bibliographies by S. B. Greenfield (New York, 1961). For the poetry alone there is C. W. Kennedy's admirable *The Earliest English Poetry* (London, 1943); nothing comparable exists for the prose.

of the literary historian is commentary on poetic and prose styles, on genres and traditions, on metrics and prosody, as well as assessment of individual works and authors. Complicating the task are chronological problems with the poetry (the major surviving manuscripts all date from around A.D. 1000), the anonymity of authors, and the like. For these reasons the first part of this book is devoted to the prose literature, mingling Latin and vernacular works as chronology and genre demand. Social and cultural history may thus less obtrusively lend their authority to the literary picture. Poetic tradition obviously flourished first: Ingeld had precedence over Christ in time, at any rate, in the Anglo-Teutonic mind, and Old English poetic style existed prior to a vernacular prose; but we can trace the development of the prose with greater precision. One final advantage accrues to this organization: the account of the poetry comes as a proper climax.

Citations from a poetic corpus that is to all effects in a foreign language also pose a problem. The reader of this *Critical History* will notice great variation in style in the necessary translations, ranging from the very literal and prosaic to the very free and somewhat "romantic." Such miscegenation will have served its purpose if it brings the reader to examine the original Old English poems for himself to determine the felicity or infelicity of the different translations.

I

The Beginnings of a Prose Tradition

AROUND THE YEAR 540, a Romanized British clergyman from his haven in Armorica composed for his hard-pressed native countrymen a document most commonly called today the *De Excidio Britanniae*. Strictly speaking, this historiographical exhortation cannot be called even Anglo-Latin because Gildas (Sapiens, or "The Wise"), the author, was not of Anglo-Saxon-Jutish lineage, but a Briton; and his sympathies, whatever his expressed horror at and sorrow for their sins, naturally lay with those earlier inhabitants of Albion who were being subjugated by tribes later to be known as *English*. But the work is in Latin, however faulty and florid the style, and it is our first extant writing from the Anglo-Saxon or Old English period.[1] Though the historian of these times finds more substantial matter in Bede's *Ecclesiastical History* and elsewhere, Gildas' account is the closest insular contemporary description of the arrival and first-hundred-years' activities of the Germanic peoples destined to inherit the island. To the Arthurian scholar, Gildas is important for the earliest reference to the British victory over the Saxons at Mount Badon and for the mention of the Roman-descended leader

1. The term *Anglo-Saxon* originally (as *Angli Saxones*) distinguished the Saxons in Britain from their counterparts on the Continent. Modern students of the language prefer the term *Old English* to stress linguistic historical continuity, but *Anglo-Saxon* is still a convenient term of reference for the people and the culture of the period. See J. W. Clark, *Early English* (London and Fairlawn, N. J., 1957), pp. 12–13.

Ambrosius Aurelianus, a prototype of the King Arthur of later legend.[2] To us, the *De Excidio* serves well as an introduction to some of the substance and methodology of the prose of the centuries to follow, ages conveniently associated with the figures of Bede (seventh and eighth centuries), Alfred (ninth century), and Ælfric (tenth and eleventh centuries), and with the successive political and cultural predominance of Northumbria and Wessex. There will be occasion later to modify the inaccuracies subsumed under these terminological conveniences.

Gildas' prose effort has been called a *chronicle*,[3] and the chronicle, along with its companion the *annal* and the related *history*, has had a long and respected career as a literary genre, at times achieving true literary interest in a Geoffrey of Monmouth or a Gibbon, at times resulting in such monumental compilations as our own *Congressional Record*. The medieval chronicle, with the Eusebius-Jerome *Chronicle* as its cornerstone, was concerned with illustrating the relation of the temporal activities of mankind to eternity. The *De Excidio* is in this tradition, but more apparent is the homiletic strain that occupies the entire third part, or Epistle, which is almost four times the length of the Preface and the History combined. The *homily* and the related *sermon* also have done long and respectable service as creative outputs of the human mind, and in English literary history have occasionally distinguished them-

2. The earliest nominal allusion to Arthur, as a famous historical chief, is in the Welsh elegy *Gododdin* (c. 600). As *dux bellorum* he later appears in the pages of Nennius' *Historia Britonum*, written c. 800. See R. H. Fletcher, "The Arthurian Material of the Chronicles," *Harvard Studies and Notes in Philology and Literature*, x (1906), 3–8 on Gildas, 8–30 on Nennius; also K. H. Jackson, "The Arthur of History," *Arthurian Literature in the Middle Ages*, ed. R. S. Loomis (Oxford, 1959), and N. K. Chadwick, *Studies in the Early British Church* (Cambridge, 1958), pp. 37–46 on Nennius. Since there is more historical matter than literary art in the *Historia*, I have relegated Nennius to this and the following note.

3. It appears under this rubric, along with Nennius' *Historia*, in the translations of J. A. Giles, *Six Old English Chronicles* (London, 1848); see also A. W. Wade-Evans, *Nennius's "History of the Britons" together with the "Story of the Loss of Britain"* (London, 1938). Gildas and Nennius have been edited by J. Stevenson for the English Historical Society, II and III (1838), and by Theodor Mommsen in *MGH: Auct. Ant.*, XIII (1894, 1898).

selves by their rhetorical effectiveness in a Wulfstan or a John Donne. But the homiletic in Gildas is not distinguished: the Epistle bristles with a short series of reprobations of British kings and judges, interminably discourses on (mostly) bad Old Testament figures, and heavily inveighs against the depraved and simoniacal British clergy through references to major prophets and to New Testament adjurations. The constant citation of authority (Gildas' is rather limited in scope, to the Bible) is, of course, a medieval commonplace, especially where ethical matters are concerned; but surely even Gildas' audience must have found this part of his work, however spiritually justified, a little tedious.

In the Preface to the *De Excidio,* Gildas disclaims his own moral and literary excellence (again, a medieval rhetorical convention) and insists that, after much inner debate, he has decided to produce the following lamentation about Britain's vicissitudes from Roman times to the present. He further disclaims the use of ornamentation, though metaphor and rhetorical colors abound. In the History itself, Gildas can make good, if conventional, use of antithesis, as in Chapters 3 and 4, where he contrasts the beauty of the island with the stiff-necked and stubborn-minded people who have so frequently rebelled against God, themselves, and foreign kings. Or in Chapter 8, forgetting the beneficence God had bestowed on the island, he refers to the land as stiff with cold and frost and remote from the visible sun in order to show the Britons receiving the light of the true Sun, Christ.

Gildas need detain us no longer, but the political, religious, and linguistic circumstances of his age must briefly be glanced at. Although Gildas is vague as to names, places, and dates in his historical matter, other Welsh, English, and Continental sources help establish the pattern of events (still conjectural at best) involving the advent, conquest, and settlement in Britain of the Germanic peoples earliest mentioned by Tacitus in his *Germania* (A.D. 98) as *Anglii,* and their related tribesmen, the Saxons and Jutes (Bede's *Iutae*). Arriving first in southeast

England about 449 as mercenaries invited by the British King Vortigern to help combat the Picts and Scots, who, after the final Roman withdrawal early in the fifth century, continued to make incursions into British territory, the Germanic tribes eventually broke more than bread with their hosts, seizing what they could of the land for themselves. By Gildas' time, some form of peace had evidently been arranged, but by 571 the "English" were again on their northward and westward expansion movement and were soon, to all effects and purposes, to make *Englaland* (a term not used regularly, however, till the eleventh century) theirs. By the year 600, some sixty years after Gildas had chastised his countrymen and seen in their disasters the punishing hand of God, ten independent English states south of the Humber and the kingdom of Northumbria (a solidification of Deira and Bernicia under Æthelfrid in 603) can be recognized.[4] Probably by this time, or shortly thereafter, the various dialects of Old English recognized by linguists as Northumbrian, Mercian (together referred to as Anglian), West Saxon, and Kentish had emerged, not as the products of the ethnic provenience of the original Germanic settlers but of their new-found insularity.[5] And the great event that was within a century and a half to lead to the first literary era among the English had just occurred: the landing of Augustine and his Christianizing mission on the isle of Thanet in 597.

The events culminating in Augustine's mission are well known to every student of Old English through Bede's unforgettable account of Gregory's fascination with the English boys for sale in the Roman marketplace and his satisfying, when

---

4. Some form of recognized superiority, or *imperium*, seems to have existed among the various kingdoms from the earliest times, on the testimony of Bede, depending on the comparative character and forcefulness of their kings. By 827 the title *Bretwalda* appears in one text of the *Anglo-Saxon Chronicle*, but real political unity in England was not achieved till the accession of Edgar in 959. See P. H. Blair (Int., 5), pp. 27 f., 44 f., 198 ff.

5. A. Campbell's *Old English Grammar* (Oxford, 1959), pp. 3–11, gives a good introductory summary of the textual evidence for the various dialects.

he became Pope, of his desire to see such Angles evangelized (*HE* II, i). Augustine's rapport with Æthelberht, king of Kent, the founding of Canterbury and establishment of the metropolitan see there, the losses in Church prestige and influence in the years that followed, and the re-establishment and reinvigoration of Christianity in the South following the arrival in 669 of Archbishop Theodore and Abbot Hadrian are part of Church history and not eminently our domain here. By the latter part of the seventh century, a Church school flourished at Canterbury[6] and produced one of the important figures in the Anglo-Saxon literary tradition: Aldhelm. Bede also, in another vivid account (*HE*, II, ix ff., esp. xiii)—that concerning Bishop Paulinus, Coefi, and the flight of the sparrow simile—informs us of the spread of Roman Christianity to Northumbria through the conversion of King Edwin in 627 in York (not till more than a century later an archiepiscopal see). But Christianity in northern England had its setbacks, too; in the seventh century, North and South, the attitude of reigning royalty toward the Church was particularly significant, and kings came and went, in many cases, with the swiftness of Bede's conversionary sparrow. Additionally in the North, Roman Christianity found itself confronted by the more ascetic Irish-inspired Christianity. The monastery at Lindisfarne had been established by Aidan of Iona in 635, and Celtic Christianity had firmly established itself in Northumbria in the next twenty years. Though the Synod of Whitby in 664 formally settled the dispute over the calculation of the date of Easter (the word *Eostre* being a linguistic legacy of Anglo-Saxon heathendom) and established more firmly the authority of Rome, Wilfrid of York (d. 709) and his

6. See V. R. Stallbaumer, "The Canterbury School of St. Gregory's Disciples," *ABR*, VI (1955–56), 389–407. The most recent Church histories are by M. Deanesly, *The Pre-Conquest Church in England* (London and New York, 1961), and C. J. Godfrey, *The Church in Anglo-Saxon England* (Cambridge and New York, 1962); on the later Anglo-Saxon Church, see F. Barlow, *The English Church, 1000–1066: A Constitutional History* (London and Hamden, Conn., 1963).

affluent Romanism continued to have difficulties well into the eighth century.[7] Nevertheless, with the founding of Wearmouth in 674 and its companion monastery Jarrow in 681 by Benedict Biscop (d. 689), who, through his six journeys to Rome, not only acquired a knowledge of Roman institutions and Church practices, especially Benedictinism, but a tremendous wealth of literary and artistic materials for his monasteries, early eighth-century Northumbria was to produce one of the greatest scholars and literary figures of Anglo-Saxon England, the Venerable Bede.[8]

Aldhelm (c. 639–709), however, will be our first consideration because he is the earliest *English* writer whose works have survived.[9] We have evidence, indeed, that he was a popular vernacular poet—King Alfred was one of his ardent admirers—though none of this poetry survives. (We shall come later to his Latin *Riddles*.) Aldhelm's prose, naturally, was in Latin, its style Celtic-inspired in its ornateness and erudition. Related by birth to West Saxon royalty, and later made first bishop of Sherborne (705), Aldhelm garnered his Hisperic style from his Irish master Maelduib at Malmesbury and nourished it at Canterbury, where he went in 671, with the near-oriental influence of Archbishop Theodore of Tarsus. Much of his cultural and literary legacy lies in his various epistles. Of these, we may cite from the Letter to Wihtfrid, a young man attracted to Ireland by its learning:

7. M. W. Pepperdene, "Bede's *Historia Ecclesiastica*: A New Perspective," *Celtica*, IV (1958), 253–262, sees as late as 731 Bede's purpose in writing the *HE* as one of combating lingering Irish asceticism and provincialism in Northumbria.

8. Benedictine practicality in its knowledge of human frailty and in its inculcation of the love of God as a positive force was to make a more lasting impression than the Celtic austerity espoused by Columba and Aidan—see A. H. Thompson, "Northumbrian Monasticism," in *Bede: His Life, Times, and Writings*, ed. A. H. Thompson (Oxford, 1935). On the history of monasticism in England, see D. Knowles, *The Monastic Order in England*, 2nd ed. (Cambridge, 1949), and J. D. Dickinson, *Monastic Life in Medieval England* (New York, 1962); on Wearmouth-Jarrow in particular, V. R. Stallbaumer, "St. Benedict Biscop's Wearmouth-Jarrow Monastic School," *BR*, XVII (1962), 11 pp.

9. R. Ehwald, ed. *Aldhelmi Opera*, in *MGH: Auct. Ant.*, XV (1919).

> Rumour has reached me, that you are going to study across the sea in Ireland. I pray you, study that you may refute the lies of pagan poetry. How foolish to stray through the tangled and winding bypaths of these legends, to turn from the pure waters of Holy Scripture that you may quench your thirst in muddy pools, swarming with a myriad of black toads, noisy with the guttural bark of frogs! What, think you, does it profit a true believer to inquire busily into the foul love of Proserpina, to peer with curious eyes into things of which it is not even meet to speak—to desire to learn of Hermione and her various betrothals, to write in epic style the ritual of Priapus and the Luperci?

and from the Letter to Wilfrid's clergy after the Council of 703 had once more exiled the controversial bishop:

> How could you forsake him who has nurtured, taught, rebuked and led you forward as sons of his love . . . ? Take a lesson from the world of Nature. . . . Do not the bees in ordered squadrons follow their king from the hive when spring has come? Do they not fly back again with him if sudden wind or rain bid him return to safe retreat? . . . What? even laymen who know nothing of Divine law are held in open scorn when in times of trouble they abandon the lord they have owned in his happy days. What, then, of you, if you send away alone and deserted the bishop who has fed and reared you?[10]

Both these passages are culturally important. The first implies the strong pull of secular literature and knowledge that Alcuin a century later was to deplore; the second bears testimony to the vitality of the *comitatus* tradition in Anglo-Saxon society (see Ch. V, "Secular Heroic Poetry"), to the fusion of the ancient Germanic ideal described by Tacitus with the Christian idealism of eighth-century England. And both further suggest the rhetorico-literary heights (whatever the apiary sexual ignorance) to which Aldhelm in his prose could rise. Perhaps the most renowned of his epistles is the Letter to "Acircius," King Aldfrid of Northumbria: after a Prologue on the mysticism of the number 7, it is devoted to a discussion of metrics and

10. Cited from E. S. Duckett, *Anglo-Saxon Saints and Scholars* (New York, 1947), pp. 39–40 and 199.

contains the famous *Ænigmata*, or *Riddles*, of Aldhelm's own devising, written in Latin hexameters.

Aldhelm can possibly be considered the first English literary critic, too. At least he was asked by others, including royalty, to criticize some of their poems, poems obviously written in imitation of the master. But his devotion was not to literature, but to enlightening his less fortunate contemporaries. He received requests from and supplied sermons for his brethren to use, and in his tractate *De Laudibus Virginitatis*, written for the community of nuns at Barking, in addition to praising the celibate life he suggests the scholarly and cultural achievements even women might attain to: knowledge of the Bible, the Fathers, history, allegory, grammar, and meter.

The School of Canterbury furnishes us with nothing further in prose of literary significance. Northumbria at this time, however, was witnessing a golden age under the beneficent rule of King Aldfrid (685–705), to whom Aldhelm addressed his famous letter. But the bulk of the literature of the Northumbrian age of letters, including Bede's work, seems to have been written in the years following Aldfrid's death, a phenomenon not surprising in view of the fact that the predominant literary form, apart from epistles, was the *saint's life*, and that the hagiographical subjects were for the most part ecclesiasts who flourished in Aldfrid's enlightened day: Cuthbert (d. 687), Wilfrid (d. 709), Guthlac (d. 714), and Ceolfrid (d. 716). An anonymous *Life of St. Gregory* by a monk of Whitby, preserved in a single manuscript in St. Gall, also survives from this time; it is perhaps the earliest of the Latin saints' lives written in England—at least it is most primitive in its literary form, based mainly on Gregory's own *Dialogues*, the Bible, and oral tradition, though the anonymous *Life of St. Cuthbert*, written early in the eighth century at Lindisfarne, may have initiated the ensuing burst of hagiographic activity in England.[11]

11. Most valuable for a study of the saint's life as a literary genre in eighth-century England are C. W. Jones, *Saints' Lives and Chronicles in Early England* (Ithaca, N. Y., 1947), and B. Colgrave, "The Earliest

The pattern for the saint's life was set by Evragius' Latin translation of the *Life of St. Antony* in the late fourth century. Here we find the typical Prologue in which the author declares the edificatory and panegyric nature of his exercise and vouches for the credibility of the narrative. From Sulpicius Severus' *Life of St. Martin* (c. 400) comes the self-deprecatory *topos* of the Prologue, which became almost universal in the later Latin lives, and the catalog of the saint's virtues. The typical life traces the saint's early days and vocation with conventional symbolic incidents, his path to the ascetic life, his trials; the subject's gaining of experience and judgment is accompanied by miracles and physical healings in the early stages and by the gift of prophecy in the later; finally there is the death warning, farewell to disciples, miracle at the tomb. These are the conventions which received infinite adaptations in the specific practices of the genre.

The Anglo-Latin lives generally follow the pattern-with-variations—Antony in his desert becomes Cuthbert on his isle of Farne, for example, or Guthlac in the East Anglian fens. But we find more of the miraculous in the *Lives* of *Cuthbert, Guthlac,* and *Gregory,* men more generally recognized as saints in Anglo-Saxon England, than in the *Lives* of *Wilfrid, Ceolfrid,* and *Benedict Biscop* (the last in Bede's *Lives of the Abbots*), men known firsthand to the writers as friends, masters, and the like. These latter may even be considered a form of historical biography, perhaps influenced by the Continental episcopal biographies of the fifth and sixth centuries. Of the many features of the individual lives of eighth-century England that

Saints' Lives Written in England," *PBA*, 1958, XLIV (1959), 35–60. Earlier works that can be consulted are G. H. Gerould, *Saints' Legends* (Boston, 1916), and B. P. Kurtz, *From St. Antony to St. Guthlac,* Univ. of California Pubs. in Modern Philology, XII (Berkeley, 1926). Jones's book contains a translation of the *Gregory,* which has been edited by F. A. Gasquet (Westminster, 1904). Colgrave's *Two Lives of St. Cuthbert* (Cambridge, 1940) contains both text and translation of the anonymous and the Bedian *Lives.* On the role of prose oral tradition in the shaping of saints' lives, see C. E. Wright, *The Cultivation of Saga in Anglo-Saxon England* (Edinburgh, 1939).

might be mentioned, we shall have to content ourselves with but a few. We may note, for example, that the Whitby *Life of Gregory* contains the earliest account of the famous medieval legend about Gregory's baptizing the soul of the pagan Emperor Trajan with his tears; that the anonymous *Cuthbert* has a certain realism in its references to specific persons and places and actions, and even humor, as in the story of the penitent ravens and the lard, or the sea's laying of the requisite twelve-foot foundational timber for the saint's privy; that Bede's prose *Cuthbert* is something of a rhetorical exercise in which Bede deliberately avoids the words of his Lindisfarne predecessor, on the one hand generalizing with romantic images and situations and on the other historicizing by putting the account of the saint's death into the mouth of Herefrid, later abbot of Lindisfarne; and that the anonymous *Life of Ceolfrid*, written between 717 and 725, emphasizes the new learning and the close connection between Wearmouth-Jarrow and the Continent.[12]

The ascetic Cuthbert, with his love of nature and animals, offers a vivid contrast to the willful Wilfrid of York, perhaps the most interesting of these saints from a modern point of view. Eddius, the author of his biography (written between 710 and 720),[13] focuses on the various temporal clashes between his admired hero and King Aldfrid and Archbishop Theodore, his exiles in Frisia and Sussex and his conversionary work there, his three trips to Rome to assert his ecclesiastical rights in York, and the rejection by the English secular and spiritual leaders of the papal decrees in his favor. Not scholarly like Aldhelm, but skillful in debate, Wilfrid was an important influence at the Synod of Whitby and in the Romanizing of northern

12. The *Life* of Ceolfrid of Jarrow has been ed. C. Plummer in *Venerabilis Baedae Opera Historica* (Oxford, 1896), I, 388–404, II, 371–377, and trans. D. Whitelock in *EHD*, pp. 697–708. It is from this *Life* that we can identify the *Codex Amiatinus* of Florence with the Latin Bible originally done at Wearmouth and Jarrow. On the whole subject of the relations of England with the Continent at this time, the best book is W. Levison's *England and the Continent in the Eighth Century* (Oxford, 1946).

13. Ed. and trans. B. Colgrave, *The Life of Bishop Wilfrid by Eddius Stephanus* (Cambridge, 1927).

Christianity, a man of strong spiritual convictions who recognized the desirability and importance of grandeur in temporal affairs.

Felix of Crowland's *Life of St. Guthlac*, written about 740 in Mercia at the request of the East Anglian King Ælfwald, and the closest to the Antonian model, is of the greatest interest to the student of Old English literature because there is an Old English prose translation in MS Vespasian D.xxi, which was also adapted for a homily extant in the Vercelli Book, and the poems *Guthlac* A and B in the Exeter Book.[14] From an esthetic point of view, the presentation of the character of the protagonist in his conversion from temporal success as a Germanic warrior to his spiritual conquests as a *miles Dei* against repeated attacks, temptations, and threats by devils is most effective. During the course of the later eighth century, other saints' lives were written by Englishmen on the Continent: Willibald's *Life of St. Boniface*, Alcuin's *Life of St. Willibrord*, and the *Hodoeporion of St. Willibald* written down by a nun of Heidenheim, the earliest extant travel literature by an Englishman.[15] But these are on the periphery of our literary history.

It is time to turn to the greatest English writer of the age, North or South, insular or continental, the Venerable Bede (c. 673–735), whose varied though Church-oriented interests and literary activities embrace hagiography, history, science, Scriptural commentary, and rhetorical matters. The medieval scholar *par excellence*, the judicious yet zealous guardian of tradition and assessor of secondary authorities, Bede began his studies at the traditional age of seven, first at Wearmouth, soon in the newly established Jarrow. There he stayed, except for brief visits to York and Lindisfarne, the rest of his life, performing his monastic duties and officiating in his rounds as a Benedictine priest. Despite some legends to the contrary, he was not a pil-

14. Felix's *Life* has been edited and translated by B. Colgrave (Cambridge, 1956) and translated by C. W. Jones (n. 11). The Old English prose is edited by P. Gonser, *Das angelsächsische Prosa-Leben des hl. Guthlac*, Anglistische Forschungen, xxvii (1909).

15. For translations and some commentary, see C. H. Talbot, *The Anglo-Saxon Missionaries in Germany* (New York, 1954).

grim to Rome; nor was he destined to be a great administrator: it was his friend Hwaetberht who was, after the custom, unanimously elected abbot when Ceolfrid retired in 716 for the journey to Rome upon which he died.

Bede's extant prose,[16] like the literature previously discussed, was written in Latin. His most famous piece, the *Historia Ecclesiastica*, also appears, however, in an Old English version of the later ninth century; and we know from his letter to Ecgberht of York that Bede himself made an English version of the Creed and the Lord's Prayer, and from the moving letter *De Obitu Baedae* by the monk Cuthbert that Bede knew native songs and composed English sacred verse even on his deathbed and that he had begun to translate into English the Gospel of St. John and extracts from Isidore of Seville's *De Natura Rerum*. Of all his English work, however, nothing survives save possibly his "Death-Song" (see Ch. X).

Among his earliest works (before 703) are treatises on grammar, metrics, and rhetoric: the *De Orthographia, De Arte Metrica*, and *De Schematibus et Tropis Sacrae Scripturae*. "Concerning Orthography" is really an alphabetical glossary with notes on grammar, evidently a textbook for elementary pupils in the monastery. "Concerning the Art of Metrics"— also a textbook, a critical synthesis from earlier grammarians— is of slightly greater interest in its exposition on the difference between rhythmical verse, new at the time, and quantitative classical meter, and in its attempt to prove the superiority of sacred to secular poetry. Copious illustration is provided, as it is in "Concerning Tropes," where, with some concentration on allegory, Bede attempts to explain the rhetorical features of the Bible.[17] Shortly after these earliest exercises, Bede's lifelong

16. J. A. Giles, ed. *The Venerable Bede's Miscellaneous Works in Latin*, 12 vols. (London, 1843–45), or Vols. xc–xcv of Migne's *P.L.* For an account of Bede's career, see E. S. Duckett (n. 10). Still the best collection of essays on Bede and his times is that edited by A. H. Thompson (n. 8). For bibliography, see W. F. Bolton, "A Bede Bibliography: 1936–1960," *Traditio*, xviii (1962), 436–445.

17. See R. B. Palmer, "Bede as Textbook Writer: A Study of His *De Arte Metrica*," *Speculum*, xxxiv (1959), 573–584; G. H. Tanenhous,

interest in chronology manifested itself in the *De Temporibus,*
where the Easter-date calculation is clarified (Chs. 11–15) in
an exposition on the six *aetates mundi,* or ages of the world.
"Concerning Times" follows Isidore's popular *Etymologiae* in
its viewing of time in units progressing from smaller to larger
and in its inclusion of a chronicle at the end, but shows an in-
dependence of judgment in its reckoning that was, to Bede's
horror, to bring a charge of heresy against him. Some twenty
years later, in the *De Temporum Ratione,* a work thirteen times
longer than "Concerning Times," Bede retraced the pattern
in more detail, constantly utilizing Biblical analogies and seeking spiritual meanings. In this more mature discussion of time,
Bede added a seventh and eighth age of eschatological nature.
He also enlarged the scope of the chronicle, making it into a
copious compendium.[18] Mention should be made here of Bede's
other scientific work, *De Natura Rerum,* based on Isidore and
on Pliny's *Natural History,* in which the various natural phenomena are "scientifically" explained, including such items as
the saltiness of the sea and the redness of the Red Sea.

The many commentaries on the Scriptures which comprise
the bulk of Bede's writings were undoubtedly of first importance
to his community and to the author. Most of them are addressed
to his dearest friend Acca, Bishop of Hexham after 709. Bede's
constant appeal to the authority of the Fathers (especially
Augustine, Jerome, Ambrose, and Gregory) and his application
of the allegorical method to both Old and New Testament
figures, names, and actions reveal Bede the scholar and theologian rather than the man of letters. An example of some
interest in the light of Old English elegiac poetry is his interpretation of Solomon's temple as a figure of the Holy Universal
Church, part of which is still exiled on earth, part of which,
having survived its peregrination, reigns with God in heaven,
where the whole Church shall reign after the Last Judgment.

"Bede's *De Schematibus et Tropis*—A Translation," *QJS,* XLVIII (1962),
237–253.
18. The works on time have been edited by C. W. Jones, *Baedae
Opera de Temporibus* (Cambridge, Mass., 1943).

Of his New Testament commentaries, probably that on Luke is Bede's greatest.[19]

Bede's interest in hagiography has previously been alluded to; his prose *Life of St. Cuthbert* (c. 721) expanded his earlier verse *Life*,[20] both based on the anonymous Lindisfarne *Life*. Bede's versions are inferior to the Lindisfarne, but his prose account is somewhat more specific and vivid than the tissue of miracles that is its hexametrical predecessor. Bede also composed a *Life* of *St. Felix of Nola* and one of *St. Anastasius*, and a *Martyrology*. The last, with its enlargement upon the bare skeletons of earlier martyrologies, transformed what were essentially calendar notices into something at least approaching a literary genre.

But to modern literary historians Bede's most attractive writings are his histories.[21] The biography-chronicle *History of the Abbots of Wearmouth and Jarrow* is a worthy forerunner of the greater *Ecclesiastical History*. Written sometime between 716 and 720, it depicts the physical, intellectual, and spiritual life of the twin monasteries founded by Benedict Biscop in 674 and 681. Most attention is devoted to Benedict (Chs. 1–14) and to the pilgrimage and death of Ceolfrid (Chs. 16, 17, 21–

19. For a recent edition of the commentaries on Luke and Mark, see D. Hurst, *Bedae Venerabilis Opera, I: Opera Exegetica, 3: In Lucae Evangelium Expositio—In Marci* . . . Corpus Christianorum, Series Latina, cxx (Turnhout, Belgium, 1960). Dom Hurst has also edited the *Opera Homiletica* in Vol. cxxii of the same series (1955). See also *Opera Exegetica 2: In Primam Partem Samvhelis Libri IIII—In Regum Librum XXX Quaestiones*, Vol. cxix (1962). For some of the "leges allegoriae" Bede subscribed to, see Plummer's edition of the *HE*, i, lix–lxi, Notes.

20. The practice of composing the same work in verse and in prose seems to have originated with Sedulius' *Carmen* and *Opus Paschale*. Aldhelm wrote his prose "On Virginity" first, then his poetic version; so did Alcuin with his *Life of St. Willibrord*. But Bede followed Sedulius in composing the poetic version first.

21. The best edition of Bede's historical works is that of C. Plummer (n. 12); see also J. E. King *Baedae Opera Historica* (London, 1930), which contains facing Latin text and English translation. Both contain, in addition to the two histories, the moving letter of Cuthbert on Bede's death and the Letter to Ecgberht. Whitelock, in *EHD*, has a translation of large portions of the *HE*, with summaries of omitted sections (item 151). The two oldest MSS (eighth century) of the *HE*, the Leningrad and the Moore, have been reproduced in facsimile in *EEMSF*, ii and ix, eds. O. Arngart (1952) and P. H. Blair, with R. A. B. Mynors (1959).

23), but among other impressive pictures is that of Easterwine, whose preference for nonpreferential treatment as a brother, despite his kinship to Benedict Biscop, had its counterpart in his great humility when he became abbot:

> Of course, as opportunity arose, he would discipline the wayward according to the Rule. But so innately gentle was he that he preferred to warn the negligent to avoid wrongdoing, so that no evil act should darken his placid countenance by the shadow of their disorder. Often as he made his rounds in overseeing the business of the monastery, he would join the groups of brothers at their work and labor with them. . . .[22]

Pathetic and moving is the scene in Chapter 13 of the two sick and dying abbots, Benedict and Sigfrid, lying on their pallets, heads on the same pillow, but so enfeebled they could not even kiss each other without the aid of the brethren. And Ceolfrid's departure and death are likewise colorful and touching episodes. There is some question as to whether this last part of the *History of the Abbots* is based on the anonymous *Life of Ceolfrid* mentioned above, or whether an annalistic logbook served as a common source. What is of significance in this history, however, is the complete absence of miracles—it is chronology made history, and hagiography has no place in it.[23] Here, framed by the picture of monastic life, is part of that larger history of the English Church Bede completed in 731.

Bede's purpose in writing the *Historia Ecclesiastica Gentis Anglorum* was to add a British and Anglo-Saxon supplement to Church history and to emphasize the unity of the English Roman Church. As model he had Rufinus' Latin translation and continuation of Eusebius' *Church History*, the first of the kind. Possibly Bede knew Gregory of Tours's *Historia Francorum*. His sources are many, including Gildas' *De Excidio*; in his prefatory material Bede lists many of them, written and

22. The translation is from Jones, *Saints' Lives*, p. 29.
23. C. W. Jones clarifies the chronicle tradition, based on the Easter table, which was ephemeral, and the hagiographic tradition, linked to the Julian calendar, which was eternal—see *Saints' Lives*, pp. 5–15. In the *History of the Abbots*, Bede first dated by the Incarnation; his similar practice in the *HE* has led to the almost universal adoption of this method of dating.

oral, and scholars have ferreted out the rest. Dedicated to King Ceolwulf of Northumbria, the *History* seems cast for a wider audience than Bede's other works. Its popularity from the Middle Ages (only Geoffrey of Monmouth's *History* surpasses it in the number of extant manuscripts) down to today is testimony to Bede's success in gauging the suitability of material to be included—a combination of history, hagiography, and storytelling—as well as to the warmth of tone and the refreshing simplicity of style.

It is the various stories embedded in the historical narrative that Old English students are most likely to be familiar with: Pope Gregory and the Anglian slaveboys in the marketplace, the conversion of Edwin of Northumbria, the gift of poetry to the cowherd Cædmon and the gentleness of his passing. But the architectonics of the *HE* are also worth noting: the general symmetry of its organization in parts and as a whole, the predominant chronological arrangement which yet allows for the insertion of small continuous biographies (such as Gregory's in ɪɪ, Fursa's in ɪɪɪ, Cuthbert's in ɪv, and Wilfrid's in v) and for a series of homogeneous narratives (such as the miracles of Oswald in ɪɪɪ and the visions of the otherworld in v) without separating simultaneous events in the different kingdoms. Bede selected pivotal dates and events for book divisions: ɪ ends just before Gregory's death in 605; ɪɪ, with the fall of Edwin and the dissolution of the first Northumbrian Church; ɪɪɪ, which includes a long recounting of the central Synod of Whitby, just before Theodore of Tarsus' arrival; ɪv, with St. Cuthbert's death in 687 (though it includes his translation and miracles); v, with the final date of writing, obviously, but with a chronological recapitulation of the whole *History* and a list of Bede's own writings. As historian, Bede is sincere and fair even with enemies like Wilfrid (though he allots space for but one miracle associated with him); as narrative artist, he knows how to animate his work with direct discourse, keeping his language lucid and sparkling, in contrast to the alliterating Hispericisms, the swollen periods, and bizarre decoration of Aldhelm, whose work he nonetheless admired and praised.

The following account from ii, ii, may serve to illustrate not only the vividness of Bede's style (insofar as this can be demonstrated in translation) but also his sense of his "Romanizing" mission and his ability to fuse miracle and historical narrative:

> Meanwhile Augustine, with the help of King Ethelbert, summoned to a conference with him the bishops and teachers of the nearest province of the Britons, . . . and began to persuade them with brotherly admonition that, preserving catholic unity with him, they should undertake for the Lord's sake the common labour of preaching the gospel to the heathens. For they did not keep Easter Sunday at the proper time, but from the 14th to the 20th of the moon . . . Moreover, they did many other things contrary to the unity of the Church. When, after a long discussion, they would not comply . . . but preferred their traditions to all the Churches which throughout the world agree in Christ, the holy Father Augustine put an end to this troublesome and long contention, saying: "Let us beseech God, 'who makes men of one manner to dwell in the house' of his Father, that he will deign to signify to us by heavenly signs which tradition is to be followed, . . . Let some sick man be brought, and let us believe that the faith and practice of him through whose prayers he shall be healed are acceptable to God, and ought to be followed by all." When the adversaries agreed to this, though unwillingly, a man of English race, who had lost the sight of his eyes, was brought. And when he was presented to the bishops of the Britons, and found no benefit nor cure from their ministry, at length Augustine, compelled by strict necessity, bowed his knees to the Father of our Lord Jesus Christ, imploring that he would restore his lost sight to the blind man, and by the bodily enlightenment of one man would kindle the grace of spiritual light in the hearts of many of the faithful. Immediately the blind man received sight, and Augustine was hailed by all as the true herald of the highest light.[24]

Throughout his life, Bede seems to have borne in mind the remarks he made early in his career in his prefatory letter to his critique on the Apocalypse of St. John:

> Thinking to consult the slothfulness of our race of the Angles, which not so long ago in the days of the blessed Pope Gregory received the seed of the Faith and cultivated it, so far as read-

24. Cited from Whitelock, *EHD*, p. 607.

ing went, lukewarmly enough, I have determined to elucidate meanings but express statements tersely, since plain brevity rather than prolix disputations is wont to stick in its memory.[25]

Bede's various prefatory letters and other epistles may be passed over here, with the exception of what was probably his last, to his friend and soon-to-be first Archbishop of York, Ecgberht. Written while Bede was very ill, in November of 734, the epistle laments the degeneracy of the Church in his times: the neglect of their duties by the bishops, their greedy and evil lives; the abuse of monastic life and the establishment of false monasteries by those who would escape secular obligations; the ignorance and deficiencies of even the well-intentioned clergy—and Bede exhorts Ecgberht to exercise control over his diocese and over himself for the salvation of all. Perhaps we should not take this Jeremiad too seriously—we can find parallels in the modern evangelistic portrait of our times or, say, in the modern critics' laments over the stagnation of our theater; for under Ecgberht, York in the years to follow was to become a famous center of learning and to eclipse the renown of Wearmouth and Jarrow. The Northumbrian School of York, in fact, was to send forth as a light to the Continent that other great eighth-century English scholar, Alcuin.

Unfortunately, Alcuin (735–804) was more the schoolmaster than the man of letters, and his reputation stems more from what he accomplished through the force of his personality, his administrative talents, his importance as a liturgist, and his influence on the culture of succeeding generations than from the literary value of his Latin prose. Charlemagne, wishing to improve education in his Frankish empire, had to seek abroad for scholars and teachers—and he garnered them from Italy, Ireland, Spain, and England. At the head of this happy band he placed Alcuin in 782, who proceeded to model the court school at Aix-la-Chapelle on the cathedral school of his native York, where he had earlier (778) been headmaster. Alcuin

25. Cited from Thompson, p. 155.

also helped establish other centers of learning throughout Charles's domains, notably at Tours, where he resided as abbot from 796 to his death.[26]

Mention has already been made of one of Alcuin's contributions to the hagiographic tradition, his *Life* of his kinsman St. Willibrord. This work is most conventional, mainly concerned with the miraculous—with the typical conceptional forecast of the saint-to-be's arrival and illuminating life (here the prospective mother has a vision of swallowing the moon and finding her bosom suffused with light), the miracles wrought by Willibrord himself among the Franks and Frisians, the miracle at the tomb (the sarcophagus, which had been six inches too short, wondrously extended itself to accommodate the saint's body), and so on. The style is no miracle, however, though the *Life* did inspire two later redactions.[27]

Alcuin's bulkiest "literary" legacy is his collection of letters.[28] The scholar and schoolmaster was an inveterate letter-writer, whose epistles harp on moral responsibility. This history opened with the most famous sentence from one of these communications, to the monks at Lindisfarne; but Alcuin had an extensive correspondence admonishing not only his fellow-ecclesiasts, high and low, but friends, lower and higher nobility, and even kings, both in England and on the Continent. Wallach goes so far as to see the elaborate *De Rhetorica et Virtutibus* (which he dates 801–804, though others have dated it earlier) as not primarily a rhetoric at all, but a moralizing political treatise or hortatory letter in the guise of a fictitious dialogue between Albinus (Alcuin) and Karlus (Charlemagne).[29]

26. On Alcuin's life and career, see E. S. Duckett, *Alcuin, Friend of Charlemagne* (New York, 1951), and A. Kleinclausz, *Alcuin*, Annales de l'Université de Lyon, iii.15 (Paris, 1948). His prose and poetry have been edited in Migne's P.L., Vols. c and ci; for special editions and translations, see following notes. For a study that falls somewhat outside the scope of this book, see G. Ellard, *Master Alcuin, Liturgist* (Chicago, 1956).

27. For a translation, see Talbot (n. 15).

28. Ed. E. Dummler, *MGH, Epistolae*, iv (1895), 1–481, with additions in *ibid.*, v (1899), 643–645.

29. L. Wallach, *Alcuin and Charlemagne: Studies in Carolingian History and Literature*, Cornell Studies in Classical Philology, xxxii

In the *Rhetoric,* mostly a compound of Cicero's *De Inventione* and Julius Victor's *Ars Rhetorica* (fourth century), are to be found many of the conventional *topoi* which appear also in Alcuin's letters: among others, the writing upon request, the writer's humility, and the feigned interest in brevity (when Albinus is asked by Karlus to give an exposition toward the end of the treatise on the four cardinal virtues, Albinus comments that "Brevity demands a few short remarks, and this difficult subject requires many," to which Karlus replies, "Then keep to the middle course, lest too many words cause weariness, and too few, ignorance").[30] As a rhetoric, Alcuin's work offers nothing original, though the use of the dialogue form is of some interest. Most of the extant manuscripts are of ninth-century provenience, and there is every evidence that scholars of the Middle Ages were going back to Cicero himself rather than to Alcuin's individual expression of the *De Inventione.*

The *De Virtutibus et Vitiis* (801–804), a compendium from many sources, including Isidore's *Sententiae* and pseudo-Augustinian homilies,[31] had a greater impact upon Alcuin's successors than the *De Rhetorica.* Ælfric, for example, included excerpts from it in his *Catholic Homilies* (see below) and it was translated into Old English, in a twelfth-century manuscript still

(Ithaca, N. Y., 1959), pp. 48 ff. The best edition of the *De Rhetorica* is that of C. Halm, in *Rhetores Latini Minores* (Leipzig, 1863), pp. 525–550; it is reproduced substantially without change and with facing English translation in W. S. Howell's *The Rhetoric of Alcuin and Charlemagne,* Princeton Studies in English, xxiii (Princeton, N. J., 1941).

30. Howell's trans., p. 145. Howell (pp. 31–32) sees Alcuin as missing the point of Cicero's ethical objectives in controversy by his appending *Virtutibus* to his title and by his dealing with Prudence, Justice, Temperance, and Fortitude *not,* as in Cicero, at the end of the topic of "Invention," but after the analysis of "Delivery," where it has no ostensible relation to that first division of rhetoric. It seems to me that Howell misses the point: that Alcuin's purpose as a Christian writer was to view the temporal as subsumed by the Eternal, as Albinus' last statement makes clear: "This dialogue of ours, which had its origin in the changing modes of civil questions, finds thus an end in talk of changeless forms. Let no one argue, then, that we have vainly conducted so long a colloquy." To this end, he undoubtedly deliberately rearranged his Cicero.

31. Wallach, pp. 236 ff., challenges Dom Rochais' contention that the florilegium of Defensor, *Liber Scintillarum,* was Alcuin's chief source.

extant. Written to Duke Wido as a moral guide for the military man and royal judge in the daily conflicts of life, the *Virtues and Vices* consists of thirty-five chapters and an epistolary peroration: the first twenty-six deal with a variety of topics embraced by the title, Chapters 27–34 with the eight principal vices, and Chapter 35 with the four cardinal virtues.

Among Alcuin's other prose works might be mentioned his commentary on Genesis, which Ælfric appropriated twice, once in his *Interrogationes Sigewulfi . . . in Genesin* and again in his *Catholic Homilies.*[32] It is on this type of influence upon subsequent literature and culture, and in his stimulation of scholarship on the Continent, that the Englishman Alcuin's fame rests today. With him, and with the Danish invasions of the ninth century, the cultural initiative in western Europe passed from England to the Continent, so that by the end of the ninth century King Alfred was moved to comment on the decline of learning in England and on the necessity to seek scholars abroad.

Such were the beginnings of the English prose tradition, in a country struggling to become a nation religiously and politically. The tongue was Latin,[33] the traditions Graeco-Roman-Celtic-Christian, but the heart and the spirit were Anglo-Saxon. Neither Aldhelm nor Bede nor Alcuin was what we would call an original thinker; but under the circumstances originality was not of the essence. These scholars and writers were the guardians, updaters, and transmitters of tradition, embodying in their loyalties to Church and country the Germanic concept of fealty to tribal chieftain. The religious education and in-

32. On Alcuin's popularity in English writings of the Middle Ages, see L. Wallach, "Charlemagne and Alcuin: Studies in Carolingian Epistolography," *Traditio,* IX (1953), 149–151.

33. Lists of words, though of lexicographical interest, hardly constitute literature, but mention should be made in this chapter of early Latin-English glosses: of the *Epinal* and *Erfurt Glosses* (pre-eighth century), and of the *Leiden, Corpus, Brussels,* and *Boulogne Glosses* (eighth century). See H. D. Meritt, *Old English Glosses* (New York and London, 1945), and *The Old English Prudentius Glosses at Boulogne-sur-Mer* (Stanford, 1959).

doctrination of the untutored and unsaved was their goal, whether they delighted in the ornate style of the southern Aldhelm or the plain style of the northern Bede and Alcuin. Chronicle-history, hagiography, and epistolography were the main literary vehicles they and their contemporaries chose to carry the burden of their messages; and while much of these writings are of more interest to the cultural and political historian than to the literary historian or critic, these early recordings of English time and reflections are not devoid of purely literary significance. Northumbria contributed most to the literary legacy of the seventh and eighth centuries—at least so far as extant documents are concerned. But Wessex-Kent with its Aldhelm and the Midlands with Felix of Crowland were also active in the realm of letters. What is perhaps most surprising and disappointing about this era is that Mercia, the most powerful and stable kingdom in England in the eighth century under the long reigns of Æthelbald (716–757) and Offa (757–796), has left us no more than Felix in the way of literature. Possibly the environment of the anti-ecclesiastical and tyrannical Æthelbald (whose accession to the kingdom, we may note, had been prophesied by St. Guthlac while the king was yet a youth and an exile) was inimical to literary endeavors;[34] possibly there was simply no Bede in Mercia. Efforts have been made to ascribe the composition of *Beowulf* to Offa's court and reign, and perhaps the greatest glory of Old English literature is testimony to eighth-century Mercia's contribution to English literature; but the ascription remains unproved. We do know that Alfred turned to Mercians in the great work of translation he embarked upon, and there is other evidence of a Mercian prose tradition in the ninth century. But that story is part of the history of the next chapter.

34. In 746–747, St. Boniface, the famous Anglo-Saxon missionary to Germany, wrote a letter of admonition to Æthelbald, charging him, among other crimes, not only with fornication and adultery but of committing these sins with nuns and virgins. The letter is translated by Talbot, pp. 120 ff.

II

Alfredian and Other Ninth-century Prose

WHILE ALCUIN OF YORK was yet pursuing his admonitory way in the Frankish empire, a new star began to rise in the firmament of English history. In 802 Ecgberht, grandfather of Alfred the Great, returned from exile in Charles's realm to ascend the throne of Wessex, establishing a firm and secure kingdom that was first to challenge successfully the political supremacy of Mercia and then to be the bulwark of English defense against the Vikings, whose piratical attacks increased in frequency and ferocity as the century progressed and many of whom, like their Anglo-Saxon predecessors in the fifth century, eventually came to settle and to stay. When Ecgberht died in 839, his son Æthelwulf inherited the crown and its thorny domestic and foreign problems. Alfred's father was not the most inspiring king: more religious than martial in his interests and endeavors, he nevertheless defended Wessex well against Danish and Welsh marauders and allied his house with Mercia by giving his daughter Æthelswith as a "peace-weaver" in marriage to its king Burgred. He sent his youngest son Alfred (849–899) to Rome twice, the second time, in 855, accompanying him himself. Young though he was on those occasions (on the first he had been anointed as a Roman consul by Pope Leo IV), Alfred could not fail to be impressed with the spiritual glory of the Church. These pilgrimages, coupled with his father's piety and his mother Osburh's diligence in and fondness for reading vernacular poetry to him as a child, fostered a religious love for wisdom and literature in the man who, with the death of his last remaining brother Ethelred, became king of Wessex in 871. Alfred's long struggles with the Danes are not part of this history,[1] but by 886, when he had concluded the famous treaty with Guthrum the Dane, Alfred was recognized as king and/or overlord by all of England south of the Humber, save for that portion settled by the Danes (Essex, East Anglia, and the Eastern Midlands), and he was for the first time free to repair his own ignorance of literature and to foster a revival of learning throughout his kingdom, a twin project that had ever been close to his heart. For the great king, soldier, statesman, and jurist[2] recognized that each man in himself is but the abstract and brief chronicle of his time, and wished for himself and his people a more enduring record here on earth and a more certain viaticum for the life hereafter.

To further his educational program, Alfred, even as had Charles the Great a century earlier, turned to other countries for a supply of teachers, for learning in England, as the king remarks in his Preface to his translation of Gregory's *Pastoral Care*, had sadly declined so that

> we now have to get them [wisdom and learning] from abroad, if we would have them [at all]. So completely had it [knowl-

1. For reading in primary sources, see *The Anglo-Saxon Chronicle*, trans. D. Whitelock, D. C. Douglas, and S. I. Tucker (London and New Brunswick, N. J., 1961), and *Asser's Life of King Alfred*, ed. W. H. Stevenson (Oxford, 1904); reprtd. with bibliographical article by D. Whitelock in 1959. For secondary accounts, see F. M. Stenton and P. H. Blair (Int., 5); also, in more detail, C. Plummer, *The Life and Times of Alfred the Great* (Oxford, 1902), B. A. Lees, *Alfred the Great: The Truth Teller* (New York, 1915), and E. S. Duckett, *Alfred the Great: The King and His England* (Chicago, 1956; London, 1957).

2. For Alfred's law code, which embraced, so the king tells us, the codes of Æthelberht of Kent, of his ancestor Ine of Wessex, and of the Mercian Offa, see F. Liebermann, *Die Gesetze der Angelsachsen*, 3 vols. (Halle, 1903–16); F. L. Attenborough, *The Laws of the Earliest English Kings* (Cambridge, 1922), edn. and trans.; *EHD*, pp. 357 ff. The *Textus Roffensis*, the MS containing the laws, has been reproduced in *EEMSF*, vii, Part i, ed. P. Sawyer (1957); Part ii, containing various charters, appeared as Vol. xi in 1962. For interesting literary comment, see D. Bethurum, "Stylistic Features of the Old English Laws," *MLR*, xxvii (1932), 263–279.

edge] fallen away among Englishmen that [when I ascended to the kingdom] there were very few on this side of the Humber who could understand their services in English, or even translate a letter from Latin into English; and I think that there were not many beyond the Humber.

From France came Grimbold, whose piety earned him sainthood, and from Saxony John, whom Alfred established as abbot of his new monastery at Athelney in the Somerset fens, a site that had served the king well in the darkest hours of his wars against the Danes. To Wessex from closer to home came the Welsh priest (and later Bishop of Sherborne) Asser, who was to record for posterity the *Life* of his king, and four Mercians: Plegmund, who became Archbishop of Canterbury in 890, Wærferth, Bishop of Worcester, and the priests Æthelstan and Werwulf. It was with the aid of these men in particular that Alfred undertook the first systematic program of translation into English of which we have any record.

Before reviewing the corpus of Alfred's achievment,[3] brief notice should be given to Asser's *De Vita et Rebus Gestis Alfredi*, written while the king still lived, in 893. Not only does Asser's *Life* supply us with most of our knowledge about Alfred as a person, but it is a literary landmark, however verbose and pretentious the Latin, as the first biography of an English layman. Einhard's *Vita Caroli* was a model, and Asser seems well informed on ninth-century events in the Frankish empire as well as in England, for the latter relying upon some version of the *Anglo-Saxon Chronicle*. But the heavy and unbalanced emphasis on the king's fine qualities, especially in the face of severe physical illness and pain, betrays the influence of the hagiographic tradition of the eighth century.[4]

3. *The Whole Works of King Alfred the Great*, ed. J. A. Giles (London, 1858).

4. The only MS of Asser's *Life* known to modern times, Brit. Mus. Cott. Otho A.xii, was burnt in the fire of 1731; Stevenson's edition (n. 1) is based on Archbishop Parker's transcripts (not his edition of 1574) and on extracts recorded by Florence of Worcester, Simeon of Durham, and the compiler of the *Annals of St. Neots*. The *Life* is translated in Giles, *Six . . . Chronicles* (1, 3) and by L. C. Jane (London, 1924); portions of it are translated in *EHD*, item 7. For the rationale of and artistic form

In Chapters 87 and following, Asser tells us how Alfred in 887 was divinely inspired to read Latin and to translate it on one and the same day, and that Asser recorded the "flowers" of learning that appealed to the king in a book which became almost as large as a psalter. This *Enchiridion*, or *Handbook*, which gave the king great comfort, unfortunately has not survived (but see the discussion to follow, on the *Soliloquies*). Also of great comfort, so Asser implies, not only to the king but to his people, was the translation of Gregory's *Dialogues*— in the main a collection of miracles and tales of wonder—made by Wærferth at Alfred's request and finished about 891.[5] But the first work from Alfred's own hand (or probably from the king's dictation to one or more scholarly amanuenses) is the translation of Gregory's *Pastoral Care*.[6]

The *Pastoral Care* was already in Alfred's day a classic: Bede had recommended it to Ecgberht of York in his Epistle of 734, Alcuin to Eanbald of York in 796, and on the Continent Hincmar of Rheims insisted that his bishops hold copies during their consecration. Gregory's work was designed to clarify his concept of the ideal bishop: it treats of his character, of his outer life with its devotion to his varied flock, and of his inner communion with God. The ideals enumerated evidently were highly compatible with Alfred's sense of his kingly responsibility

in the *Life*, see M. Schütt, "The Literary Form of Asser's 'Vita Alfredi,'" *EHR*, LXXII (1957), 209–220.

5. Ed. By H. Hecht in *BAP*, v (1900–1907); there is an unpublished translation by R. M. Lumiansky (Ph.D. thesis, Univ. of North Carolina, 1942). For textual discussion, see P. N. U. Hartung in *Neophil*, XXII (1937), 281–302, and for more general commentary, B. J. Timmer, *Studies in Bishop Wærferth's Translation of the Dialogues of Gregory the Great* (Groningen, 1934).

6. There is some question about the chronology of Alfred's works, since all postdate Asser's *Life* or at least are not mentioned therein—see G. K. Anderson (Int., 5), p. 264; also Bromwich (n. 18), p. 302. For text and translation of Alfred's *Pastoral Care*, see H. Sweet, ed., EETS 45, 50 (1871–72). On textual transmission and authority, see K. Sisam, *Studies in the History of Old English Literature* (Oxford, 1953), pp. 140–147. For sympathetic contextual and critical treatment of this and most of the Alfredian translations, see E. S. Duckett, *Alfred the Great*, pp. 142 ff. For a cogent analysis of the Preface, see F. Klaeber, "Zu König Ælfreds Vorrede zu seiner Übersetzung der Cura Pastoralis," *Anglia*, XLVII (1923), 53–65. The MSS roughly contemporary with Alfred have been reproduced in *EEMSF*, VI, ed. N. R. Ker (1956).

to God and to his people; and the book must have seemed an essential plank in his scheme of educational reform: for how could men learn without properly disposed and educated teachers? In the famous Preface, Alfred laments the decline and fall of learning in England and underscores the necessity for translation into English of Latin writings. There also he outlines his plan to have capable young freemen taught to read their mother tongue, with those specially apt for holy orders further instructed in Latin. As for his method of translation, he comments that he has done it "sometimes word by word, sometimes sense for sense," as he learned the *Pastoral Care* from Plegmund, Asser, Grimbold, and John (the variety of national origins of the four teachers named is perhaps significant). In the translation, the "sense by sense" paraphrase predominates; but the text is closely adhered to nevertheless, with few additions save for brief clarifying remarks.

The Old English version of Bede's *Ecclesiastical History* was for long attributed to Alfred himself, and by many scholars placed chronologically after the *Pastoral Care*; but at best it may have been part of his large educational plan, executed by one of his Mercian translators, because the dialect has many Anglian forms and stylistically the translation differs from the known works of Alfred.[7] Here once again, this time in a somewhat tortured and unidiomatic but at times comfortable, even inspired, Old English prose, are the stories of the religious conversion of the English and the overnight miracle of Cædmon's poetic conversion; but about one quarter of the original Latin is omitted: papal letters, poems in honor of saints, and the paschal controversy. Presumably epistolary documents would not interest a wider lay audience, and the Easter issue was no

7. In the extant MSS (four and a fragment), Alfred is not named as author—the ascription rests with Ælfric (*Catholic Homilies* II, 116–118) and with William of Malmesbury, the early twelfth-century historian (*De Gestis Regum Anglorum*), but Alfred's reputation may have been responsible for the attribution, even as it was for the ascription to him of the later *Proverbs of Alfred*. See esp. D. Whitelock, "The Old English Bede," PBA, 1962, XLVIII (1963), 57–90. Further, see Bromwich (n. 18), p. 302, n. 2; also J. J. Campbell, "The Dialect Vocabulary of the OE Bede," JEGP, L (1951), 349–372, and Vleeskruyer (n. 25).

longer current. The translator made his omission judiciously, however, and in orderly fashion, with narrower interests than Bede had had. Bede's passion for precision and authority are not in evidence, nor is his concern for geography, chronology, and etymology. But the Old English translator had something of a poetic turn of mind, exhibited in a vocabulary rich in poetic diction, in metaphoric creativity—he translates, for instance, the bald *paruissimo spatio* of the conversion-of-Edwin sparrow simile into *an eagan bryhtm* 'the twinkling of an eye'—and in a poetic sense of economy that nevertheless renders the Latin text closely and faithfully, with little extraneous matter.[8]

The translation of Orosius' *Universal* or *Compendious History*[9] is less faithful to its Latin original and more wide-ranging. Unlike the Bede, it may well have been written by Alfred himself, though less probably than the *Pastoral Care*, the Boethius, and the *Soliloquies*. Orosius, an Iberian priest, had been asked by Augustine to write a history disputing the notion that the barbarian invasions of Rome were due to Christianity; and his *Historiae adversum paganos* (418), accentuating the greater evils of pre-Christian times, was the result. The Orosius took Alfred far from home in its historical and geographical details; and this ranging evidently sanctioned in the king's mind departures from the text. Among the most famous is the early insertion which enumerates the tribes and regions of northern and central Europe and then relates the voyages of the Norwegian Ohthere and the Anglo-Saxon or Danish Wulfstan, who visited Alfred's court and reported respectively on their journeys into the White and Baltic Seas. This account of Germanic geography and navigation, in a book originally by a Mediterranean writer, appears appropriately after Orosius' brief allusion to the

8. Text and translation of the OE Bede by T. Miller, EETS 95, 96, 110, 111 (1890–98); text alone by J. Schipper, in *BAP*, iv (1899); translation alone by T. Stapleton (Oxford, 1929).

9. The text of the Lauderdale MS has been edited by H. Sweet, with the Latin original, in EETS 79 (1883); J. Bosworth's *King Alfred's Version of the Compendious History* . . . (London, 1859) is based on the Cotton MS and contains a translation; B. Thorpe's translation of Pauli's *Life of Alfred the Great* also contains a translation of Alfred's Orosius.

Scandinavian countries. The voyages of the two sea captains are first-rate narrative. From Ohthere we learn about the far North and about the existence and subsistence of the Lapps (Finns), of whale and walrus hunting (the walruses being highly valued for the very fine "bones in their teeth"), and of friendly and hostile inhabitants of the Arctic waste. From Wulfstan emerges an account of the strange burial custom of the Esthonians: of their "refrigerating" of the dead man for as long as six months, of the feasting and carousing around the bier, of the horse racing for portions of the dead man's possessions, and of the final cremation of the body. The prose in which these narratives are couched is economical and suggestive; as R. W. Chambers comments, in two or three pages

> we get a shrewd idea of the traveller's [Ohthere's] character: the mixture of curiosity and more practical ends which prompted his exploration; the caution which led him to stop it; a caution which also prevented him dwelling on the many tales which he heard of the lands beyond, "but which he knew not the truth of it, for he saw it not himself."[10]

Alfred reduced the original seven books of Orosius's *History* to six. The still-considerable bulk is not exactly exciting, though there are curiosities of a literary-critical nature to be gleaned here and there. For example, the translation of the passage describing the first elephants brought against the Romans by Pyrrhus in aid of the Tarentines contains the sentence, "He [Minutius, a Roman] ventured under an elephant so that he stabbed it in the navel." The Latin reads to the effect that "With his sword he sliced off the beast's trunk stretched out against him." There was obviously some confusion in Alfred's mind about the unusual Latin *manus* for 'trunk' and about elephantine physiognomy; just possibly the Old English sentence is a delightful echo of Wiglaf's coming to Beowulf's aid and searching for the dragon's soft underbelly into which he

---

10. *On Continuity* (Int., 4), p. lx. On the navigational problems involved in Ohthere's voyage, see A. Binns, "Ohtheriana vi: Ohthere's Northern Voyage," *EGS*, vii (1961), 43–52; note, p. 43, gives further bibliography. Geographical problems are discussed by R. Ekblom, "King Alfred, Ohthere and Wulfstan," *SN*, xxxii (1960), 3–13; also see n. 11 and G. K. Anderson (Int., 5), p. 301.

plunged his sword.[11] A further interest of Alfred's Orosius: for the historian of the language, the Tollemache (or Lauderdale) MS of this work is one of the three basic sources of our knowledge of early West Saxon, the dialect on which many students of Old English have been nurtured (see end of this chapter).[12]

From historical works, many scholars reason, Alfred turned to his philosophical translations, those of Boethius' *Consolation of Philosophy* and St. Augustine's *Soliloquies*. Boethius' Latin work was written in 524, while the Christian author was in prison, accused of treason by the Ostrogoth king Theodoric, who shortly had him murdered. To Boethius, who had held the highest honors under Theodoric, the sudden turn of fortune seemed calamitous; the *De Consolatione Philosophiae* was his reasoned answer to his undeserved misfortune. It reviews by means of a dialogue between Lady Philosophy, who appears in Boethius' cell, and the author the vagaries of Fortune and the falseness and instability of the happiness she brings; it moves through a discussion of free will and predestination to a Platonic understanding of the source of true felicity in the one and only and immutable Good. Despite its noncommitment to Christianity in any specific way, the *Consolation* became one of the most popular books in the Middle Ages. In Anglo-Saxon England it may have influenced the *Beowulf* and *Wanderer* poets, among others, and in fourteenth-century England it not only was translated by Geoffrey Chaucer but left an indelible impress upon his poetry, especially upon his *Troilus and Criseyde*.[13] To Alfred, who had known so intimately the

11. P. 156, ll. 10–11 of Sweet's edition (n. 9). S. Potter, "Commentary on King Alfred's Orosius," *Anglia*, LXXXI (1953), 385–437, gives many such tidbits in his comparison of the OE and Latin texts; n. 2 furnishes bibliography to 1943 on the Ohthere and Wulfstan voyages.

12. The Tollemache MS has been reproduced in *EEMSF*, III, ed. A. Campbell (1953).

13. See H. F. Stewart, *Boethius: An Essay* (Edinburgh, 1891), and H. R. Patch, *The Tradition of Boethius* (New York and Oxford, 1935). For a modern translation, see R. H. Green, *Boethius: the Consolation of Philosophy* (New York, 1962). There is no proof that the *Beowulf* and *Wanderer* poets knew Boethius; as clerics they may well simply have

vicissitudes of war and the wracking of bodily pain, Boethius was the inevitable choice for translation.

William of Malmesbury informs us—and we may well believe him in this matter—that Alfred requested aid from Asser in understanding Boethius. That he finally penetrated to Boethius' meaning his translation makes clear enough; but that he remade the *Consolation* in his own image is also apparent. He changed the five books of Latin prose with alternating rhyming sections into forty-two chapters of Old English prose with proem and epilogue; later, from this prose, he made another version translating all but nine of the Boethian meters into verse.[14] He saw in the Boethian Good the Christian God. Despite his dependence upon Latin commentaries,[14a] he personalized paraphrases throughout by the addition of or substitution for illustrations, comments, metaphors, and similes. Among the most notable changes or additions are references to Christ, Christians, angels, and the devil. The hymn to the universal obedience of the Creation to the Creator, for example, reminds Alfred of the outstanding exception of the rebellious angels; and his simple but engaging expansion of the Orpheus and Eurydice story of Boethius III, meter 12, makes the moral allegory explicitly Christian. Orpheus, for Alfred, represents the penitent turning toward the light who looks back at his old sins (poor Eurydice!) and thus loses all he had hoped to gain; or the Titans piling Pelion on Ossa suggest Nimrod and the Tower of Babel. Lady Philosophy is metamorphosed into Wisdom, and Boethius himself occasionally becomes *Mod*, or Mind, as in Chapter XVII (Boe. II, prose 7), where the king

---

known the "consolatio" genre, of which Boethius' work is but one example —see J. E. Cross, *Neophil*, XLV (1961), 63–75.

14. Two MSS and a fragment survive: the Bodleian MS, containing the prose version, is of twelfth-century provenience—it is edited by W. J. Sedgefield, *King Alfred's Old English Version . . . Philosophiae* (Oxford, 1899), and translated by him into modern English (Oxford, 1900); the Cotton MS, containing the Old English *Meters*, is early tenth century— see under poetry.

14a. For recent discussion, see B. S. Donaghey, "The Sources of King Alfred's Translation of Boethius's *De Consolatione Philosophiae*," *Anglia*, LXXXII (1964), 23–57.

is clearly speaking on his own behalf about the duties of a monarch: of how he must have abundance for his "tools' (his men) of gifts, weapons, food, ale, and clothes; of how all must be ruled by Wisdom in a service which is freedom, not slavery; of how he desires to live so that after his life his memory will continue in the good works he has accomplished. The fusion of Germanic and Christian elements in this last passage may be seen elsewhere in the translation; for example, in the expansion of Boethius II, meter 7 (Alfred's Ch. XIX), the famous "Where now are the bones of Fabricius?" is supplemented by "What now are the bones of the famous and wise goldsmith, Weland? I call him wise, for the skillful man can never lose his skill, nor can he more easily be deprived of it than the sun may be moved from its place." The simple simile frequently becomes more fully developed, as in Chapter XXXIX, paragraph 7 (Boe. IV, prose 6), on the wheel of destiny:

> Just as on the axle of a wagon the wheels turn and the axle stands still and yet bears all the wagon and controls all the motion, so that the wheel turns around and the nave next to the axle moves more firmly and securely than the rim does; so the axle is the highest good, which we call God, and the best men move next to God just as the nave moves next to the axle. . . . [The simile continues, comparing the middle sort of men to the spokes, one end in the nave, and the other in the rim, now thinking of this life below, now looking upward toward the Divine, etc.]

Alfred's free rendering of Boethius did indeed make his translation more than either a "word by word, or sense by sense" version of the *Consolation*; it made it a literary and philosophical document in its own right.

The *Soliloquies* of St. Augustine of Hippo is the last translation generally ascribed to Alfred.[15] Mentioned by none of the

15. But see n. 6. The *Soliloquies* has been edited and translated, with a Latin text, by H. L. Hargrove, *King Alfred's Version of the Soliloquies of St. Augustine*, Yale Studies in English, XIII and XXII (1902, 1904); for criticism of this edition, see K. Jost, *Beiblatt zur Anglia*, XXXI (1920), 259–272, 280–290; XXII (1921), 8–16. Edited also by W. Endter in *BAP*, XI (1922).

English medieval chroniclers, including the indefatigable William of Malmesbury, this work is nonetheless attributed to Alfred in the sole surviving manuscript of twelfth-century provenience (the first of the two codices bound together in the famous Cotton Vitellius A.xv—see Ch. IV); and its subject matter and style are similar to those of the Alfredian Boethius.[16] Augustine's work, in the form of a dialogue between himself and Reason in two books, is a search for God and for belief in the eternal life of the soul. At the end, Augustine questions Reason about the growth of the intellect after death, and is referred to his own work *De Videndo Dei* (*On Seeing God*). Alfred, with his passion for knowledge and belief in the temporal efficacy of wisdom, was dissatisfied with the somewhat inconclusive ending of the Latin *Soliloquies*. He therefore turned to the Augustinian piece alluded to and made a third book, describing in some measure the life of the soul after death—the good soul in glory and the wicked damned, according to the merits of each while they inhabited bodies on this earth—and including arguments for the eternal value of wisdom attained on this earth in the growth of the intellect and its contribution to the happiness in heaven. In his translation, Alfred begins by following the Latin text fairly closely, but soon he is wandering afield, drawing not only upon Augustine's *De Videndo Dei* but upon his *De Civitate Dei*, upon Gregory's *Dialogues, Moralia*, and *Homilies*, and upon Jerome's *Vulgate* and *Commentary on Luke*. In this sense his *Soliloquies* is a chrestomathy, or a gathering of blooms or flowers, as the *explicits* designate Books I and II; and some scholars have tried to associate this work with the lost *Enchiridion*, or *Handbook*.

Among the memorable additions to his source in Book I is Alfred's elaboration, in Augustine's long prayer to God near the beginning, of the passage on the rule of God through cyclical alternation: Augustine talks about the seasons and the stars,

16. See F. G. Hubbard, "The Relation of the 'Blooms of King Alfred' to the Anglo-Saxon Translation of Boethius," *MLN*, IX (1894), 321–342.

but Alfred adds the seas and the rivers, and then comments that some things in their cycles become not exactly what they were:

> but others come in their place, as leaves on trees; and apples, grass, and plants and trees grow old and sere and others come, wax green, and bloom, and ripen; wherefore they in turn begin to wither. And so all the beasts and birds. . . . Yea, even men's bodies grow old, just as other created things age; but as they formerly more worthily live than trees or other beasts, so they also more worthily shall arise on Judgment Day. . . .

There is also an elaborate metaphor on the ship (man) and the anchor (the virtues), and on the many paths to the king's palace (wisdom). But perhaps the most interesting of all the Alfredian contributions is the Preface, where in the form of a parable of driving his wagon into the forest to gather wood from the finest trees for making tools and dwellings, the king describes his own lifetime search for knowledge and his translation of books; and he exhorts others who are capable and "who have many wagons" to go into that forest and collect fair beams wherewith to build "many a fair wall, to set up many a peerless house, and to build a fair town" where they may dwell happily and easily in winter and in summer "as I have not yet done."[17] Alfred, in short, explicitly recognizes that he has made but a start for himself and for his people, and urges others in the path of temporal and spiritual wisdom that he sought out and found. It is tempting to see in this Preface a humble yet noble conclusion to the hopes Alfred had expressed for English learning in his Preface to the *Pastoral Care*.

Of other works attributed to the king, the prose Psalms (nos. 1–50) in the unique manuscript of the Paris Psalter can with most probability be so credited, for not only does William of Malmesbury tell us that Alfred left at his death an unfinished translation of the Psalter but the vocabulary, phraseology, and syntax of the unfinished prose psalms show close similarity to

17. For commentary, see S. Potter, "King Alfred's Last Preface," in *Philologica: the Malone Anniversary Studies*, eds. T. A. Kirby and H. B. Woolf (Baltimore, 1949), pp. 25–30.

the style of the Boethius and the *Pastoral Care*.[18] The rendering varies from close translation to translation with commentary (e.g., *Ps.* 44), the text generally based on the Roman Psalter, but occasionally on the Gallican, which gradually, though not completely (e.g., the *Eadwine Psalter* of c. 1150), supplanted the Roman in English churches with the Benedictine Reform of the later tenth century (see Ch. III). The *Proverbs of Alfred*, unlike the *Psalms*, are not really Alfredian: they are a twelfth-century compilation ascribed to the king who, like Solomon in religious tradition, embodied for the English the high ideal of wisdom. The proverbs seem to be drawn from Old Testament Books of Wisdom and the popular Latin *Distichs of Cato*.[19]

Alfred's contribution to English history and literature extends beyond his translations and those he directly inspired. The *Anglo-Saxon Chronicle* (*Old English Annals*), various versions of which survive in seven manuscripts,[20] is usually, though not confidently, attributed to Alfred's instigation; at least the rapid dissemination of the work to centers of learning in the kingdom probably can be laid to his encouragement of the project. The oldest manuscript, the Parker, or Winchester, MS (the "A" version of the editions), is written up to almost

18. The Psalms have been edited by J. W. Bright and R. L. Ramsay, *Liber Psalmorum: the West-Saxon Psalms* (Boston and London, 1907). The entire *Paris Psalter* has been reproduced in facsimile in *EEMSF*, VIII, ed. B. Colgrave et al. (1958). For commentary, see J. I'a. Bromwich, "Who was the translator of the prose portion of the Paris Psalter?" in *The Early Cultures of North-West Europe*, eds. Sir C. Fox and B. Dickins (Cambridge, 1950).

19. See H. P. South, *The Proverbs of Alfred* (New York, 1931); and esp. O. S. A. Arngart, *The Proverbs of Alfred*, 2 vols. (Lund, 1942, 1955), and "The Distichs of Cato and the Proverbs of Alfred," *KHVL Arsberättelse* 1951–52, pp. 95–118.

20. All the versions are edited and translated by B. Thorpe, in 2 vols. (London, 1861), but the most used edition is C. Plummer's *Two of the Saxon Chronicles Parallel*, 2 vols. (Oxford, 1892, 1899), reprtd. 1952 with bibliographical note, etc., by D. Whitelock. For separate editions of the different MSS, see p. xxv of *The Anglo-Saxon Chronicle*, trans. D. Whitelock et al. (n. 1). The best translation is the one just mentioned; it puts into parallel columns and footnotes the variations of the several MS traditions. Also good is the translation of G. N. Garmonsway (Everyman's Library, corrected ed., 1955).

the end of the 891 entry in one hand of the late ninth century or early tenth, and presumably drew upon earlier annals as well as upon the epitome at the end of Bede's *Ecclesiastical History*, an epitome of an unidentified "universal" history, some genealogies, and the like. Of particular interest is the entry for 755, in which the feud between Cynewulf and Cyneheard is detailed in an archaic prose that suggests an oral narrative tradition or an earlier written source.[21] Whereas most of these early entries simply characterize the years they represent, the Cynewulf-Cyneheard story is epic or dramatic in nature, in its stress on *comitatus* loyalty vs. blood relationships and in its political overtones. Alfred's wars against the Danes after the resumption of hostilities in 893, till 896, written in a different hand, are less dramatically but nonetheless eloquently narrated. Among other fine accounts in this more-than-pedestrian journalism are the "D" and "E" renditions of the difficulties Edward the Confessor had in 1051 with Godwine and his sons over Eustace of Boulogne (Edward's brother-in-law) and the actions of his men in Dover. Both texts are northern recensions of the *Chronicle* till 1031, but after that, while "D" continues to be northern (probably compiled at York), "E" seems to have found its way to Canterbury; as a result, the "D" text shows a decided partisanship for Edward, while the "E" is more favorably disposed to Godwine, who held the earldom of Kent, Sussex, and Wessex; yet the sense of an English nationality in both versions is remarkable.[22] The poems inserted in the *Chronicle*, especially *The Battle of Brunanburh*, the entry for the year 937, will be dealt with later, but mention of them here will indicate something further of the heterogeneity of tastes and styles incorporated in the *Chronicle* by its many contributory hands.

Perhaps also inspired by the translating activity of Alfred's

21. On the possibility of an oral prose saga, see C. E. Wright (I, 11). The description of the prose as "archaic" is D. Whitelock's, in *The Anglo-Saxon Chronicle*, p. xxii; the latest commentator, T. H. Towers, "Thematic Unity in the Story of Cynewulf and Cyneheard," *JEGP*, LXII (1963), 310–316, describes it as "vigorous and living" prose.
22. See R. W. Chambers, *On Continuity* (Int., 4).

reign was the late ninth- or early tenth-century medical text known today as *Bald's Leechbook*.[23] The connection with Alfred comes near the end of the second book, where a number of prescriptions are said to have been ordered told to King Alfred by Elias, Patriarch of Jerusalem from about 879 to 907—we know from other sources that Alfred received gifts from Elias and probably had other communications with him. The first thirty chapters of Book I of the physician Bald's text give prescriptions for infections of the body in descending order, from head to feet; the rest of the chapters deal with various ailments, one whole chapter being devoted to bloodletting. Book II is more learned than I, containing symptoms and diagnoses as well as prescriptions for internal disorders. Book III, largely repeating the first, contains many more charms or magic incantations (on these, see the discussion following on poetry). The *Leechbook* hardly qualifies as literature, but occasionally a dry medical humor seeps through, as in the comment at the end of a prescription for adder bite that entails the use of bark from Paradise: "then he that wrote this book said that it was difficult to obtain."

One last work may be mentioned as possibly connected with the Alfredian circle: the Old English *Martyrology*, five fragments of which survive.[24] This is a ninth-century translation of an unknown Latin text; the dialect is clearly Mercian, and there is a slight possibility that the translation was carried out by one of Alfred's imported Mercian scholars (but see below). Also of late ninth-century and of Mercian provenience is *The Life of St. Chad*, extant only in the twelfth-century MS Hatton 116, transcribed in Worcester, the last important stronghold of Anglo-Saxon learning and culture in Norman England. This

23. The MS is possibly from about 950. Text printed in O. Cockayne, *Leechdoms, Wort-Cunning, and Star-Craft of Early England* (London, 1864–66), II, 2–364. Reproduced in facsimile in *EEMSF*, v, ed. C. E. Wright (1955). See also G. Storms, *Anglo-Saxon Magic* (The Hague, 1948).

24. Four of these are edited by G. Herzfeld, EETS 116 (1900), the fifth by C. Sisam, "An Early Fragment of the Old English *Martyrology*," *RES*, N. S. IV (1953), 209–220.

homily is translated ultimately from the account of the Bishop of Mercia from 669–672 in Bede's *Ecclesiastical History*, IV, 2 and 3. It incorporates certain stereotypes from the saints' lives, however, the most important of which are the introductory and concluding lines taken from Sulpicius Severus' *Life of St. Martin*.[25]

Alfred has usually been acclaimed as the father of English prose; and certainly the vigorous activity of translation associated with his name, as well as the original vernacular *Chronicle*, suggests his right to that title. In addition, Alfredian prose, as represented in the Hatton MS of the *Pastoral Care*, the Parker MS of the *Chronicle*, and the Tollemache MS of the Orosius— all contemporaneous or early tenth century—has been used to establish early West Saxon as "standard" Old English for many an Old English grammar.[26] But there seem to be valid objections to accepting Alfred's claim to prosaic paternity, as well as to considering early West Saxon as a norm for Old English. On the latter point, Alfred's dialect is anything but "pure" West Saxon—the earlier political ascendancy of Mercia, along with the amanuenses from various locales employed by Alfred, may in part account for the admixture of Anglian forms in Alfred's West Saxon. Further, Alfred was no grammarian, unlike his literary heir Ælfric a century later; and Ælfric's language (late West Saxon) is for this reason and for others now preferred by many linguists as the norm for the study of the language.[27] On the former point, translations into English were made before Alfred's time: Bede, we remember, undertook several, though nothing survives, and his efforts we can be sure were nothing so programmatic as Alfred's. The great king's

25. See *The Life of St. Chad*, ed. R. Vleeskruyer (Amsterdam, 1953), containing parallel texts of the Tanner MS of the OE Bede and the Moore MS of the Latin Bede. An earlier edition, by A. Napier, in *Anglia*, x (1888), 131–156, is still valuable.

26. E.g., *The Elements of Old English* by S. Moore and T. A. Knott, 10th ed. (Ann Arbor, Mich., 1955).

27. E.g., Quirk and Wrenn (I, 5). See C. L. Wrenn, " 'Standard' Old English," in *Transactions of the Philological Society for 1933* (London, 1933), pp. 65–88.

importation of many Mercian scholars, however, does seem to imply that a Mercian "school" of translation may have existed earlier in the ninth century: the *Martyrology* and *Chad* point in this direction. The most recent scholarship in this area, moreover, would link the Mercian Wærferth's translation of Gregory's *Dialogues* and the Tanner MS of the Old English Bede with these two works, and even see ninth-century Mercian originals behind such pieces as the prose *Guthlac*, *The Blickling Homilies*, the *Leechbook*, and the prose texts in the *Beowulf* MS.[28] Whether or not we accept the notion of a Mercian tradition of vernacular prose antedating Alfred, there is no question that the vocabulary and style, as well as the dominant phonological features, of the Mercian texts differ from those of the more strictly Alfredian. Particularly noticeable in the former is more consciously rhythmic phrasing and more extensive use of the poetic device of alliteration, a style that was to find its finest flowering in the works of two rather different practitioners of the late tenth and early eleventh centuries, Ælfric and Wulfstan.

Before turning to these two men and to other significant works of the third and final period of Anglo-Saxon literary prose, we might briefly review the literary continuity and change from the Age of Bede to the Age of Alfred. First we may note that the two dominant literary genres, chronicle-history and hagiography-biography, continue, both in translations of Latin literature and in "original" vernacular prose. Religious edification in tractates and in the Bible itself finds continuance in translations like the *Pastoral Care* and the *West Saxon Psalms*. And scientific writing, now not on time computation or on the "nature of things" but on medical prescriptions, flourishes also. But the large volume of epistolary correspondence seems to have shrunk

---

28. R. J. Menner, "The Anglian Vocabulary of the Blickling Homilies," in *Philologica*, pp. 56–64, and R. Vleeskruyer, esp. pp. 39–71. See also O. Funke, "Studien zur Alliterierenden und Rhythmisierenden Prosa in der älteren altenglischen Homiletik," *Anglia*, LXXX (1962), 9–36. For some reservations about Vleeskruyer's Mercian and early-dating enthusiasm, see C. Sisam, *RES*, N. S. VI (1955), 302–303.

(though many of the letters of Alfred's time, being in the vernacular, may not have survived), and there seems, at least on the basis of surviving manuscripts, to have been little interest in grammar and rhetoric—a deficiency that Ælfric was to recognize. But a philosophical interest emerges with Alfred, in the Boethian and Augustinian translations—an intellectual refinement and sophistication that goes beyond the more practical and political ideological disputations and admonitions of the seventh- and eighth-century Anglo-Latin writers.

III

Ælfric, Wulfstan, and Other Late Prose

ALFRED's immediate political heirs consolidated and expanded his territorial gains, but though they made gifts to the Church and were not hostile to learning, they did not advance his educational and cultural program. Edward the Elder (d. 924) succeeded in uniting the whole kingdom as far north as the Humber under his rule, though it cost him unceasing vigilance and campaigning to do so, first against some of his own rebellious subjects and then against the Danes. Edward's son Æthelstan (d. 939) climaxed tenth-century English martial prowess with his victory at the Battle of Brunanburh in 937. But in these years the only "literary" activity we can be sure of was the continuance of the *Anglo-Saxon Chronicle,* and the only datable piece of much literary value was the poem celebrating Brunanburh and included therein. It was not till the peaceful reign of Edgar (959–975), Alfred's great grandson, that the advent of religious reform laid the foundation for a cultural renascence, a quickening that was to produce the outstanding scholar and prose stylist of the late Old English period, Ælfric, monk of Cerne(1) and Abbot of Eynsham (c. 955–c. 1012).[1]

1. The usual date given for Ælfric's death is c. 1020–25, but P. A. M. Clemoes, in "The Chronology of Ælfric's Work," in *The Anglo-Saxons: Studies Presented to Bruce Dickins,* ed. P. Clemoes (London, 1959), p. 245, makes a good case for an earlier date; see also D. Whitelock, "Two Notes on Ælfric and Wulfstan," *MLR,* xxxviii (1943), 124, and, as a corollary, K. Sisam (II, 6), pp. 170–171. On the question of Ælfric's

The monastic reform of the later tenth century was long overdue. Since the "golden age" of Wearmouth-Jarrow and York had departed with the onslaught of the Danish invasions at the end of the eighth century, the moral and cultural force of monasticism and of the Benedictine discipline had languished in England.[2] The extent to which spiritual dissolution had set in may be seen in Ælfric's perhaps somewhat exaggerated account of the condition of the community of Winchester in 963: "There were at that time in the Old Minster, the seat of its Bishop, clerics of evil habits, so lost in pride, arrogance, and indulgence that some of them refused to celebrate Mass in their order. Wives they had taken unlawfully, and these they cast off to take others. Constantly they gave themselves to gluttony and drunkenness."[3] But with the accession of Edgar and his raising of Dunstan, Abbot of Glastonbury, to the post of Archbishop of Canterbury, the English Church became revitalized.[4] With Dunstan (d. 988), two other clergymen were prominent in the English monastic reform: Æthelwold, Abbot of Abingdon and Bishop of Winchester (d. 984), and Oswald, Bishop of Worcester and Archbishop of York (d. 992). Æthelwold translated the Benedictine Rule and

---

identity, there has been no change in critical opinion from C. L. White's conclusions that he was neither the Ælfric who was Archbishop of Canterbury nor the one who was Archbishop of York: see her *Ælfric: A New Study of His Life and Writings* (Boston, 1898), pp. 88–100.

2. See Dom D. Knowles (I, 8), 1st ed. (1940), pp. 24, 31–36. For a view that the Church itself, as distinct from monasticism, was firmly rooted in the English social order, and of not-inconsequent moral force in these times, see J. V. Fisher, "The Church in England between the Death of Bede and the Danish Invasions," *TRHS*, 5th ser., 2 (1952), 1–19.

3. *Chronicon Monasterii de Abingdon*; translation quoted from E. S. Duckett, *Saint Dunstan of Canterbury* (New York, 1955), p. 119. It should be noted that a parallel dissolution had occurred on the Continent; the English clergy were not alone in their iniquity.

4. On Dunstan's life and times, see J. A. Robinson, *The Times of Saint Dunstan* (Oxford, 1923), and more recently E. S. Duckett (n. 3). A facsimile of Dunstan's Glastonbury classbook has been edited by R. W. Hunt in *Umbrae Codicum Occidentalium*, iv (Amsterdam, 1961); it contains the well-known full-page picture of Dunstan kneeling at Christ's feet, a drawing perhaps by the saint himself.

probably executed the *Regularis Concordia*, the outgrowth of the Synodal Council of Winchester, about 970.[5] It is to Ælfric, his pupil at Winchester, that we look, however, for the literary embodiment of this religious and educational reformation.

In the face of—or perhaps because of—a resurgence of Viking activity in the late tenth century, that was to lead to ultimate Danish conquest of England in the eleventh, Ælfric labored to strengthen his people by book learning against the horrors and temptations of the perilous times. His educational program was double-pronged: he wanted to keep alive the Latin tradition of the Church, hence his Latin *Grammar*, *Glossary*, and *Colloquy* for the oblates in the monasteries; he wanted also to help those in the present clergy who did not know Latin well enough to perform their duties with a clearer understanding of the Christian *Weltanschauung* embracing the Creation, Fall, Redemption, and Judgment—an objective that gave rise to his translations into English of homilies, saints' lives, Old Testament books, and canonical letters designed for the clergy's guidance. This program bears a similarity to Alfred's of the century previous, but it was more systematized and devoted to a specifically religious cause.

Ælfric's accomplishments may be viewed in three stages: the first concludes with the publication of his *Lives of the Saints* in 1002; it begins with the two series of *Catholic Homilies* (989, 992) and includes a translation of Bede's *De Temporibus Anni* and of the *Heptateuch*, the Latin works mentioned above, and the *Letter to Wulfsige* (in which Ælfric attempted to clarify for the Benedictines whom Wulfsige had invited to Sherborne essential doctrine and incumbent duties). The second stage, 1002–1005, consists of more homilies and "occasional" pieces, the result of his reputation by this time; these pieces he used to expand his instructions to parish priests, to state the fundamentals of monastic life, to offer moral guidance, and to synthesize his earlier themes. The last stage, after his

5. For the Latin text and English translation of the *Concordia*, see Dom Symons, *Regularis Concordia* (Edinburgh, 1953).

establishment as Abbot of Eynsham, contains still more homilies, the Latin *Vita Sancti Æthelwoldi*,[6] two pastoral letters to
Archbishop Wulfstan (in Latin and in English), and the *Letter
to Sigeweard* ("On the Old and New Testament").[7] Those
works which have most engaged the attention of students and
critics of Old English literature have been the *Catholic Homilies*,
the *Lives of the Saints*, the *Heptateuch*, and the *Colloquy*, and
it is to these that we now turn.[8]

The two series of *Catholic Homilies* and the *Lives of the
Saints*[9] may be commented on together for at least two reasons.
First, they were viewed by Ælfric as something of a continuum,
whereby he first made accessible in English an account of and
commentary on the facts and doctrines of Christianity, including the Scriptures, the origins and spread of Christianity, and
the lives of its saints. Many of the "Homilies" are really saints'
lives and many of the latter incorporate homilies; and Ælfric's
Preface to the latter work explains that he is now devoting himself to saints celebrated among the monks themselves, whereas
formerly he had been concerned with those honored on festival
days. Second, they reveal a development in Ælfric's methodology
and style; and it is Ælfric's mature style for which he is celebrated as a literary figure, a style which, as we observed in
Chapter II, is taken by many scholars as the standard not only
of late West Saxon, or classical Old English, but as the norm
for the teaching of the language.

These three series of homilies and saints' lives consist of
approximately forty sermons each. Their sources are named by

6. There are two versions of this *Life*, the longer attributed to
Wulfstan, the precentor of Winchester. Critical disagreement exists as
to which has precedence in point of time; see the Introduction to the
translation of the shorter Life (Ælfric's) in *EHD*, pp. 831–839.

7. I have followed the dating indicated by Clemoes (n. 1). For
a somewhat different chronology, see Sisam (II, 6).

8. C. L. White's *Ælfric* is still the most comprehensive study. For
more recent bibliographical material and considerations, see G. K. Anderson (Int., 5), pp. 308–339, and Clemoes.

9. For the best edition of the former, see B. Thorpe, ed. *The
Homilies of the Anglo-Saxon Church*, I (London, 1844); of the latter,
see W. W. Skeat, ed. *Ælfric's Lives of the Saints*, EETS 76, 82, 94, 114
(1881–1900).

Ælfric himself: mainly Gregory the Great, St. Augustine, St. Jerome, and Bede—though Ælfric may have found the homilies of these forerunners conveniently collected in some version of the popular homiliary of Paul the Deacon.[10] But Ælfric, though no innovator or speculative philosopher or theologian, was also no mere translator: he expanded, condensed, embroidered in the light of his specific purpose to expound to Englishmen the truths of Christianity. Sometimes these truths were controversial: Ælfric preached the Eucharistic belief of Ratramnus, for example, that the bread and wine were mystically symbolic of the body and blood of Christ, a view that was to be condemned, ultimately, at the Synod of Vercelli in 1050 in favor of the doctrine of transubstantiation. Yet Ælfric was extremely conservative and careful in his teachings, never asserting dogma (such as the Assumption of the Virgin) that he had doubts about. In handling his Biblical material, Ælfric condensed his sources to make effective narrative and to heighten dramatic potentialities as well as to remove unfamiliar elements which might cause confusion in the faithful.[11] To this end, too, he, like the Old English poets before him, used Old English social, political, and legal nomenclature to translate Biblical relationships and even the smallest features of daily life of Scriptural times. He used similes from these areas, too, as had Alfred, though the sources of his similes were more likely Patristic rather than "life," as when he compares the joys in heaven over the conversion of a sinner to "the greater love which a chieftain feels in battle for the soldier who after flight boldly overcomes his adversary, than for him who never took to flight, nor yet in

10. See C. J. Smetana, "Ælfric and the Early Medieval Homiliary," *Traditio*, xv (1959), 163–204, and J. E. Cross, "Ælfric and the Mediæval Homiliary—Objection and Contribution," *Studier utg. av KHVL: Scripta Minora* (1961–62: 4). Father Smetana observes that Ælfric does not maintain a strict distinction between *sermon* (a discourse on a dogmatic or moral issue for instructional purposes) and *homily* (a commentary and exegesis on Scriptural text). Of the eighty-five actual homilies in the *Catholic Homilies*, he further points out, fifty-six may properly be termed exegetical; twelve are topical sermons and expanded Gospel texts; seventeen are saints' lives. See also his "Ælfric and the Homiliary of Haymo of Halberstadt," *Traditio*, xvii (1961), 457–469.

11. See Charles R. Davis, "Biblical Translations in Ælfric's *Catholic Homilies*," unpubl. diss. (New York University, 1949).

any conflict performed any deed of valor" (*CH*, ɪ, p. 343).[12]
Still, Ælfric followed in his methodology the typological-alle-
gorical-symbolic tradition of exegesis that he found in his originals. In *CH*, ɪɪ, page 282, for example, he explains the crossing
of the Red Sea on a fourfold level of meaning: literally, the
crossing of the Israelites from servitude to the promised land;
allegorically, the passage of Christ from the "middle-earth" to
the heavenly Father; tropologically, the moving in this present
life from sin to virtue; and anagogically, the crossing in the next
life after our resurrection to eternal life in Christ.[13]

The first series of *Catholic Homilies* is largely Scriptural
and exegetical in content, while the second is more legendary,
less didactic, and more concerned with the appearance of
Christianity in England. In the latter and in the *Lives of the
Saints*, the narrative assumes greater prominence than the
moralizing, the saints' lives in particular resembling later medieval tales of wonder. Stylistically in these three series, Ælfric
moves from a prose heightened occasionally by alliteration and
other rhetorical effects to an almost regularly metrical style:
balanced, antithetical, synonymic, and richly alliterative—so
much so that earlier critics disputed as to whether the *Lives*
was not meant to be poetry (Skeat printed many of the *Lives*,
or portions of them, as such, and Jost has reverted to this practice in his edition of Wulfstan's *Institutes of Polity*—see below). Whether Ælfric derived this style which, though found in
other Old English prose, even to some extent in Alfredian prose,
has come to be his hallmark, from the rhymed Latin prose of
the time (his familiarity with it is evidenced by his Latin *Vita
Sancti Æthelwoldi*), with a substitution of alliteration for the
rhyme and even an attempt to capture Latin rhythm, particularly the *cursus*; or whether he drew mainly upon his native Eng-

12. Ælfric's source for this simile was Gregory, *Hom. XXXIV in
Evang.* §4. I gratefully acknowledge Dr. J. E. Cross's identification of this
source and his many helpful comments on other portions of this text.
13. See H. Schelp, "Die Deutungstradition in Ælfrics Homilæ
Catholicæ," *Archiv*, cxcvɪ (1960), 273–295. On the fourfold method of
interpretation, see B. Smalley, *The Study of the Bible in the Middle
Ages* (London, 1941).

lish poetic and prose heritage, however inspired he was by Latin literature, is still a matter of debate among literary historians.[14]

The *Heptateuch* (so named by Thwaites, its first editor, in 1698) is a translation of and commentary on the Pentateuch, Joshua, and Judges. Ælfric's actual share in the Pentateuch translation is still not conclusively established.[15] But we know he was not as happy translating the Old Testament Vulgate as he had been in his work on the New. He was afraid, for one thing, that *sum dysig man* 'some foolish man' might think he could live under the New Law as the patriarchs had lived under the Old. Still, he acceded to the request of his powerful patron Æthelweard that he do the job, and he performed in his typical fashion, interchanging epitomes of the history in the Old Testament with more extensive translation, and omitting "catalogs" and abstruse passages. At the end of his paraphrase of Judges, which treats in detail only of Samson, Ælfric updates his material by expounding the typology-allegory of Samson, commenting on the consuls and Caesars of Rome, especially on Constantine and the elder and younger Theodosius, and concluding with a paean of praise for Alfred, Æthelstan, and Edgar, the three "victorious" kings of Wessex and England.

Finally we must look at the *Colloquy*, with which most students of Old English become acquainted early in their study of the language, despite the fact that the Old English gloss they read is not Ælfric's but presumably the work of a cleric of a generation or two later. Written as a supplement to his Latin *Grammar* and *Glossary*, the *Colloquy* is the first use of the

14. The former view is enunciated by G. H. Gerould, "Abbot Ælfric's Rhythmic Prose," *MP*, xxii (1925), 353–366; the latter by D. Bethurum, "The Form of Ælfric's *Lives of the Saints*," *SP*, xxix (1932), 515–533. A more recent commentator, R. Vleeskruyer (II, 25), stresses the use of Old English poetic formulas and alliteration as the basis of Old English prose style, and sees Ælfric (and Wulfstan) as continuing and developing a Mercian (rather than Alfredian) vernacular prose tradition of the ninth century. For differences of opinion among literary historians, see K. Malone, p. 101, and G. K. Anderson, pp. 311–312 (Int., 5).

15. See J. Raith, "Ælfric's Share in the Old English *Pentateuch*," *RES*, N. S. iii (1952), 305–314.

"direct method" of language instruction. It is the most engaging and literarily effective example of a type of medieval dialogue that "became the drudge of monastic pedagogues, and in the role of a literary Cinderella laboured in obscurity in monastic classrooms to help boys learn their lessons."[16] The realism of this work has often been noted, as has its sociological picture of the occupational strata of Old English society. Less noted has been its fine organization and structure, dramatic in effect, with its pairing and contrasting, for example, of the king's bold hunter and the independent, timid fisherman who would rather catch fish he can kill than hunt those (whales) which can destroy him and his companions; and with its lively disputation toward the end about which occupation is the most essential. Ælfric's work is a good illustration of how even the most unpromising material, from a modern point of view, can become "literature" in the hands of a master craftsman.

Ælfric has until recently received much more attention than his colleague and contemporary Wulfstan. But the great administrator and adviser to kings (Æthelred and Cnut), the legalist and homilist, has fully received his due in the researches of the last fifteen years.[17] His first appearance on the religious scene is as Bishop of London from 996 to 1002; from 1002 to his death in 1023 he was Archbishop of York and Bishop of Worcester, though he relinquished the latter see in 1016, or at least had it ruled by a suffragan. Though there is no record of his belonging to any of the well-known eleventh-century monastic houses, Wulfstan was a Benedictine and was buried at Ely, as the one medieval account of his life, in the twelfth-

16. G. N. Garmonsway, "The Development of the Colloquy," in *The Anglo-Saxons* (n. 1), p. 249. The best edition is Mr. Garmonsway's (London, 1939).

17. The most significant works: D. Bethurum, *The Homilies of Wulfstan* (Oxford, 1957); K. Jost, *Wulfstanstudien*, Swiss Studies in English 23 (Bern, 1950), and *Die "Institutes of Polity, Civil and Ecclesiastical,"* Swiss Studies in English 47 (Bern, 1959); D. Whitelock, ed. *Sermo Lupi ad Anglos*, 3rd ed. (London, 1964); A. McIntosh, "Wulfstan's Prose," PBA, 1949, xxxv (1950), 109–142. For earlier editions and further bibliography, see these works and the following notes.

century *Historia Eliensis,* informs us.[18] During his tenure as Bishop of London he established his reputation as a preacher, probably with his eschatological homilies—the approach of the millennium and the incursions of the Danes gave rise to a rash of such homilies; in this period his nom de plume *Lupus* appears on documents for the first time. As Archbishop of York, he instituted reforms in the northern Church, which had suffered severely from Danish depredations, and probably helped rebuild the York library by encouraging manuscript collection. As adviser to and lawmaker for Æthelred from 1008 to 1012, he concerned himself with the problem of moral regeneration; Codes V–X *Æthelred,* for example, attempt to provide legal sanctions for the infringement of Christian ethics. The presence of heathen Danes in England made Wulfstan conscious that the amalgamation of civil and ecclesiastical laws, such as existed in the Continental Carolingian laws, would not suffice for England; and in his legal writings—the *Canons of Edgar,* the *Peace of Edward and Guthrum,* the *Institutes of Polity,* and *I* and *II Cnut*—the concept of the division yet interrelation between divine and civil obedience and jurisdiction becomes more and more explicit.[19]

The *Institutes of Polity* is Wulfstan's greatest accomplishment in the fields of law and politics. Three main manuscripts survive, indicating a first (*I Polity*) form and a greatly expanded revision (*II Polity*).[20] This work defines the duties of all classes of men, though it does not include the specific lay obligations of thegns, *ceorlas,* and slaves except as they impinge upon their religious duties. Beginning with the responsibilities of the king,

18. Wulfstan, Archbishop of York and Bishop of Worcester and homiletic writer (Wulfstan II of York), should not be confused with St. Wulfstan, Bishop of Worcester (d. 1095) (Wulfstan II of Worcester), the last of the Anglo-Saxon bishops in Norman England.

19. The *Canons* was Wulfstan's first major work, a learned and comprehensive set of instructions to his secular clergy to combat the abuses he had earlier preached against. See R. G. Fowler, " 'Archbishop Wulfstan's Commonplace-Book' and the *Canons of Edgar,*" *MÆ,* xxxii (1963), 1–10.

20. Jost, *Polity;* a valuable critical summary and review by D. Whitelock appears in *RES,* N. S. xii (1961), 61–66.

Wulfstan moves to the doctrine (taken from Ælfric's *Letter to Sigeweard*) of the three supports of the throne: preachers, workers, and warriors—then to the duties of those in authority, starting with the highest ecclesiasts, and moving to secular government in the persons of such as earls, reeves, judges, and lawyers. By defining the limits of power, Wulfstan tries to clarify the interrelationship of the Church and the secular state. Probably also by Wulfstan, at least as a rewriting—an attribution made by a study of style—is the *Rectitudines Singularum Personarum* and its second part *Gerefa*.[21] If this attribution is correct, it would nicely complement the *Institutes*, treating as it does of the lay duties of tenants of a great fief to their temporal lord and in more detail of the manorial duties of the reeve.

Students of English literature, however, have rightly been most interested in Wulfstan as a homilist. Unlike Ælfric's, Wulfstan's sermons (they are really more sermon than homily —see n. 10) were not written around the calendar of saints' days; Miss Bethurum (n. 17) groups them around subjects: eschatology, the Christian faith, archiepiscopal functions, and evil days. It is one of the last group (Miss Bethurum's xx) that has made the greatest impression upon readers, the famous *Sermo Lupi ad Anglos*.[22] This "Sermon of Wolf to the English," extant in five manuscripts, was preached in the troublesome times between Æthelred's expulsion in 1013 and his death in 1016, most likely in 1014. The pulpit orator is nowhere more thunderous than in this denunciation of the English for their sins, sins which had occasioned their destructive persecution by the Danes. Toward the end of his sermon, Wulfstan makes specific mention of Gildas' earlier excoriation of the Britons for their sinful responsibility for the Anglo-Saxon persecutions; actually, he took this Gildas reference from Alcuin, who had

21. See D. Bethurum, "Episcopal Magnificence in the Eleventh Century," in *AGB*, pp. 162–170. The text is edited by F. Liebermann (II, 2), I, 444–455.

22. In addition to her separate edition (n. 17), Miss Whitelock furnishes a translation in *EHD*, item 240, from which I cite below.

used it to point the same moral to the monks at Lindisfarne after the Viking raids of 793! Wulfstan begins:

> Beloved men, realize what is true: this world is in haste and the end approaches; and therefore in the world things go from bad to worse, and so it must of necessity deteriorate greatly on account of the people's sins before the coming of Antichrist, and indeed it will then be dreadful and terrible far and wide throughout the world.

Over and over again he calls attention to treachery and disloyalty as the cardinal sin: "There has been little loyalty among men, though they spoke fair enough"; "For now for many years, as it may seem, there have been in this country many injustices and wavering loyalties among men everywhere"; "Nor had anyone had loyal intentions toward another as justly he should, but almost everyone has deceived and injured another by word or deed"; "For here in the country, there are great disloyalties both in matter of Church and State . . . [he proceeds to some detail, including mention of the death of Edward the Martyr and the expulsion of Æthelred]"; "Many are forsworn and greatly perjured, and pledges are broken again and again." And, in somewhat atypical fashion for Wulfstan, he resorts to realistic detail to characterize the evil days that have befallen the English; for example, "And often ten or a dozen, one after another, insult disgracefully the thegn's wife, and sometimes his daughter or near kinswoman, whilst he looks on, who considered himself brave and mighty and stout enough before that happened."

In this sermon as in others, Wulfstan's method of composition was careful and painstaking: he collected Latin selections on the topic from the most authoritative sources and then translated and expanded them into a sermon, pausing in the development to reflect on religious or ethical truths suggested by his sources. Rhetorical questions or exclamations frequently introduce such reflections.

Realistic detail, or specificity, which Wulfstan generally felt unsuitable for his sermons (perhaps he had a "Puritan" fear that the audience would enjoy the details for their own sake?), is more characteristic of Ælfric. In other ways, too, the archbishop's subject matter and style differ from the abbot's. In line with his avoidance of realism and his practical morality, he does not use metaphors, similes, or analogical interpretation of Scripture. He eschews the lives of saints, and except where his sources make it requisite, he avoids straight narrative technique. Though he uses a rhythmic prose which superficially resembles that developed by Ælfric from his *Lives of the Saints* onward, Wulfstan intensifies his rhythms into a strong two-stress system based on independent syntactic units, or at least on breath groups, that somewhat resembles that of classical Old English verse.[23] He heightens the emotional pitch of his sermons still further by a profusion of intensifying adjectives and adverbs; and he uses more alliteration and rhyme and a greater parallelism of word and clause than Ælfric. Rhetorically, he depends heavily on the repetitive devices prescribed in medieval manuals of rhetoric, such as Alcuin's, which were mainly based on Cicero. And he has certain pet phrases and tricks of expression, as well as favorite vocabulary items, that distinguish him from Ælfric (for example, the "beloved men" salutation at the beginning of the *Sermo Lupi ad Anglos*, and the use of *dryhten* 'Lord' where Ælfric has *haelend* 'Savior').[24] A short passage from Ælfric's *De Falsis Deis* ("On Heathen Gods"), and Wulfstan's rewriting of it for *his* sermon, will illustrate various of these differences:

Ælf.:   *An man waes eardigende/ on þam eglande Creta,// Saturnus gehaten,/ swiðlice and wælreow,// swa þæt he abat his sunan,/ þaþa hi geborene wæron,// and unfæderlice macode/ heora flæsc him to mete;// he læfde swaþeah/ ænne him to life,// þeahþe he abite/ his gebroðra onær.*

23. This style has been carefully analyzed by A. McIntosh (n. 17). For expansion and modification, see O. Funke, "Some Remarks on Wulfstan's Prose Rhythms," *ES*, XLIII (1962), 311–318. Jost edits major portions of the *Institutes of Polity* in two-stress lines to give reality to McIntosh's findings. See reservations in n. 25, below.

24. For a thorough study of Wulfstan's stylistic traits, see the sections on "The Canon" and on "Style" in Bethurum, *Homilies*. On pp. 93–94 Miss Bethurum gives a fine detailed analysis of a Wulfstanian sentence.

(There was a man dwelling on the Island Crete, called Saturn, cruel and bloodthirsty, so that he ate his sons as soon as they were born, and in an unpaternal way made their flesh his meat; he left, nevertheless, one alive, though he had eaten his brothers formerly.)

Wulf.: *An man wæs on geardagum// eardiende on þam iglande/ þe Creata hatte// se wæs Saturnus gehaten;// ond se wæs swa wælhreow// þæt he fordyde// his agene bearn// ealle butan anum// ond unfæderlice macode// heora life to lyre// sona on geogoðe.// He læfde swaþeah uneaðe// ænne to life,// þeah ðe he fordyde// þa broþra elles.*

(There was a man in days of yore, dwelling on the island which is called Crete, who was called Saturn; and he was so bloodthirsty that he destroyed his own children all except one, and in an unpaternal way brought their life to loss straightway in youth. He left, however, unwillingly one alive, though he had destroyed the brothers otherwise.)

I have attempted in the markings of the above passages to indicate the difference in breath groups, phrasing, and alliterative patterns in the two men: Ælfric's phrasing is longer, and its two halves are often bound by alliteration, whereas Wulfstan's are shorter (two-stress) with alliteration predominantly within the two-stress phrasings. Wulfstan's characteristic softening of realistic detail appears, moreover, in his handling of Saturn's eating of his children. His use of intensifying adjectives and adverbs is not revealed, however, in these sentences.

The difference between Ælfric's and Wulfstan's rhythms and Alfred's may be seen by viewing the above lines side by side with the following from the voyage of Ohthere that Alfred inserted into his translation of Orosius' *History:*

Ohthere sæde his hlaforde, Ælfrede cyninge, ðæt he ealra Norðmonna norðmest bude. He cwæð ðæt he bude on ðæm lande norðweardum wið ða Westsæ.

(Ohthere told his lord, King Alfred, that he dwelt furthest north of all the Norsemen. He said that he dwelt in that land (which is) northwards along the West [i.e., North] Sea.)

Alliteration and phrasing in the Alfredian sentence have not been marked; the sentence can be read in several ways. But the style exhibits a simplicity, limpidity, and periodicity that is very attractive.[25]

Of Wulfstan's other works, the prose portions of *The Benedictine Office* are of some significance. The *Office* is the English liturgy adapted from the Benedictine Rule, with introductory material from Hrabanus Maurus, the Carolingian expositor, and metrical paraphrases in the native Cædmonian tradition. The latest editor[26] believes that Wulfstan rewrote an existing vernacular text, which he postulates was Ælfric's translation; but the attribution of such a hypothetical text to Ælfric is dubious, and much still remains to be clarified about the literary relationship of the two most eminent prose stylists of early eleventh-century England.[27]

Ælfric and Wulfstan, as I have noted, are most memorable in literary history as homilists. Among the surviving works of the millennial era we also find anonymous homilies and fragments of homilies and saints' lives.[28] Two collections of such material are worth brief attention, the so-called *Blickling Homilies* (named after the former residence of the manuscript in Blickling Hall, Norfolk) and the homilies in the Vercelli Book. The former[29] consists of nineteen homilies, mostly arranged in the order of the liturgical year, beginning with "The Annunciation of Saint Mary." Some of the pieces are really

25. I cannot agree with O. Funke (n. 23), that "neither speaker nor hearer would feel any rhythmical movement in these periods [he pauses after *hlaforde, cyninge,* and the first *bude* only]; it is ordinary non-metrical prose." By pausing additionally and naturally after *Norðmonna,* the second *bude,* and *norðweardum,* I can even obtain satisfying two-stress groups! The point so far as Wulfstan's rhythms is concerned is that we should not inflexibly try to fit his prose into the Procrustean two-stress phrasing, nor call that which does not fit "bad" prose. MS pointing may be a good guide, but when we are left "unpointed" we should proceed with extreme caution.

26. J. M. Ure, *The Benedictine Office* (Edinburgh, 1957).

27. See P. Clemoes, "The Old English Benedictine Office, CCCC MS 190, and the Relations between Ælfric and Wulfstan: a Reconsideration," *Anglia,* LXXVIII (1960), 265–283.

28. For bibliography on this miscellaneous homiletic prose, see G. K. Anderson (Int., 5), pp. 348–349, 358–364.

29. Edited and translated by R. Morris, EETS 58, 63, 73 (1874–80); reproduced in facsimile in *EEMSF,* x (1960), ed. R. Willard.

saints' lives, notably the nineteenth, a *Life of St. Andrew* which
parallels the poetic *Andreas*. One of them (the tenth) is a
monitory sermon which Morris entitles "The End of the World
is Near"; it contains passages which bear some resemblance to
portions of the elegiac poems *The Wanderer* and *The Seafarer*.
Most famous is the seventeenth Blickling homily, on the "Dedi-
cation of St. Michael's Church," because it incorporates a vision
of St. Paul which is remarkably similar to the description of the
haunted mere in *Beowulf:*

> As St. Paul was looking towards the northern region of the
> earth, from whence all waters pass down, he saw above the
> water a hoary stone; and north of the stone had grown woods
> very rimy. And there were dark mists; and under the stone
> was the dwelling-place of monsters and execrable creatures.
> And he saw hanging on the cliff opposite to the woods, many
> black souls with their hands bound; and the devils in likeness
> of monsters were seizing them like greedy wolves; and
> the water under the cliff beneath was black. And between the
> cliff and the water were about twelve miles, and when the
> twigs brake, then down went the souls who hung on the twigs
> and the monsters seized them. [Morris translation]

In general, the theology of the *Blickling Homilies* is sober and
not given to the miraculous; it is millennially oriented, drawing
upon the Apocrypha to a considerable extent.[30] Occasionally the
prose has a lyrical quality, but it does not rise to Wulfstan's
impassioned heights nor does it possess the cool clarity of
Ælfric's writings. The eleventh homily, on "Holy Thursday,"
declares that the date is 971 years from the Incarnation of
Christ, but this is more likely to be the date of compilation of
the manuscript than the date of composition.[31]

The homilies in the Vercelli Book are intermingled with

30. For some remarks on the apocalyptic OE literature, see
M. Förster, "A New Version of the Apocalypse of Thomas in Old
English," *Anglia*, LXXXIII (1955), 6–36; for the Gospel of Nicodemus,
which received an OE translation and which contains the important Harrowing of Hell legend and lays the foundation for the Grail story in its
reference to Joseph of Arimathea, see S. J. Crawford, *The Gospel of
Nicodemus* (Edinburgh, 1927), and W. H. Hulme, *PMLA*, XIII (1898),
457–541, and Hulme, *MP*, I (1904), 579–614.
31. On dialect and dating, see Menner and Vleeskruyer (II, 28).

the Old English Christian epics *Elene* and *Andreas* and other poems, including the beautiful *Dream of the Rood.* There are twenty-three homiletic pieces in the collection[32] on such conventional calendar topics as "The Passion of Christ," "The Last Judgment," and "Epiphany," and on monitory and hortatory themes like the evils of gluttony and extravagance and the need for moderation. Also included in these pieces are some saints' lives: the twenty-third and last homily is a version of the prose *Guthlac* found in MS Vespasian D.xxi (see I, 14). The manuscript arrangement of this material seems haphazard; perhaps, as dialectal differences and groupings suggest, the scribe was copying seriatim from sheaves of different provenience, without bothering to impose any order upon his collection.[33]

In addition to the Old English saints' lives of Andreas, Guthlac, and others included in the *Blickling* and *Vercelli Homilies,* a few Latin lives of the late tenth century and early eleventh century may be mentioned. Earlier in this chapter reference was made to Ælfric's and Wulfstan's (the precentor of Winchester's) *Lives of St. Æthelwold* (n. 6). The two other leading reformers of the Benedictine Revival likewise found their biographical sanctifiers. A Continental Saxon priest, known only as "B" and claiming personal knowledge of St. Dunstan of Canterbury, composed a *Life* of that Church dignitary around the year 1000.[34] In typical hagiographic fashion, this *Life* exploits its subject's sanctity more than his political sagacity. A second early *Life,* by Adelard, a monk of Ghent, written between 1005 and 1012, expands even further the miraculous

32. Ed. R. Wülker, *Codex Vercellensis* (Leipzig, 1894); M. Förster, *Die Vercelli-Homilien,* I, in *BAP,* xii (1932), and *Il Codice Vercellese* (Rome, 1913)—a facsimile edition. The Vercelli MS was deposited in Vercelli, Italy, probably in the eleventh century, where it remains to this day; for a conjecture on its arrival at the town, see K. Sisam (II, 6), pp. 116–118.

33. See P. W. Peterson, "Dialect Grouping in the Unpublished Vercelli Homilies," *SP,* L (1953), 559–565.

34. See W. Stubbs, *Memorials of St. Dunstan,* Rolls Series (1874), pp. 3–52. Parts of this earliest life have been translated by Miss Whitelock, *EHD,* item 234.

element. St. Oswald, who became Archbishop of York in 972, is commemorated in an anonymous *Life* written between 995 and 1005.[35] As in the *Lives* of St. Dunstan, the wonder-working aspects of the churchman's life predominate.

A good case has been made for assigning the authorship of the *Life of St. Oswald* to Byrhtferth of Ramsey.[36] But Byrhtferth is more important for his scientific writings. Not only did the scientific works of Bede find a commentator in this Benedictine monk, who studied at Ehternach and read such writers as Macrobius; but in his *Enchiridion*, or *Manual* (A.D. 1011), Byrhtferth gives us something of an attempt at a cosmic philosophy based on science.[37] It is the first work of its kind in English (though parts of the text are in Latin, particularly the section dealing with number symbolism). The *Manual* presents a synthesis of humanistic and religious convictions, reflecting the late Old English view of man as the microcosm of the macrocosm.[38] Basically a scientific text, with a mathematical and astronomical orientation, it also includes an account of different kinds of poetry and rhetorical tropes.

Byrhtferth was the closest to a modern scientist that the Old English period produced. In Chapter II, I called attention to a different kind of scientific writing in *Bald's Leechbook*. Medical theory and practice, from the evidence of this text and of others, especially the *Lacnunga*, was primarily a curious mixture of degenerated knowledge of Greek medicine, Teutonic pagan charms, and Latin Christian overlay that merits more

35. Edited in J. Raine, *The Historians of the Church of York and its Archbishops*, I, Rolls Series (1879), pp. 399–475. Parts are translated in *EHD*, item 236.

36. S. J. Crawford, "Byrhtferth of Ramsey and the Anonymous Life of St. Oswald," *Speculum Religionis* (London, 1929), and D. J. V. Fisher in *Camb. Hist. Journ.*, x, Part III (1952).

37. The *Manual* is edited and translated by S. J. Crawford, EETS 177 (1929); see also H. Henel in *JEGP*, XLI (1942), 427–433, and in *Speculum*, XVIII (1943), 288–302.

38. On the appearance of this concept in the OE period, see J. E. Cross, "Aspects of Microcosm and Macrocosm in Old English Literature," *AGB*, pp. 1–22; on Byrhtferth in particular, see J. H. G. Grattan and C. Singer, *Anglo-Saxon Magic and Medicine* (London, 1952), pp. 39, 93.

the name of magic than of medicine. The texts of most of these pieces have been edited and translated by Cockayne (II, 23), including the *Peri Didaxeon* ("Concerning Doctrines [of Medicine]") and the *Herbarium Apuleii*.[39] We shall consider the poetic charms embedded in such works in a later chapter.

Homilies, hagiography-biography, scientific writing—these prose genres flourished in the classical Old English period. But perhaps the most interesting feature of this era is the introduction of Oriental themes and stories in translations. Of the works showing Eastern influence, by far the most attractive and engaging is the Old English version of the Greek-Latin romance *Apollonius of Tyre*.[40] This translation survives in one manuscript, the mid-eleventh-century CCCC MS 201, along with some of Wulfstan's homilies, and presumably was composed in the first quarter of that century. The story's continuing popularity is attested to by the many earlier manuscripts of the Latin text, by two Middle English versions (one of which is John Gower's, in his *Confessio Amantis*), and of course by Shakespeare's *Pericles, Prince of Tyre*. Strange and wonderful are the adventures of the hero: his wooing of the tyrant Antiochus' daughter and his solving of the incest riddle that makes him an exile from his own land; his shipwreck and regaining of fortune in a manner reminiscent of Odysseus' adventure in Phaeacia (save that he, being unmarried, is free to accept Arcestrate-Nausicaä's "proposal"); the "death" of his wife at sea after giving birth to a girl; his daughter's later adventures in a brothel, chastity miraculously preserved; and the final reunion of Apollonius, Arcestrate (now a priestess of Diana) and daughter Thasia. But the tale is more than a romance-adventure; and the Old English version—the central part is unfortunately missing —translates sensitively and understandingly, capturing the very human characters and relationships of the Latin version with a

39. See also Storms (II, 23), which further provides a good bibliography, and Grattan and Singer (on *Lacnunga*, especially).

40. P. Goolden, ed., *The Old English Apollonius of Tyre* (London, 1958); J. Raith, ed. *Die alt- und mittelenglischen Apollonius-Bruchstücke* (Munich, 1956).

humor and deftness of touch unique in Old English prose literature. As a sample, we may observe the passage where first
Apollonius, now friend to King Arcestrates and tutor to his
daughter, and then the king, who is confronted by three suitors
for Arcestrate's hand, perceive from the young girl's letter that
she loves Apollonius. The king asks Apollonius if he under-
stands whom his daughter means by her statement that she
loves "the shipwrecked man":

> *Apollonius cwæð: "Ðu goda cyning, if þin willa bið, ic hine*
> *wat." Ða geseah se cynge þaet Apollonius mid rosan rude*
> *wæs eal oferbræded, þa ongeat he þone cwyde and þus*
> *cwæð to him: "Blissa, blissa, Apolloni, for ðam þe min dohtor*
> *gewilnað þæsðe min willa is. Ne mæg soðlice on þillicon*
> *þingon nan þinc gewurþan buton Godes willan." Arcestrates*
> *beseah to ðam þrym cnihtum and cwæð: "Soð is þæt ic eow*
> *ær sæde þæt ge ne comon on gedafenlicre tide mynre dohtor*
> *to biddanne, ac þonne heo mæg hi fram hyre lare geæmtigan,*
> *þonne sænde ic eow word." Ða gewændon hie ham mid þissere*
> *andsware.*

> (Apollonius said: "You good king, if it is your desire, I know
> him." When the king saw that Apollonius was all suffused
> with the redness of the rose, he understood the words [his
> daughter had written] and so said to him: "Rejoice, rejoice,
> Apollonius, because my daughter desires that which is my
> desire. Truly nothing in such matters can take place without
> God's will." Arcestrates turned to the three young noblemen
> and said: "It is true what I said to you earlier, that you have
> not come at a suitable time to ask for my daughter ['s hand],
> but when she can free herself from her studies, then I shall
> send word to you." Then they went home with this answer.)

The smooth Old English prose, so suitable to narrative and so
different from anything by Alfred, Ælfric, or Wulfstan, is a
taste of a narrative style that might have been developed if
William had lost at Hastings. We may notice particularly the
delightful word play on *þin willa, min dohtor gewilnað, min
willa,* and *Godes willan,* and the humor (in the implicit identification of the *lar* with the *lareow*—of the studies with the in-
structor) in the king's dismissal of the three suitors; neither of
these felicities is present in the Latin.

The interest of the Anglo-Saxons in the strange and marvelous, and especially in Oriental wonders,[41] manifested itself
less felicitously in certain other prose documents: the prose
Salomon and Saturn, The Wonders of the East, and *The Letter
of Alexander to Aristotle.* These three works appear in MS
Cotton Vitellius A.xv. The manuscript consists of two parts,
and the last two works, along with a *Life of St. Christopher,*[42]
are part of the second, or *Beowulf* codex. These three texts are,
in fact, in the same hand that (c. A.D. 1000) transcribed the first
1939 lines of the Old English epic. Kenneth Sisam has cogently
argued that the *Beowulf* codex was compiled as a book about
monsters (II, 6, pp. 65–96). *St. Christopher,* a late accretion
(after c. 950) to the earlier works, probably found its place in the
collection by virtue of its presentation of the saint as a giant—
twelve fathoms tall in the Old English as compared to twelve
cubits in the Latin. *The Wonders of the East* is found additionally in MS Tiberius B.v. (c. A.D. 1000), where each section
is preceded by the Latin text;[43] illustrations in oil colors adorn
this manuscript. This description of marvels traces its ancestry
to a compilation made in England probably in the eighth
century, though the Old English version of the fictitious Latin
Letter of Fermes to the Emperor Hadrian may be no earlier
than the first quarter of the tenth century, and of Mercian
provenience. Among the wonders rather boringly detailed in the
collection is an account of hirsute women thirteen feet tall, with
boars' tusks and asses' teeth and oxen's tails, who are the color
of marble and who possess eleven feet. Alexander destroyed
them.

Alexander's Eastern conquests became popularized in the

41. Non-Oriental monster-interest may be found, of course, in
Beowulf and in the eighth-ninth century Latin *Liber monstrorum,* which
was compiled in England.

42. See S. Rypins, ed., *Three Old English Prose Texts,* EETS 161
(1924). For facsimiles of the three, see *EEMSF,* xii (1963), ed. Kemp
Malone.

43. F. Knappe, *Die Wunder des Osten* (Berlin, 1906), collates both
OE texts and the Latin. For facsimiles, see M. R. James, *Marvels of the
East* (Oxford, 1929).

Middle Ages through Julius Valerius' Latin translation (and through the *Epitome* of this translation) of the Greek Pseudo-Callisthenes. *The Letter of Alexander to Aristotle,* as it is called, is a fictitious letter in which Alexander purportedly greets his mentor from India, reciting the many wonders he has encountered on his military expeditions to the East. Among the more straightforward narrative accounts are the campaigns against Darius and Porrus. Of greatest interest to the Old English translator is a passage in which Alexander recounts with relish his disguised meeting, as a servant, with the tyrant Porrus, and of his tricking Porrus by telling him that his master Alexander is so old that he cannot warm himself anywhere save by the fire—a narrative visitation that has analogues in William of Malmesbury's accounts of King Alfred's disguised visit to the Danish camp and of the Dane Anlaf's similar one to Æthelred's camp before the Battle of Brunanburh. The Old English translator seems to have considered the military campaigns more important than the wondrous sights, since he abruptly brings his version to a conclusion after the prophecy of Alexander's early death by the speaking tree, though the Latin continues with more marvelous sights and prodigies encountered by the Greek potentate. Stylistically, *The Letter* does not measure up to the Old English *Apollonius,* being heavy and ponderous in its somewhat shaky translation and in its excessive use of Old English doublings for single Latin words. Both in style and in spirit this translation may well go back to the late ninth century, though it is common to speak of this and the other Oriental Old English pieces as appearing on the English scene only as the Anglo-Saxon period drew to its close.[44]

The prose *Salomon and Saturn*[45]—there is a poetic version, to be considered later—is a part of the midtwelfth-century manuscript which was bound with the *Beowulf* codex sometime in the sixteenth or seventeenth century. Among other pieces,

44. See Sisam (II, 6), pp. 65–96.
45. Edited in J. M. Kemble, *The Dialogues of Salomon and Saturnus* (London, 1848).

this manuscript contains Alfred's translation of Augustine's *Soliloquies*. *Salomon and Saturn* is a catechistic dialogue that also received a Middle English translation known as *The Maister of Oxford's Catechism*. It consists of exchanges between the two disputants, representing Eastern and Western wisdom. Questions are asked by Saturnus, and answered by Salomon, concerning such subjects as the creation of man and the universe, the life of Adam and his children, and the nature of flowers and of the stars. Of the total fifty-nine questions, twenty are common to another Old English catechism, *Adrian and Ritheus*.[46]

The somewhat esoteric Biblical and scientific lore represented in such dialogues as those just mentioned had a complement in popular proverbial wisdom collected in the so-called *Distichs of Cato*, as well as in poetic maxims and gnomes. The Old English *Distichs*, which translates sixty-eight of the one hundred and forty-four Latin proverbs dating back to the third or fourth century, concerns itself with such gnomic meat as the seizing of opportunity by the forelock, the guarding against praise going to one's head, the teaching of one's son a trade if one can't leave him wealth, and the accepting of responsibility for one's own poor judgment rather than blaming fortune.[47]

With the *Distichs* we reach the end of this review of the major pieces of late Old English prose. Mention may be made of various glossed psalters, fourteen of these appearing between 975 and 1075, six of them based primarily on the Gallican text and eight on the Roman.[48] Of linguistic interest especially, as exhibiting the later tenth-century Northumbrian dialect, is the gloss of the famous late seventh-century *Lindisfarne Gospels*

46. For commentary, see F. L. Utley, "The Prose *Salomon and Saturn* and the Tree Called Chy," *MS*, XIX (1957), 55–78. See also M. Förster, "Zu Adrien and Ritheus," *Englische Studien*, XXIII (1897), 431–436.

47. The OE version of the *Distichs* is edited by J. M. Kemble, *op. cit.*, pp. 258–269. For discussion, see J. Nehab, *Der altenglische Cato* (Berlin, 1879) and R. D. N. Warner, EETS 152 (1917); also O. Arngart (II, 19).

48. For editions of these, see J. Rosier, *The Vitellius Psalter*, Cornell Studies in English, XLII (1962), pp. xii–xiii.

made by Aldred of Chester-le-Street. And finally there is an early eleventh-century Old English version of the Gospels, *The West Saxon Gospels*, that one of the six manuscripts in which it survives attributes to Ælfric.[49] Bede, we will remember, is supposed to have made a translation of the Gospel of St. John in the eighth century, but this eleventh-century version is the earliest Old English translation (apart from glosses) that has survived. In style it does not measure up to the great prose pieces of the late Old English period nor to the later fourteenth-century translation of Wyclif.

As Anglo-Saxon England moved toward its rendezvous at Hastings, entries continued to be made in the famous *Chronicle* begun in Alfred's reign. A notable contributor toward the end of the tenth century was Ælfric's patron Æthelweard, who most probably wrote the entry for the year 983 and who continued to take an active interest in the *Chronicle* throughout the next decade. In a Latin that is the despair of historians, Æthelweard also wrote a *Chronicon* between 976 and 980, relying heavily for three of his four sections on the *Anglo-Saxon Chronicle* and on Isidore and Bede.[50] I referred in Chapter II to the exciting events of the year 1051, those concerned with the difficulties between Edward the Confessor and Godwine and his sons. And the *Chronicle* continued to be added to even after the accession of William, until it transformed itself in *The Peterborough Chronicle*, which runs to 1154, into Middle English.[51] A final continuity between the earliest Old English prose and the latest, between Old and Middle English, may be found in legal codes and writs. These, while not strictly literature, used from earliest times such literary techniques as two-stress lines,

49. On Aldrediana, see G. C. Britton and R. L. Thomson, *EGS*, VII (1961), 1–19, 20–36. For edition of the various Gospels, see W. W. Skeat, *The Holy Gospels in Anglo-Saxon* (Cambridge, 1871–87).

50. See L. Whitbread, "Æthelweard and the Anglo-Saxon Chronicle," *EHR*, LXXIV (1959), 577–589. For an edition of the *Chronicon*, with translation, see A. Campbell, *The Chronicle of Æthelweard* (London and New York, c. 1962).

51. *The Peterborough Chronicle, 1070–1154*, ed. C. Clark (Oxford, 1958).

rhyme, alliteration, assonance—no doubt as aids to memory and for oral recitation; and they achieved a high degree of literacy and polish in the *Codes* and in the *Institutes of Polity* drawn up by Archbishop Wulfstan. Eleventh-century writs are especially rich in the variety of their formulaic linkings: in their use of two different words alliterating (*sacu and socu, mid lande ond mid læse*), of two contrasting words alliterating (*binnan byrig ond butan*), of rhyme (*be lande ond be strande*), of assonance (*mid mæde ond mid læse*), and so on.[52] It is these techniques, and others, which I have referred to casually in the course of this survey of prose, that we must now examine in more detail, since they lie at the heart of Old English poetry.

52. See F. E. Harmer, *Anglo-Saxon Writs* (Manchester, 1952), pp. 61–73, 85–92.

IV

Some Remarks on the Nature and Quality of Old English Poetry

OLD ENGLISH, Old Icelandic, Old Saxon, and Old High German poetry derive from a common verse form still clearly discernible behind the separate developments of the surviving poetic corpora. That form is keyed to a dominant linguistic fact: the Germanic fixing of stress upon the initial syllable of a word, exclusive of most prefixes. A concomitant of such stress was the tendency to aid continuity of discourse—not to mention continuity of hereditary lineage—by the use of initial rhyme, or alliteration; and it is these two features, intensified or heightened, that contributed to the stabilized Germanic verse pattern. We find this pattern as early as the fourth- or fifth-century runic declaration of pride in craftsmanship inscribed on the golden horn of Gallehus:[1]

Ek HlewagastiR HoltijaR   horna tawido

(I, Hlewagast, Holt's son,   made [this] horn.)

Differences in the verse forms of the individual Germanic languages may be attributed to, among other things, differing degrees of retention of initial stress, with consequent loss of or increase in the number of short syllables in the poetic line. The earliest Icelandic poetry, with its tightly packed line, exhibits the result of strong initial stress, the looser Old Saxon and Old High German line the result of weakened initial stress;

---

1. On runes, see Chapter X.

Old English poetry seems to stand somewhere between these alliterative verse extremes.[2]

The Germanic poetic line, as the Gallehus inscription suggests, consists of two half-lines or verses divided by a caesura, with two major stresses or lifts in each verse: Ek Hlēwăgăstir HŏltijaR   hŏrnă tăwidŏ.[3] The a- or on-verse may have its two lifts alliterating, as in the inscription, but the important consideration is the binding of the b- or off-verse to its antecedent verse by alliteration of its first lift. The number of weak or secondary stresses (dips) in each foot or measure is variable within certain limits; there is even the possibility of anacrusis, that is, of dips before the first foot or measure begins. In Old English poetry, the accepted pattern of alliteration in a verse-pair demanded that an initial consonant alliterate with itself whatever the following vowel or consonant, except that the paired consonants sc, sp, and st could alliterate only each with itself. A vowel commonly alliterated with any other vowel, less commonly with itself. Verse-binding alliteration was recognized only as it coincided with major stresses, and stress alliteration was most likely to fall upon nouns and adjectives. The phonetic quantity of syllables was also significant, lifts normally being reserved for long syllables, though light verses, with the stress on short syllables, were permissible in the first foot of the verse, and resolution of two short syllables for stress purposes was common, as in line 2425a of Beowulf: Bēowŭlf măðeladĕ. Occasionally we find verses, especially a-verses, that seem to have only one stressed syllable, as in The Wanderer, line 11a:

2. On the importance of linguistic features in the patterning of the poetic line, see W. P. Lehmann, The Development of Germanic Verse Form (Austin, Tex., 1956).

3. ⌣ indicates a long, heavily stressed syllable, ⌣ or x̆ secondarily stressed long or short syllable, and x an unstressed syllable. Resolved stress, where a short-stressed syllable is rhythmically yoked with a following very lightly stressed syllable as a single stress, is marked ⌣x. (A long syllable is one which contains either a long vowel or diphthong, or a short vowel or diphthong closed by two immediately following consonants; a short syllable is one containing a short vowel or diphthong left open by a single following consonant.)

þæt biþ in eorle, and others that are hypermetric, with more than two stresses, as in *Beowulf*, line 1168a: árfæst æt ecga gelácum.

The recognition of stress and alliteration in Old English is one thing; the actual reading of the verses is another. Basically, there are two schools of thought on the latter: the isochronous and the nonisochronous. Eduard Sievers formulated the latter, with his hypothesis of five basic kinds of poetic verses of at least four syllables, consisting of two feet with a major stress in each. He based his categories upon observable lift-dip patterns. Since even the dissidents from his theory refer to these five types, I shall briefly enumerate their patterns: Type A: $\_$ x / $\_$ x; Type B: x $\_$ / x $\_$; Type C: x $\_$ / $\_$ x; Type D: either $\_$ / $\_$ x x or $\_$ / $\_$ x x; Type E: $\_$ x x / $\_$.[4] Even in these basic patterns, without introducing allowable extra dips, there is obvious inequality of duration between some feet in the verse, unless one goes to exaggerated lengths to draw out or to hurry through the feet in the D and E types. This difficulty has led to successive assaults on Sievers' hypothesis by, among others, Leonard, Heusler, Pope, and Nist,[5] and the resorting to musical analogy of equal time per measure. John Pope in particular, with his brilliant theorizing about the use of the harp as a musical "rest" to eke out measures not superficially conforming to the 4/8 time he postulates for normal, 4/4 time for hypermetric verses, has revolutionized our ideas about Old English meter; but recently A. J. Bliss, attacking the isochronous theory as an unwarranted imposition upon an era unfamiliar with the concept, has returned to a some-

4. See Eduard Sievers, *Altgermanische Metrik* (Halle, 1893), for a full explanation of this system; for a cogent synopsis, see Appendix I of *Bright's Anglo-Saxon Reader*, rev. and enlarged by J. R. Hulbert (New York, 1935).

5. W. E. Leonard, "*Beowulf* and the Niebelungen Couplet," *Univ. of Wisconsin Studies in Lang. and Lit.*, XI (1918), 99–152, and "Four Footnotes to Papers on Germanic Metrics," *Studies in English Philology: A Miscellany in Honor of Frederick Klaeber* (Minneapolis, Minn., 1929), pp. 1–13; A. Heusler, *Deutsche Versgeschichte*, I (Berlin, 1925); John C. Pope, *The Rhythm of Beowulf* (New Haven, Conn., 1942); John A. Nist, *The Structure and Texture of Beowulf* (São Paulo, Brasil, 1959), Ch. VII.

what modified Sievers position.[6] The subtleties of the various hypotheses concerning the metrics of Old English poetry are beyond the scope of this history, though we may illustrate a few verses scanned or read as Sievers suggested and as Pope suggests to note the difference between the system governed by "natural" stress and that governed by the concept of measured time and the use of the "rest" with accompanying chords on the harp:

Næs hearpan wyn,   B

gomen glēobēames,   D

nē gōd hafoc   C

geond sæl swingeð,   C

nē se swifta mearh   B

burhstede bēateð.   E

Bealocwealm hafað   A

fela feorhcynna   D

forð onsended.[7]   A

delight of the gleewood,
sweeps through the hall,
stamps in the courtyard.
forth dispatched

(Not at all [is there] joy of the harp,
nor the good hawk
nor the swift horse
Cruel death has
many of mortal race.)

[*Bwf.* 2262b–66]

There seems to be little doubt that the harp was a formal accompaniment of the recitation of the oldest English verse. In *Widsith* (ll. 103–105), the fictitious scop who is speaker of the poem declares that "We two, Scilling and I, with clear voice delivered song before our liege-lord, loud to the harp the voice resounded"; in *Beowulf* (ll. 89–90), the poet describes the sound of revelry in Heorot as "There was the sound of the harp, clear

6. A. J. Bliss, *The Metre of Beowulf* (Oxford, 1958).

7. It must be remembered that the musical analogy systems do not deny stress, but that they do not equate stress with *duration* of sound. Notice, too, that in Pope's system, unlike Sievers', place is found for a light first measure with a stressed rest, so that both lifts, alliterating or not, are in the second measure—e.g., 1. 2264a; such scansion is almost invariable in B- and C-type verses. The second measure in Pope's system is always heavy.

the song of the scop"; and Bede's story of Cædmon informs us of the illiterate cowherd's embarrassment when he saw the harp, that should accompany his own verse-making, approach him at the dinner table. But our knowledge of how the harp was used in connection with verse recitation—did it accompany the chanting or was it plucked only during "rests"?—and even of how it was played—with the fingers or with a plectrum?—is imprecise, though admirable attempts at reconstruction have been made on the basis of the Sutton Hoo discovery.[8]

In addition to investigating the rhythmic and phonemic principles and practices of Old English poetry, scholars have devoted considerable attention to the nature of its diction and to aspects of its style. Despite the limited number of extant writings in Old English, it seems certain that poetry utilized not only the language of prose but also a special vocabulary of its own. Some archaic words evidently acquired poetic status by their perpetuation only in verse: *mece* 'sword' and *guð* 'battle' are two such words. But more important were metaphoric, especially metonymic, words like *ceol* 'ship' (literally "keel") and *lind* 'shield' (literally "linden-wood"); and compounds or combinations of basic nouns plus limiting genitives that periphrastically designated persons or objects by one of their attributes. Such compounds as "heath-stepper" for the referent *stag*

8. Among the artifacts unearthed in the royal burial mound at Sutton Hoo, in southeastern Suffolk, England, in 1939, were the remains of a small harp. For discussion of the nature of the harp and its use in connection with the recitation of OE poetry, see J. B. Bessinger, Jr., "Beowulf and the Harp at Sutton Hoo," *UTQ*, xxvii (1958), 148–168, and esp. "The Sutton Hoo Harp-Replica and Old English Musical Verse," in Creed, *New Approaches* (Int., 2); also C. L. Wrenn, "Two Anglo-Saxon Harps," *AGB*, pp. 118–128. There is an interesting recording, on Caedmon Records, by Mr. Bessinger of Cædmon's *Hymn* and other OE poems recited to the accompaniment of a replica of the Sutton Hoo harp. For bibliography on Sutton Hoo till 1958, see bibliographical articles by F. P. Magoun, Jr., and J. B. Bessinger, Jr., in *Speculum*, xxix (1954), 116–124, and xxxiii (1958), 515–522; the most recent volume is by Chas. Green, *Sutton Hoo, The Excavation of a Royal Ship Burial* (London and New York, 1963). On the relationship of *Beowulf* to Sutton Hoo, see C. L. Wrenn's Supplement to Chambers' *Beowulf: An Introduction*, 3rd ed. (Cambridge, 1959), pp. 508–523, and his "Sutton Hoo and Beowulf," in *Mélanges de Linguistique et de Philologie, Fernand Mossé in Memoriam* (Paris, 1959), pp. 495–507.

or "spear-tree" for *warrior* illustrate this last concept and are usually referred to as *kennings,* though it is perhaps better to distinguish the former as a *kent heiti*—a more direct periphrasis identifying the referent with something it *is* (the stag is actually a "stepper")—and the latter as a true *kenning,* wherein the referent is identified with something it is *not* except in a very special metaphoric sense—a warrior is not a "tree" except as both stand tall and straight and unshrinking under blows.[9]

The Old English poets utilized their word hoard formulaically. Originally at least of oral composition, Anglo-Saxon poetry was fashioned by the scops from a stock of verse or verse-pair formulas; that is, from stylized syntactically related collocations of words in regular rhythmic patterns.[10] The poet could find among his formulaic resources almost any semantic values he needed for the immediate sense or ornamentation of the poem he was creating. Conveniently, he could substitute individual words within the grammatical and rhythmic patterns either for contextual or alliterative purposes. Thus we find the *Beowulf* poet at line 2765a talking about *gold on grunde* and again, in line 3167a, about *gold on greote.* In the former instance the "ground" or "earth" occurs in a context condemning gold as overpowering to men's souls, even when buried; in the latter, the more specific "dust" suggests Beowulf's grave barrow, in which the useless gold is being reburied along with the hero. Or we find the exiled Adam *duguðum bedæled* 'of joys deprived' in *Genesis,* line 930a, and Satan similarly deprived in *Christ and Satan,* line 121a, while the Wanderer is *eðle bedæled* 'of native land deprived' in *The Wanderer,* line 20b, and mankind, through Adam and Eve, are *eðle bescierede* 'from native land cut off' in *Christ,* line 32b. These formulas and formulaic sys-

9. For some studies of Old English diction and figurative language, see H. C. Wyld, "Diction and Imagery in Anglo-Saxon Poetry," *E & S,* XI (1925), 49–91; H. Marquardt, *Die altenglischen Kenningar* (Halle, 1938); E. G. Stanley, "Old English Poetic Diction and the Interpretation of *The Wanderer, The Seafarer,* and *The Penitent's Prayer,*" *Anglia,* LXXIII (1956), 413–466; and esp. Brodeur, *Art of Beowulf* (Int., 2), Ch. I.

10. See F. P. Magoun, Jr., "Oral-Formulaic Character of Anglo-Saxon Narrative Poetry," *Speculum,* XXVIII (1953), 446–467.

tems were, further, useful in combination to present fixed themes, such as that of the beasts of battle, which appears in twelve passages in nine poems, or that of exile, which appears not only in the elegies but in some unexpected contexts.[11] We can readily recognize the convenience of these systems for oral composition, but the formulaic-thematic habit also carried over into written compositions as well, as definitely attested by the works of Cynewulf and by the *Phoenix*.[12]

We might expect that a poetry so constructed, so formulated, would become dull and conventional in the pejorative sense of the term; and so it did in the hands of lesser poets. Yet the better scops could and did use their stocks of words, formulas, and themes individualistically. One of the methods by which the Old English poets achieved originality was the coining of compounds, as the *Beowulf* poet's immense wealth of newly minted compound words attests. In a larger way, originality in the use of formulas and themes depended upon the degree of tension created between the traditional associations evoked by these stylizations and the unique applicability they had in their specific contexts. The *Beowulf* poet, for example, hoards the "beast of battle" theme, not using it in the traditional way in scenes describing the battles against either demons or hostile armies, but reserving it uniquely and climactically for the end of the Messenger's great speech prophesying doom to all of the dead Beowulf's people.[13] Or the poet, working on the degree of expectancy set up by the

11. On the former, see F. P. Magoun, Jr., "The Theme of the Beasts of Battle in Anglo-Saxon Poetry," *NM*, LVI (1955), 81–90; on the latter, S. B. Greenfield, "The Formulaic Expression of the Theme of 'Exile' in Anglo-Saxon Poetry," *Speculum*, XXX (1955), 200–206.

12. There has been great controversy among scholars over the oral vs. written provenience of extant OE poetry. The chief spokesman for the oral composition theory has been Magoun (see n. 10); also, R. P. Creed, "The Making of an Anglo-Saxon Poem," *ELH*, XXVI (1959), 445–454. The chief proponent of the written theory for most of the poetry has been Brodeur (see n. 9); for a pre-Magoun statement in favor of written theory, see R. Girvan, "The Medieval Poet and His Audience," *English Studies Today* (Oxford, 1951), pp. 85–97.

13. See A. Bonjour, "*Beowulf* and the Beasts of Battle," *PMLA*, LXXII (1957), 563–573.

traditional collocations, or by his own creation of habitual patterns, could deliberately extend or frustrate that expectancy in various ways.[14] In *The Wanderer*, for example, the opening line temporarily suspends the conventional association of "wretchedness" and "lone-dwelling" (*earm anhaga* is the traditional pattern) when the poet says: "Oft him anhaga   are gebideþ" (Often the lone-dweller experiences mercy), suggesting by the syntactic and alliterative-metrical pattern the possibility that God's mercy may be extended to an exile—a key idea in the poem that is brought to a resolution in its conclusion. It is not till line 2b that the traditional collocation with wretchedness is brought in through the adjective *modcearig* 'weary in spirit.' In a somewhat different way, the poet could achieve a semantic linking via the metrical pattern despite an absence of syntactic dependency, as when the *Beowulf* poet comments of the Danes that

	Swylc wæs þeaw hyra,
hæþenra hyht;	*helle gemundon*
in modsefan,	*Metod hi ne cuþon . . .*

(Such was their custom, the hope of heathens; they remembered hell in their hearts, they knew not the Lord . . .)

[ll. 178 ff.]

where the hope of heathens is equated through alliteration and stress with hell (*hæþenra, hyht, helle*).[15]

This brief sampling of the possibilities of individuality within the Old English formulaic convention verges on the subject of style. Of various Anglo-Saxon stylistic elements, none has received more attention than the device called *variation*.[16]

14. See R. Quirk, "Poetic Language and Old English Metre," *Early English and Norse Studies*, eds. A. Brown and P. Foote (London, 1963), pp. 150–171.

15. For this last illustration, see Quirk, p. 159. For the suggestion that OE poets used syntax and word order for significant poetic effect, see S. B. Greenfield, "Syntactic Analysis and Old English Poetry," *NM*, LXIV (1963), 373–378.

16. On the use of *litotes*, or understatement, see F. Bracher, "Understatement in Old English Poetry," *PMLA*, LII (1937), 915–934; on rhetorical patterns, see A. C. Bartlett, *The Larger Rhetorical Patterns in Anglo-Saxon Poetry* (New York, 1935); for one suggestion about the

This device may be seen at its simplest in such a line as "Beowulf maðelode, bearn Ecgðeowes," where "son of Ecgtheow" *varies* the noun *Beowulf;* and more complexly in the opening lines of the epic:

> *Hwæt, we Gar-Dena   in geardagum,*
> *þeodcyninga   þrym gefrunon,*
> *hu þa æþelingas   ellen fremedon,*

where both *þrym þeodcyninga* 'glory of people-kings' and 'how the princes valor performed' are variational objects of *gefrunon* 'heard.' Variation, then, is a double or multiple statement of the same idea, each restatement suggesting through its choice of words either a general or more specific quality, or a different attribute of that concept; and such statements may, as in the first example, or may not, as in the second, be grammatically parallel. The importance of this stylistic device in Old English poetry, its potentialities and limitations, have been well summarized by Arthur Brodeur:

> Variation is . . . the chief characteristic of the poetic mode of expression. . . . [It] restrains the pace of Old English poetic narrative, gives to dialogue or monologue its leisurely or stately character, raises into high relief those concepts which the poet wishes to emphasize, and permits him to exhibit the object of his thought in all its aspects. But it could be a dangerous instrument in the hands of an inferior poet: it could impart on the one hand an effect of sheer redundancy, on the other an unpleasing jerkiness of pace; it could stiffen the flow of style, and clog the stream of thought.[17]

We shall encounter this stylistic trait again and again in the individual poems discussed in the following chapters. But before turning to specifics, it might be best to say a few words

---

use of Latin rhetorical figures in OE poetry, see J. E. Cross, "On *The Wanderer* Lines 80–84: A Study of a Figure and a Theme," *VSL Arsbok,* 1958–59, pp. 77–110. On end-stopped and run-on lines, see K. Malone (Int., 5), pp. 26–28, and *RES,* xix (1943), 201–204. Valuable also are D. Slay, "Some Aspects of the Technique of Composition of Old English Verse," *TPS,* 1952, pp. 1–14, and A. Rynell, *Parataxis and Hypotaxis as a Criterion of Syntax and Style, especially in Old English Poetry* (Lund, 1952).

17. *The Art of Beowulf,* p. 39.

here about the dating of Old English poetry, about the poetic subject matters and genres, and about the manuscripts containing the poetry.

Almost all of the surviving Old English poetry has been preserved in four manuscripts, known familiarly as the *Beowulf* MS (Cotton Vitellius A.xv), the Exeter Book, the Junius MS, and the Vercelli MS.[18] The first three reside in England, in the British Museum, the Chapter Library of Exeter Cathedral, and the Bodleian Library at Oxford respectively; the fourth somehow crossed the Alps during the Middle Ages, where it remains to this day in the Cathedral Library at Vercelli (see III, 32). All four manuscripts date from around the year 1000; their dialect is mainly late West Saxon, the language of Ælfric, with an admixture of Anglian and Northumbrian forms that undoubtedly survived as part of the common poetic vocabulary from the earlier centuries.[19] The dates of composition of the poems in these manuscripts, whether of oral or written provenience, cannot be determined with precision; but critics generally agree upon an early period, ranging from the late seventh to the early ninth century, which includes the composition of *Beowulf* and the Cædmonian poems; the period of Cynewulf, ninth

18. Facsimiles have been made of all four: J. Zupitza, *Beowulf*, 2nd ed., EETS 245 (London, 1959)—this does not include *Judith* and the prose pieces, but K. Malone's recent facsimile edition does: *EEMSF*, xii (1963); R. W. Chambers, M. Förster, and R. Flower, *The Exeter Book of Old English Poetry* (London, 1933); I. Gollancz, *The Cædmon Manuscript of Anglo-Saxon Biblical Poetry, Junius XI in the Bodleian Library* (Oxford, 1927); M. Foerster, *Il Codice Vercellese . . .* (Rome, 1913). The complete poetic corpus has been edited by G. P. Krapp and E. V. K. Dobbie in *The Anglo-Saxon Poetic Records* (New York, 1931–53): I. *The Junius Manuscript*; II. *The Vercelli Book*; III. *The Exeter Book*; IV. *Beowulf and Judith*; V. *The Paris Psalter and the Meters of Boethius*; VI. *The Anglo-Saxon Minor Poems*. *The Exeter Book* has been specially edited by I. Gollancz and W. S. Mackie, as EETS Vols. 104 and 194 (London, 1895 and 1934). For literal prose translations of most of the poetry, see R. K. Gordon, *Anglo-Saxon Poetry*, rev. ed. (New York, 1954). Editions of individual poems, and other translations, are mentioned where appropriate.

19. On the dialect of the poetic vocabulary, see Sisam, *Studies* (II, 6), Ch. 8. Sisam argues that the poetry of the seventh—early ninth century was neither Anglian nor West Saxon, but of common stock.

century; and a ninth-tenth–century period, which saw the making of *Genesis B, Judith,* and the late battle poems, among others. It must be stressed, however, that there is critical disagreement about the dating of individual poems, the elegies, for example, having been located in every century from the seventh to the tenth by one critic or another, and *Beowulf* itself having both early and late dating enthusiasts.

The four main manuscript collections of Old English poems, and others containing one to several pieces, offer a variety of poetic genres, from lyric through epic and allegory, from riddles to didactic verses. Some of the poems are exclusively secular in their thought and content, others are devotionally or doctrinally oriented. Some have their roots in Germanic pagan antiquity, some in Christian Latinity. Because of the difficulty of dating, and for other reasons, it has seemed best in the following chapters to consider the poems according to subject matter. We shall begin with the secular hero, proceed to the Christian saint, then to poems about Christ, poems about Old Testament figures, poems dealing with miscellaneous Christian and secular subjects, lore and wisdom in verse, and finally the elegies.

V

Secular Heroic Poetry

THERE IS ample evidence in Old English poetry that the common fund of narrative material associated with the Teutonic Heroic Age of the fourth–sixth centuries survived in the songs of the Germanic tribes who settled in Britain. Poems like *Widsith* and *Deor*, through their very allusiveness in presenting this material, attest to the vitality that stories about Continental heroes like Eormanric, Theodoric, and Ingeld must have had in the early English oral tradition, though these songs are now lost to us. Perhaps more important for Old English poetry as a whole than the particular figures of the Heroic Age were the spirit and code of conduct they embodied, for these were to endure down to the Norman Conquest. This heroic spirit manifested itself most strongly in the desire for fame and glory, now and posthumously; the code of conduct stressed the reciprocal obligations of lord and thanes: protection and generosity on the one part, loyalty and service on the other, a mutuality that was the core of the *comitatus* relationship described as early as A.D. 98 by the Latin historian Tacitus in his *Germania* and demonstrated as late as the tenth century in the historic English poem *The Battle of Maldon*. Interestingly enough, this spirit and code of conduct, with suitable transmutation, also found accommodation in Old English poetic representations of Old Testament narrative, saints' lives, and the figure of Christ Himself—as we shall see later.

HƿÆT ƿE GARDA

na ingeardagum. þeod cyninga
þrym gefrunon huða æþelingaſ ellen
fremedon. oft ſcyld ſcefing ſceaþen
þreatum monegū mægþum meodo ſetla
ofteah egſode eorl ſyððan æreſt ƿearð
feaſceaft funden he þæſ frofre geba
ƿeox under ƿolcnum weorð myndum þah
oðþ him æghƿylc þara ymbſittendra
ofer hronrade hyran ſcolde gomban
gyldan þæſ god cyning. ðæm eafera ƿæſ
æfter cenned geong ingeardum þone god
ſende folce tofrofre fyren ðearfe on
geat þþie ær drugon aldorleaſe lange
hƿile him þæſ liffrea ƿuldreſ ƿealden
ƿorold are forgeaf beowulf ƿæſ breme
blæd ƿide ſprang ſcyldeſ eafera ſcede
landum in . . . .
. . . . ƿilcean gromum . . . .

For the moment we are concerned with the Germanic secular hero as he appears in Old English poetry; and pre-eminent stands the figure of Beowulf. Though Beowulf has his analogues in such Scandinavian heroes as Boðvarr Bjarki and Grettir the Strong,[1] he seems to be unique to the Old English epic to which, in modern editions, he gives his name. His origins, that is, along with those of the monsters he fights, are more to be found in folktale than in heroic story. But in the hands of the *Beowulf* poet he has become epically proportioned like the Homeric and Vergilian heroes of an earlier Heroic Age, and he has been given, along with other epic accoutrements, an historical setting involving him with the fates of two dynasties, the Danish Scyldings and the Geatish Hrethlings.[2] As an additional layer in *Beowulf*, there is the Christian ethos, undoubtedly the contribution of the monastery which probably produced the written poem,[3] though certain Christian elements may already have "lain in solution," as it were, in oral songs about *Beowulf* utilized by the religious poet.[4] The fusion of these three levels by the more-than-capable anonymous author

1. See *The Saga of Hrolf Kraki*, trans. Stella M. Mills (Oxford, 1933), and *The Story of Grettir the Strong*, trans. E. Magnússon and W. Morris (London and New York, 1900). On the relation of *Beowulf* to the widespread "Bear's Son Tale," the eminent authority is F. Panzer, *Studien zur germanischen Sagengeschichte, I, Beowulf* (Munich, 1910). For more recent attempts to relate the poem to folktale and myth, see Rhys Carpenter, *Folk Tale, Fiction and Saga in the Homeric Epics* (Berkeley and Los Angeles, 1946), and A. B. Lord, *The Singer of Tales* (Cambridge, Mass., 1960).

2. On *Beowulf* as an epic poem, see S. B. Greenfield, "*Beowulf* and Epic Tragedy," AGB, pp. 91–105; on heroic aspects, see H. M. Chadwick, *The Heroic Age* (Cambridge, 1926), esp. Ch. XV; on Vergilian parallels, see T. B. Haber, *A Comparative Study of the Beowulf and the Aeneid* (Princeton, N.J., 1931). For a study of the historical and non-historical elements in the poem, see R. W. Chambers, *Beowulf: An Introduction*, 3rd ed. with Suppl. by C. L. Wrenn (Cambridge, 1959), W. W. Lawrence, *Beowulf and Epic Tradition* (Cambridge, Mass., 1928), reprtd. 1961, and the introductions to editions listed in n. 8, below.

3. See A. Campbell, "The Old English Epic Style," *English and Medieval Studies: Presented to J. R. R. Tolkien* (London, 1962), pp. 14–15. An older theory is that the poet was a chaplain in a royal or noble household.

4. See R. D. Stevick, "Christian Elements and the Genesis of *Beowulf*," MP, LXI (1963), 79–89.

leads to the richness and complexity of this sole complete surviving Germanic epic.

It is remarkable that even the one manuscript text of this heroic poem has survived, and some account of its history and transmission may serve to indicate the perils to which Anglo-Saxon manuscripts were subject. Whether the *Beowulf* as we have it was orally composed or not—and I incline to the latter view[5]—a written text in the Anglian or Mercian dialect probably existed by the middle of the eighth century.[6] This text, or a copy of it, must have survived the Danish invasions of the ninth and tenth centuries; but the extant manuscript is a further copy in the same late West Saxon *koiné*, or artificial literary dialect, that includes some Anglian and other non-West Saxon forms, of the other three chief codices of Old English poetry. It is transcribed in two hands: the first copyist did the three prose pieces preceding *Beowulf* (see III, p. 64) as well as up to line 1939 of the poem; the second, the remainder as well as the fragmentary *Judith* that completes the *Beowulf* codex. In the course of the centuries, the codex survived the sixteenth-century dissolution of the monasteries,[7] became bound in the early seventeenth century with the twelfth-century manuscript containing Alfred's *Soliloquies* (see II, p. 37), and came to rest on the first shelf beneath the bust of the Emperor Vitellius in the famous library of the antiquarian Sir Robert Cotton (d. 1631). Fate kindly spared it when in 1731 fire swept the library and destroyed or badly mutilated many of the Cottonian collection, though the scorching it received then has caused some deterioration around the edges of the vellum leaves, and some fading and crumbling elsewhere in the parchment. Fortunately the Icelander Thorkelin had two copies of the text made on his visit to England in 1786–87: one by an unknown copyist who knew

5. See IV, 9, 10, 12.
6. On dating and dialect, see D. Whitelock, *The Audience of Beowulf* (Oxford, 1951), Brodeur, *Art of Beowulf* (Int., 2), and Chambers-Wrenn (n. 2).
7. The sixteenth-century Anglo-Saxonist Laurence Nowell, Dean of Lichfield, apparently had something to do with the MS at this time, since his name appears on the first page of the *Beowulf* codex.

no Old English (Thorkelin Transcript "A"), and one by himself (Transcript "B"). These transcripts, plus the facsimile edition of Zupitza and ultraviolet light readings of the manuscript itself, have been invaluable in establishing the present text of the poem as represented, with individual variations, in the great modern editions of Chambers, Klaeber, Wrenn, Dobbie, and E. von Schaubert.[8]

Whatever the disagreements about details and about the interpretation of small passages and large sections, and whatever the disagreements about the ultimate unity of the poem and about its *significatio*,[9] the narrative movement of *Beowulf* is clear enough. It revolves around the three great monster fights in the hero's career: against Grendel, Grendel's mother, and finally against the dragon. The setting of the first two inter-related engagements is Denmark. Beowulf, nephew to King Hygelac of the Geats, comes to offer his aid to King Hrothgar of the Danes, whose princely hall Heorot has been nightly ravaged for twelve years by the troll-like yet Cain-descended Grendel, aroused to fury by the sound of revelry by night. After a series of verbal confrontations with the coast guard, the hall warden Wulfgar, and climactically with the *þyle* (orator? jester?[10]) Unferth, in which he displays his skill and wisdom in debate, Beowulf meets Grendel in a hand-to-hand encounter in the dark night of Heorot. The hero's physical prowess is equal to his impressive appearance and verbal acumen, and Grendel is forced to flee despairing of life, having left his arm as "life-ransom" in Beowulf's powerful grasp. The second en-

8. F. Klaeber, *Beowulf and the Fight at Finnsburg*, 3rd ed. (Boston, 1936), with supplements in 1941, 1950; C. L. Wrenn, *Beowulf: With the Finnesburg Fragment*, rev. and enlarged (London, 1958); E. V. K. Dobbie (IV, 18); E. von Schaubert, *Heyne-Schückings Beowulf*, 18th ed. (Paderborn, 1963–). For facsimiles, see EETS 77 and 245 (1882 and 1959), and EEMSF, XII (III, 42). A very important ultraviolet reading is *Geatisc meowle*, l. 3150: see Pope (IV, 5), pp. 232–234.

9. For some of the major bibliographical items concerning the unity of *Beowulf*, see pp. 307–308 of Zesmer-Greenfield Guide (Int., 5). A convenient florilegium is *An Anthology of Beowulf Criticism*, ed. L. E. Nicholson (Notre Dame, Ind., 1963).

10. See J. L. Rosier, "Design for Treachery: the Unferth Intrigue," *PMLA*, LXXVII (1962), 1–7.

counter derives from the first, for the monster's mother, on the following night, avenges her son's death by snatching and eating Hrothgar's dearest counselor Æschere. Beowulf once again undertakes the adventure, but this time he must seek out his antagonist in her own lair, which is described by Hrothgar in the famous haunted mere passage:

> "They live in secret places, windy
> Cliffs, wolf-dens where water pours
> From the rocks, then runs underground, where mist
> Steams like black clouds, and the groves of trees
> Growing out over their lake are all covered
> With frozen spray, and wind down snakelike
> Roots that reach as far as the water
> And help keep it dark. At night that lake
> Burns like a torch. No one knows its bottom,
> No wisdom reaches such depths. A deer,
> Hunted through the woods by packs of hounds,
> A stag with great horns, though driven through the forest
> From faraway places, prefers to die
> On those shores, refuses to save its life
> In that water."[11]

Strength of arm is not enough to assure the hero victory in this battle beneath the water: nor does the sword Hrunting, lent him by a now-chastened Unferth, avail. Only an old sword, the work of giants, which the hero spies in the monster's cave, enables him to kill the female of the species, thus finally and effectively cleansing the Danish kingdom of this external evil. The third confrontation takes place in Beowulf's old age. King of the Geats for fifty years, the hero must now save his own kingdom from the fiery depredations of a dragon, whose anger has been roused by the stealing of a cup from the treasure hoard it has been guarding for three hundred years. Not without foreboding, Beowulf challenges the monster in its barrow, and

11. Cf. with *Blickling Homily* 17 (p. 59 in this book). Citations from *Beowulf* in this chapter are from the recent "free" translation by B. Raffel (New York, 1963). For an older standard poetic translation, see C. W. Kennedy's *Beowulf* (New York, 1940); an excellent prose translation is that by D. Wright (Baltimore, 1957). On the nature of the mere, see K. Malone, "Grendel and His Abode," *Studia Philologica et Litteraria in Honorem L. Spitzer*, eds. A. G. Hatcher and K. L. Selig (Bern, 1958), pp. 297–308.

battle ensues. The hero ultimately needs the aid of his kinsman Wiglaf, but even with it, receives his own death wound in the killing of the dragon. He is given a hero's funeral pyre; his ashes, along with the dragon's hard-won hoard, are placed in a splendid tumulus atop a seaside cliff; and twelve chieftains ride round the barrow lamenting and praising their fallen lord.

Such a bare outline of the major action tells little about the magnificence of *Beowulf* as an epic or heroic poem. Even so, I have tried to suggest something of the anonymous poet's sense of structure in the "movements" of the three contests: in the differing natures and motivations of the antagonists; in the progressive difficulties Beowulf has in conquering his foes; in the shift of locales from the friendly confines of Heorot to the submerged cavern to the windy headland. Also involved in the structural movement is the progressive isolation of the hero: in the Grendel fight his band of retainers draw their swords in an attempt, however vain, to help their leader; in the second contest this band can only sit on the shore of the mere—the Danes already having departed in despair—suffering and yet hoping for the reappearance of their beloved chieftain; and in the dragon fight, Beowulf's *comitatus*, with the exception of Wiglaf, deserts him, abandoning him to the ultimate isolation of death. This last structural variation clearly impinges upon theme, the concept of loyalty vs. disloyalty that pervades the poem and that was integral to the Germanic secular ethos. As the ethical norm we are given Beowulf's almost unparalleled loyalty to his uncle and lord, Hygelac, in his refusal to accept the crown in lieu of Heardred, Hygelac's son, after the king has been killed in Frisian fields; and as one of several contrasts we find suggested the latent treachery in Heorot, in the character of Unferth, who has killed his kinsmen in battle, and in Hrothulf, Hrothgar's nephew and co-ruler, who will one day usurp the Danish throne.

The complexity and richness of the poem may perhaps be best summarized in the concept of *contrast*. For contrasts (and parallels) are what bind the poem into a unity, operating in the larger structural elements, character presentations, theme, and even in the most detailed stylistic matters. It is this unifying technique that allows the poet to bring into his poem the many apparent digressions, whether they be legendary—as they largely are in the first part of the poem—or historical—as in the second part. And it permits the Christian and pagan elements to co-exist meaningfully within the framework of the poem.[12]

The two major structural divisions provide the over-all contrast of youth vs. age: with youth in Part I is connected the ideal of the perfect retainer, in Beowulf's strengths of mind, body, and character, and in his conception of service to both Hrothgar and to his proper lord, Hygelac; with old age in Part II, in the ideal of the Germanic king, in Beowulf's attempt not only to protect his people but to provide them with treasure as part of the *comitatus* bond. One of the critical problems in this respect is whether the aged Beowulf is indeed "perfect," either as a secular hero or as an exemplar of the Christian hero, receiving the "doom" of the righteous as his eternal reward; or whether he is "flawed" in his eagerness for treasure, thus tragically exemplifying the degeneration and sinful pride which Hrothgar in his homily (ll. 1735 ff.) had warned him of; or whether Beowulf, though admirable by the "inner" secular standards of the poem, falls short from the "outer" Christian perspective of the poet, being subject to the curse and damnation laid upon the dragon's hoard, with only the "hope of heathens" for an afterlife reward—the hope which is hell.[13]

The youth-age structural contrast is also related to success and failure and, in a widening sense, to the rise and fall of nations.[14] In Part I, the rise of the Scylding dynasty in Denmark is outlined as a prelude to the story proper, and the glory of

12. Cf. A. Bonjour, *The Digressions in Beowulf* (Oxford, 1950).

13. See the chapter "Beowulf, Christian Hero," in M. B. McNamee's *Honor and the Epic Hero* (New York, 1960); M. E. Goldsmith, "The Christian Perspective in *Beowulf*," AGB, pp. 71–90; E. G. Stanley, "Hæthenra Hyht in *Beowulf*," AGB, pp. 136–151.

14. The concept of the youth-age symbolic unity was first clearly formulated by J. R. R. Tolkien in the seminal article, "*Beowulf*: The Monsters and the Critics," PBA, 1936, XXII (1937), 245–295; it was reprinted separately in 1959, and is reproduced in *An Anthology* . . . (n. 9).

the hall and court of Hrothgar at the peak of its opulence, with its Germanic aura of singing, feasting, and drinking, gift-giving and magnanimity of spirit is set scenically and directly before our eyes. Indeed the panorama of heroic life is suggested by the allusions to and digressions on heroic stories from the whole realm of Germania. In Part II the focus is on the end of the Geatish nation. The setting, in contrast to that of Part I, is the desolate headland and barrow where Beowulf fights the dragon, his own hall having already been destroyed by the dragon's breath. The panorama is now historical rather than legendary, unfolding in flashbacks by the poet himself, then by Beowulf, and finally by Wiglaf's messenger: it reveals the progressive elimination of the members of the Hrethling dynasty—the eldest son of King Hrethel accidentally slain by bowshot at his brother Hæthcyn's hands, Hæthcyn killed by the Swedes, and the last brother, Hygelac, humbled in Frisia and his son Heardred later killed by the Swedes; and Beowulf, the last survivor, is childless.[15] The messenger prophesies the final defeat and dispersal of the Geats in a memorable passage incorporating the "useless treasure" theme:

> "No one living
> Should enjoy these jewels; no beautiful women
> Wear them, gleaming and golden, from their necks,
> But walk, instead, sad and alone
> In a hundred foreign lands, their laughter
> Gone forever, as Beowulf's has gone,
> His pleasure and his joy. Spears shall be lifted,
> Many cold mornings, lifted and thrown,
> And warriors shall waken to no harp's bright call
> But the croak of the dark-black raven, ready
> To welcome the dead, anxious to tell
> The eagle how he stuffed his craw with corpses,
> Filled his belly even faster than the wolves."
>
> [ll. 3015–27]

The rise and fall of nations that is the extension of the youth and age of the hero is emphasized further in the contrast

15. On the poetic manipulation of the historical material, see S. B. Greenfield, "Geatish History: Poetic Art and Epic Quality in *Beowulf*," *Neophil*, XLVII (1963), 211–217.

between the *tones* of the two halves of the poem. The heroic dominates in the first part, with the evocation of such a concept as that of the good king, or in the heroic resolution Beowulf exhibits in confrontation with Wyrd or Fate, or in Beowulf's advice to Hrothgar upon Æschere's death that

> "It is better for us all
> To avenge our friends, not mourn them forever.
> Each of us will come to the end of this life
> On earth; he who can earn it should fight
> For the glory of his name; fame after death
> Is the noblest of goals."

The elegiac dominates the second part, from the elegy of the last survivor (ll. 2247 ff.) who buries the hoard the dragon takes possession of, to the lament of Hrethel for his son Herebeald and the elegy of the old man whose son hangs on the gallows, to the final lament around Beowulf's funeral mound.

On the one hand, the larger contrasts just mentioned are modified by such matters as the arrival and ship burial of Scyld, which serves as a prolegomenon to the whole poem and which enhances both the heroic and elegiac within itself as well as affording a larger parallelism to the burial of Beowulf at the poem's conclusion; the seeds of downfall in the Danish dynasty sown in the significant allusions to future treachery and to the burning of Heorot; age in the figure of King Hrothgar himself; and the central helplessness of the Danes under the ravages of the Grendel clan. Further, there is the *historical* allusion in Part I to the death of Hygelac,[16] an allusion made at the moment Wealhtheow bestows the necklace upon Beowulf; and Hygelac's fall serves to unify the impending doom of both Danish and Geatish nations.[17] In Part II the elegiac is qualified somewhat by the heroic actions recounted, and especially by Wiglaf's behavior in coming to Beowulf's rescue in the face of the flight of the other retainers; but though his aid is not too

16. The historicity of this incident is attested by Gregory of Tours, the *Liber Historiae Francorum*, and the *Liber Monstrorum*; see Chambers-Wrenn (n. 2), pp. 2–4, 381–387.
17. See Brodeur, *Art of Beowulf*, pp. 71–87.

little it is too late, serving only to heighten the *lif is laene* 'life is transitory' theme that is so central to the epic.

On the other hand, the larger structural contrasts are rein-forced by lesser antitheses throughout the poem, as the qualifi-cations in the preceding paragraph have already suggested. To these might be added the use of character contrasts, as in Hroth-gar's scop's allusions to Sigemund (good) and Heremod (bad) in connection with his "improvised lay"[18] about Beowulf on the way back from the mere, or in the Thryth (niggardly, wicked)-Hygd (liberal, gentle) contrast. There are, furthermore, sym-bolic contrasts, good and evil finding their correspondences in light and darkness, joy and sorrow.[19] And, on the most detailed stylistic level, within the semantic and syntactic collocations of the poetic line, we find such moments as the one in which Beowulf comes, the morning after the celebration of Grendel's death, to ask whether Hrothgar has spent the night pleasantly. "Ne frin þu æfter sælum! Sorh is geniwod/Denigum leodum. Dead is Æschere," replies the king. ('Ask not after joys! Sorrow is renewed to the people of the Danes. Dead is Æschere.') The opposition of joy and sorrow is suggested in one way by the syntactic break in the line, yet the alliterative connection of *sælum* and *sorh* underlies the confluence of the emotions. Simi-larly, in the passage in which Grendel stalks Heorot: "Com on wanre niht/ scriðan sceadugenga. Sceotend swæfon," (In the dark night the walker in shadows came striding. The shooters slept), the moving Grendel and the sleeping warriors are effectively contrasted through the syntactic severance and the chiastic use of the verbs, yet brought into their soon-to-be-realized association by the alliterative and metrical pattern.[20]

These are but samples of the range of the *Beowulf* poet's

18. A skeptical attitude toward the improvisation of heroic lays has been urged by N. E. Eliason, "The 'Improvised Lay' in *Beowulf*," *PQ*, xxxi (1952), 171–179.

19. H. G. Wright, "Good and Evil; Light and Darkness; Joy and Sorrow in *Beowulf*," *RES*, N. S. viii (1957), 1–11.

20. See Quirk, "Poetic Language" (IV, 14), p. 160; S. B. Green-field, "Grendel's Approach to Heorot: Syntax and Poetry," in *New Approaches* . . . (Int., 2).

accomplishments in drawing the many disparate elements of his poem into one of the triumphs of English poetry. One further example, at a little greater length, will have to suffice for this critical history. The Finn Episode (ll. 1068–1159), a sample of the entertainment provided by the scop in Heorot after the defeat of Grendel, is an excellent tragedy in itself, focusing as it does on the conflicting claims imposed upon Hengest: to revenge his dead leader Hnæf on the one hand, and to keep the peace pact he has been forced to make with Hnæf's slayer, King Finn of Frisia, on the other. The final resolution, with Hengest and the Danes slaughtering Finn and his retainers in their hall, and thus exacting revenge, is presented by Hrothgar's scop as a Danish victory, and on this level alone would find its *raison d'être* in the context of *Beowulf*. But the Episode operates on more subtle lines in the over-all unity of the poem. For though the scop has concentrated on Hengest, the *Beowulf* poet himself gives another perspective through Hildeburh's wretchedness: her loss of brother (Hnæf), son, and finally of husband (Finn), so that the heroic-elegiac pattern of the whole poem is reflected in miniature in this story. On another level, the theme of treachery is emphasized at the beginning, in the litotical comment that Hildeburh, Finn's wife, had "little reason to speak well of the loyalty of the Jutes," and the theme of treachery runs throughout the piece, to be picked up after the scop finishes his song when the *Beowulf* poet alludes to the future treachery in Heorot itself. In another way, the Episode reveals the failure of human attempts to achieve peaceful compromise, a theme echoing throughout the *Beowulf*; and the unenviable position of Queen Hildeburh has its immediate parallel in Wealhtheow, who will be the loser when nephew Hrothulf usurps, and a more distant parallel in Wealhtheow's daughter Freawaru, whose future suffering will be adumbrated by Beowulf in his report to Hygelac. Finally, the Finn Episode is balanced in Beowulf's report by the Ingeld Episode, for the former treats of a past triumph within the perspective of disaster, while the latter foretells future disaster within the perspective of triumph (at least we know from *Widsith* that Ingeld, though he burned Heorot, was defeated by Hrothgar and Hrothulf).[21] In this balanced presentation of past and future, we can see one more way in which the poet has gained epic scope for the folk-tale contests that are the narrative basis upon which he so expertly and admirably built.[22]

The Finn Episode in *Beowulf* presents a part of what must have been a series of stories about the Danish-Frisian conflict. Another segment is preserved in the fragmentary *Fight at Finnsburg,* now extant only in Hickes's transcription in his *Linguarum Vett. Septentrionalium Thesaurus* (1705), the manuscript having subsequently been lost.[23] Only some forty-seven lines of this probably early oral poem remain, recounting an earlier stage in the hostilities, when the Frisians began the attack on Hnæf. From what can be pieced together from the Fragment and the Episode, Hnæf and his band of sixty Danes evidently had been paying a visit to Hnæf's sister Queen Hildeburh and her husband King Finn, when through the treachery of the Eotens (Jutes?) in the service of Finn, Hnæf's party was attacked in their quarters by the Frisians. The Fragment's beginning is missing, but clearly a sentinel for the Danes spots the moonlight (or torchlight) glittering on swords as the treacherous attack is about to be launched. The Danes, after taking up positions at the two doors of the Germanic hall, hold out against the besiegers for five days without losing a man. As the Fragment ends, a Dane—some critics say a Frisian—is

---

21. For interpretations of the Finn Episode, see R. A. Williams, *The Finn Episode in Beowulf* (Cambridge, 1924); A. G. Brodeur, "The Climax of the Finn Episode," *Univ. of California Pubs. in English,* III, no. 8 (1943), 285–362, and "Design and Motive in the Finn Episode," *ibid.,* XIV (1943), 1–42; K. Malone, "Hildeburg and Hengest," *ELH,* x (1943), 257–284. For one view on the Ingeld Episode, see K. Malone, "The Tale of Ingeld," in *Studies in Heroic Legend . . . ,* eds. S. Einarrson and N. E. Eliason (Copenhagen, 1959), pp. 1–62; for another, see pp. 157–181 of A. G. Brodeur's *Art of Beowulf.*

22. For further, illuminating comments on the *Beowulf* poet's expertise, see A. Bonjour, *Twelve Beowulf Papers* (Int., 2).

23. The text is edited in most editions of *Beowulf;* for bibliography, see Klaeber's edition, pp. 239–243.

wounded severely and is queried by Hnæf—or Finn?—as to how the warriors are surviving their wounds. From the Episode, we know that in the continuation of the fighting Hnæf died, and was succeeded by Hengest, who ultimately made a truce with Finn when both forces were decimated. The Episode's concentration, as we have seen, was on the tragedy of Hengest and Hildeburh, and the final revenge on Finn.

The emphasis and the style of the Fragment are quite different from those of the Episode, and from the epic *Beowulf*. The *Fight at Finnsburg* is no curtailed epic, but a bona fide *lay*, a brief narrative with compressed description and rapid conversation.[24] The poem must have opened with the sentry's questions about the meaning of the light he sees, for Hnæf replies: "This is no daylight dawning from the east, nor dragon flying, nor gables of this hall on fire; but here they bring forth (arms), the birds (of prey) sing, the gray-coated one [i.e., the wolf] shrieks, the battle wood resounds, shield answers shaft." The narrative progresses in a series of *then* announcements: "Then arose many a gold-adorned thane, girded on his sword"; "Then yet Guthhere tried to restrain Garulf"; "Then was the noise of battle in the hall"; "Then a wounded warrior departed"; "Then the guardian of the people straightway asked him." The movement jerks along powerfully, as the poet commends the small band for their courage and devotion in repaying their leader for the "white mead" (meed?) he had dealt out in more prosperous days. Although the *Fight* is mainly valued for the light it throws on the whole complex of the Finnsburg story, and particularly on the *Beowulf*ian Episode, it is in its own right a moving account of stark, unvarnished heroic action in the best spirit of ancient Germanic poetry, such a lay as might well have delighted the audience in a Germanic chieftain's hall.

Among other fragments shored against the ruins of extant Germanic heroic poetry are two Old English manuscript leaves, discovered in 1860 in the Royal Library of Copenhagen, con-

24. On stylistic and verse differences between OE epic and lay, see A. Campbell (n. 3).

taining portions of the Walter of Aquitaine story.[25] The legend itself, varied in its surviving forms in different languages, basically recounts the history of Hagen, Walter, and Hildegund (-gyth) after they were sent as hostages to the court of Attila the Hun by their respective nations. When Gunther succeeds to the Burgundian throne and refuses to continue payments for his countryman Hagen, the latter escapes, as later do Walter and Hildegund, who have become betrothed. Loaded with treasure they have taken from Attila, the lovers are accosted on their way to safety by Gunther, covetous of the treasure, and his unwilling vassal Hagen, who in the Hunnish court had become a brother-in-arms of Walter's. A peace offer of some of the treasure is rejected by Gunther, and the Burgundian party attack Walter who, protected in a narrow defile, defeats them one by one till only Gunther and Hagen, who has hitherto refused to fight, remain. In the Latin *Waltharius*, the conflict ends after Hagen, finally drawn into the fight by Gunther's shame and by the death of his nephew in the earlier fighting, and Gunther attack Walter in the open, each of the heroes being maimed but not killed in the encounter, and being reconciled at last.

The Old English fragments, consisting of sixty-odd lines which modern editors entitle *Waldere*,[26] include three speeches evidently connected with the final combat between Guthhere and Hagena, and Waldere. Only the speaker of lines 11 and following of Fragment II, in which the Burgundian King Guthhere is taunted, is identified, as Waldere himself; there has been great critical controversy over the attribution of the other two speeches. The speech of Fragment I, urging Waldere on to combat, has been attributed to either Hildegyth or Hagena; the first speech of Fragment II (ll. 1–10), praising a sword, has been attached by some to Hildegyth or Hagena, by most to Guthhere. Critical uncertainty also exists as to the order of the

25. See F. P. Magoun, Jr., and H. M. Smyser, eds. and trans., *Walter of Aquitaine: Materials for the Study of his Legend*, Conn. College Monograph, No. 4 (New London, Conn., 1950).
26. Edited in *ASPR*, VI, and by F. Norman, 2nd ed. (London, 1949).

fragments, at least two recent scholars believing they should come in reverse sequence, though they differ on their attributions of the speeches.[27] The relation of *Waldere* to the Latin epic *Waltharius*, formerly ascribed to Ekkehard I of St. Gall and thus dated about 930 but now ascribed to a "Brother Gerald" and variously dated, has been a problem, though the consensus sees the Old English lines as the remnants of an earlier (eighth century?) independent version. Even the nature of the original Old English poem has been called into question: formerly critics considered it, from its leisurely style, an epic approaching the proportions if not the quality of *Beowulf*; recently it has been suggested to have been more on the order of the shorter epic like *Maldon* (see below). Miss Brady aptly summarizes the quality of the fragments:

> They are too short to reveal anything of this poet's narrative technique and methods of characterization and motivation, but they do exhibit a surprising number of the salient characteristics of Old English poetic style: the literal and metaphorical bipartite appellatives and adjectival compounds, direct in their reference and often vivid in their descriptiveness; the literal characterizing periphrases; the variations, appositions, and parallelisms; the *maðelode*-formula, with its variation *gyddode wordum*; even a good example of the characterizing *se þe* clause which the *Beowulf* poet uses with telling effect.[28]

In brief, it is a pity that we do not possess more of *Waldere*; what survives is largely interesting only as it relates, however puzzlingly, to the Walter saga as a whole and as it exemplifies common traits of Old English heroic conduct and poetic style.

Of much greater interest among early Old English verse reflecting the Germanic heroic tradition is *Widsith*, not in itself a heroic poem but a poetic *tour de force* which presents allusively the raw materials for many such poems. The text is

27. See B. H. Carroll, Jr., "An Essay on the Walther Legend," *Florida State University Studies*, v (1952), 123–179, and G. Eis, "Waltharius-Probleme," in *Britannica: Festschrift für Hermann M. Flasdieck* (Heidelberg, 1960), pp. 102–107. For arguments for the usual order of the fragments, see J. D. Pheifer, "*Waldere* I. 29–31," *RES*, N. S. xi (1960), 183–186.

28. C. Brady, review of Magoun and Smyser (n. 25), *Speculum*, xxvi (1951), 400.

preserved only in the Exeter Book.[29] The lay or epic material is embodied in three *thulas,* or mnemonic poetic lists, which comprise the main body of the poem, around and through which is woven the lyric-narrative "history" of the fictitious *scop* Widsith "far-journey(er)."[30] The whole poem is carefully conceived and fashioned, though there are a few obvious interpolations by a later poet or scribe in the process of transmission down to the Exeter Book.

Nine lines of prologue set forth the fictitious Widsith's lineage and penchant for travel, particularly emphasizing his visit to the chief figure of the Germanic Heroic Age, Eormanric, king of the Ostrogoths, fl. 375[31] (a hero to be eclipsed in later legend by the sixth-century Visigothic King Theodric, d. 526— the Dietrich von Bern of German story). The scop then speaks for himself, in lines 10–134, reciting in detail the knowledge of kings and kingship and nations he has garnered in his long-lived career as a court poet. The first thula, possibly the earliest surviving bit of Old English verse, is patterned on an "A ruled B" scheme, with suitable stylistic variation; it culminates in line 35 with "Offa ruled the Angles, Alewih the Danes," and a subsequent expansion on the prowess of Offa and then of the Danish co-rulers Hrothwulf and Hrothgar of *Beowulf* fame. If, as some have suggested, *Widsith* was composed in its present form in Mercia, this expatiation on the Anglian King Offa I, king while the Angles still resided on the Danish peninsula, would have special point as analogous praise for his English descendant Offa II (eighth century)—compare the Offa-Thryth digression in *Beowulf,* lines 1931b–62. Most observers, however, date *Widsith* in the late seventh century.[32]

29. The great early twentieth-century edition is R. W. Chambers' *Widsith: A Study in Old English Heroic Legend* (Cambridge, 1912); the definitive modern edition is K. Malone's *Widsith,* rev. ed. (Copenhagen, 1962). Malone has an exhaustive bibliography on the poem.

30. On scops, see L. F. Anderson, *The Anglo-Saxon Scop,* Univ. of Toronto Studies in Philology, 1 (1903).

31. See C. Brady, *The Legends of Ermanaric* (Berkeley, 1943).

32. So Chambers and Malone; for arguments for a tenth-century dating, see R. L. Reynolds, "Le Poème anglo-saxon *Widsith:* Réalité et Fiction," *Le Moyen Age,* LIX (1953), 299–324, and G. Langenfelt, "Studies in *Widsith,*" *Namn och Bygd,* XLVII (1959), 70–111.

At line 50 the scop reintroduces his personal affairs in several lines with a strong elegiac flavor but concluding with an emphasis upon his success in singing. The second thula follows, principally in the pattern "With C-tribe I was," with interruptions to praise the liberality of the Burgundian King Guthhere and the Lombard Ælfwine (Alboin), reserving the greatest praise for Eormanric's gift of a precious ring (*beag*) — which he gave to his own lord, the Myrging Eadgils, in return for the regranting of his ancestral estate—and for Ealhhild's (Eormanric's Queen = Swanhild?) similar gift, for which he sang her praises throughout many lands. The famous lines:

> Đonne wit Scilling   sciran reorde
> for uncrum sigedryhtne   song ahofan,
> hlude bi hearpan   hleoþor swinsade,

(When we two, Scilling and I, with clear voice before our liege-lord raised up song, loud to the [accompaniment of the] harp the song resounded)

suggesting the practice of singing in tandem,[33] lead into the third thula, whose basic pattern is "D sought I" with extrapolations on the figures of Wulfhere and Wyrmhere and on Wudga and Hama. Widsith's first-person speech ends with further words of political wisdom about the nature of kingship. Nine lines of epilogue echo the nine lines of the prologue, but now the concern is not with the single scop Widsith but with all gleemen who wander till they find discriminating and generous lords who wish to win fame on earth through poetic praise, performing noble deeds "till all passes, light and life together." The poem's stress on the liberality of kings in rewarding scopic endeavor has suggested to one modern critic that *Widsith* was a real scop's plea for patronage.[34]

The subtleties of the architectonics and stylistics of *Widsith* cannot be explored here; the reader is warmly recommended to Malone's edition of the poem. Nor is this the place to con-

33. See C. L. Wrenn, AGB, pp. 119–120. It is possible that Scilling is the name of the scop's harp rather than of another singer.
34. W. H. French, "*Widsith* and the Scop," *PMLA*, LX (1945), 623–630.

sider the many problems relating to the provenience of the poem and its parts. On this score perhaps the words of R. W. Chambers are most judicious:

> Excluding this catalogue of kings (18–49) and . . . the later interpolations [of Oriental and Biblical references in certain lines], the poem seems homogeneous enough. It is of course quite possible. . . . that between our poem, and the mass of lays of the Eormanric and other cycles which lie behind it, there may intervene some heroic catalogues of champions or of peoples. But . . . it is not clear that the same poet who depicted the figure of Widsith the traveller could not have drawn up these lists for himself from the lays which he knew.
> [p. 141]

Although *Deor*, like *Widsith*, employs a fictitious scop as narrator and also alludes to Germanic heroic story, its tone is overridingly elegiac, and we shall consider it in the section on the elegies. Two poems of the tenth century, however, deserve consideration in this chapter, for, though they do not concern themselves with Germanic story, they nevertheless reflect the continuing vitality of and esteem for the secular heroic values of the Age of Bede and earlier. These are the two historical poems, *The Battle of Brunanburh* and *The Battle of Maldon*. The former is a *Chronicle* poem; that is, it appears as the entry for the year 937 in four of the manuscripts of *The Anglo-Saxon Chronicle*—there are five other such poems, which will be dealt with under miscellaneous verse. The latter is extant only in the transcript of about 1724 by John Elphinston, the manuscript (which also included the unique text of Asser's *Life of Alfred*) having perished in the Cottonian fire that scorched the *Beowulf* manuscript in 1731.[35]

Brunanburh is a panegyric on the heroism of King Æthelstan and his young brother Eadmund, who was but sixteen at the time of the battle celebrated. These grandsons of Alfred the Great defeated and put to flight near Brunanburh the combined

---

35. Both *Brunanburh* and *Maldon* are edited in *ASPR*, VI; a separate edition of the former is by A. Campbell (London, 1938), of the latter by E. V. Gordon (London, 1937) reprtd. 1960. For prose translations, see *EHD*, items 1 and 10.

forces of King Constantine II of Scotland, King Eugenius (Owen) of the Strathclyde Britons, and Anlaf, son of the Viking king of Dublin. Precisely where the historic battle site was is a matter of conjecture, though it was certainly somewhere on the west coast between Chester and Dumfries, possibly the city of Bromborough in Wirral.[36] To the Old English poet, this victory was the most glorious occasion in English history:

> since the Angles
> And Saxons arrived in England out of
> The East, brave men trying a broad
> And dangerous sea, daring warriors
> Who swept away the Britons, seized
> The land and made it theirs alone.[37]

The poem is a tissue of heroic formulaic clichés, themes, and stylistic variation:

> *Her Æthelstan cyning,   eorla drihten,*
> *beorna beahgifa*   . . .

"In this year[38] Æthelstan the King, lord of earls, ring-giver to men . . ." it begins. And toward the end it introduces the "beasts of battle" to whom the victorious English leave the bloodstained field. But the conventional heroic epithets and stylistic mannerisms are nevertheless infused with a vitality and spirit that is hard to analyze; perhaps it lies partly in the specificity of the occasion, perhaps partly in the poet's shifting of point of view from the English to the enemy to the passing of time (as "God's, the eternal Lord's, bright candle rose up in the morning, the glorious star, and glided over the earth until that noble creation sank to rest") to the dead and the dying to the fleeing Scots and Vikings, and so on. The panoramic sweep of the poem may not bring us *vis-à-vis* individual heroes, but it admirably suggests the heroic virtues embodied in their actions.

36. The most recent advocate of Bromborough is J. McN. Dodgson, "The Background of Brunanburh," *SBVS*, xiv (1956–57), 303–316.
37. Cited from B. Raffel, *Poems from the Old English*, 2nd ed. (Lincoln, Neb., 1964).
38. N. Isaacs, "Battlefield Tour: *Brunanburg*," *NM*, LXIII (1962), 236–244, suggests that *her* in this instance means "in this place," emphasizing the 'homeland' concept, the need to maintain by triumph that which was originally wrested by triumph.

Maldon, on the other hand, is in the more scenic style of the older epics, and its heroes in defeat, especially Earl Byrhtnoth, spring wonderfully to life—so much so that many scholars have felt the poet must have been an eyewitness to the battle. Most critics, indeed, have at least taken the poem as an accurate depiction of the historical event reported more laconically in the *Chronicle* entry for the year 991:

> In this year Olaf came with 93 ships to Folkstone, and ravaged round about it, and then from there went to Sandwich, and so from there to Ipswich, and overran it all, and so to Maldon. And Ealdorman Brihtnoth came against him there with his army and fought against him; and they killed the ealdorman there and had control of the field;[39]

and with embellishments of the marvelous in Byrhtferth's *Vita Oswaldi,* about 1000 (see III, 36) and in the *Liber Eliensis,* about 1170. But recently J. B. Bessinger has cautioned against the "equation of poetic verisimilitude to historical verity";[40] and I am inclined to heed his *caveat.* For though an historical battle was the occasion of the poem, under the scop's handling of the traditional heroic formulas its real heroes merge with legendary ones,[41] and their conduct reflects the traditions of the heroic code embodied in the *comitatus:* obedience, loyalty, truthfulness, fortitude, self-sacrifice in a just cause—with the addition of the Christian virtues of trusting in God and submissiveness to His will.

Unfortunately, the beginning and end of *Maldon* are missing, though it seems unlikely that much has been lost at either point. The poem represents the English army, specifically the Essex *fyrd* under the leadership of the old earl Byrhtnoth, drawn up against the Viking invaders along the Blackwater estuary, called the Panta in the poem. Dramatically highlighted

---

39. From the A version, as translated by D. Whitelock in *The Anglo-Saxon Chronicle* (II, 1), p. 82; see Whitelock, n. 3 on this dating of A (ostensibly written for the year 993) and the disputed presence of Olaf Tryggvason at this battle.

40. "*Maldon* and the *Olafsdrapa:* An Historical Caveat," *AGB,* p. 31.

41. See E. B. Irving, Jr., "The Heroic Style in *The Battle of Maldon,*" *SP,* LVIII (1961), 457–467, esp. pp. 459–460, though he, unlike Bessinger, takes the poem as an authentic record of the battle.

is the demand of the Viking messenger for tribute to buy off
the invaders, and the earl's scathing reply:

"Listen, sailors. Can you hear what we say?
We offer a tribute of tempered steel,
Javelins and spears with poisoned points,
Weapons and armor you'll wear only
In death. Messenger, this is your answer:
Tell your leaders the unlucky news
That this earl and his army don't shake at their boasts,
But will stand and defend their homes and fields
And all this land and these people, who belong
To Ethelred, my king . . .
We forge our peace on the points of our spears
And they're yours for the asking: blood not gold."
[Raffel trans.]

The loyalty evinced here by the earl to even so "unready" a
king as Æthelred has its counterpart in the second part of the
poem (ll. 205 ff.) when Byrhtnoth lies dead and his *comitatus*,
related by kinship and friendship, utter their heroic vows one
by one and fight till they drop beside their lord. But two crucial
actions intervene: first, when the Vikings, repulsed by the tide
and the English defense of the bridge or causeway, *lytegian*, or
deceive, Byrhtnoth into allowing them to cross the river and
engage in full combat—it is *for ofermode*, says the poet, that
the earl succumbs to the Danish deceit, and whether *ofermod*
is excessive pride that is "magnificent, perhaps, but certainly
wrong" or magnificent and right,[42] Byrhtnoth's action leads
with the inevitability of tragedy to the moving denouement;
second, when the earl lies dead and the battle stands paused
and poised, some unheroic soldiers precipitate the ultimate
disaster by fleeing to the shelter of the nearby woods. The contrast between the cowards' action, reminiscent of the flight of
Beowulf's retainers in the dragon fight, and the heroism of the
loyal *comitatus* following, is the heart of the poem's representation of the heroic mode, culminating in the oft-quoted lines

42. See R. W. V. Elliott, "Byrhtnoth and Hildebrand: A Study in
Heroic Technique," AGB, pp. 57–59.

that have summed up that way of life for all readers of Old
English literature:

> "*Hige sceal þe heardra,   heorte þe cenre,*
> *mod sceal þe mare,   þe ure mægen lytlað*"

(Mind must be the stronger, heart the braver, courage must
be the greater, as our strength dwindles).

VI

The Christian Saint as Hero

THE RELATION between the Germanic secular hero and the Anglo-Saxon saint as the latter appears in the Old English Christian epic has for the most part been oversimplified. This Christian epic hero has been viewed as garbed in the borrowed robes, or rather armor, of his Germanic counterpart, as a warrior venturing into battle against spiritual evil and the forces of Satan even as the secular lord and his *comitatus* engaged the armed forces of predatory enemies. There is, of course, much truth in this picture: as we shall see in this chapter and the next, Christ and His saints come marching in with many of the qualities of a Beowulf or a Byrhtnoth. And the phraseology and tone in which these qualities and the actions are depicted in the poetry are similar to those arraying the heroes of the Anglo-Saxon secular world. These "lives" are quite different from the Latin saints' lives written in the Age of Bede (see Ch. I). But recent understanding of verse composition by theme and formula, whether in oral or written form, has caused many scholars to discard earlier notions of explicit borrowing or dependence of one poem upon another based upon similarity of word hoard or phrasing. We have also been recently reminded of the rather complex overlapping in the two kinds of heroes: Old English poetic saints' lives are not just Christian themes treated in the spirit of secular heroic poetry; indeed, the stories of saints' lives may well have conditioned some of the concepts appearing in what is generally considered *echt-germanisch*. Grendel's cannibalism, for example, is not typical of the Germanic *eoten*, or giant, even if it is of the later troll (cf. the ON *Grettissaga*), but rather like one of the customs of the Anthropophagi, who are the antagonists in the Apocryphal story of St. Andrew; and the *Beowulf* poet may have acquired this idea from a Christian source or from a classical source in a monastic library.[1]

The Old English poetic version of the life of St. Andrew, the late-ninth–century (?) *Andreas*, beautifully illustrates the complexity just mentioned. This 1722-line poem, which is extant only in the Vercelli Book,[2] though there is an Old English prose version in the *Blickling Homilies* (see Ch. III) and another in MS CCCC 198, was long thought to be directly indebted to *Beowulf*. Based on a nonextant Latin recension of the Greek *Acts of St. Andrew and St. Matthew*, it sets forth the story of Andrew's journey to Mermedonia to free Matthew from the Anthropophagi, who had imprisoned and blinded him, reserving him along with others for their feasting festival on the thirtieth day. The sea journey to a foreign land with a band of "thanes," the rescue from man-eating fiends, and so on, are reminiscent of Beowulf's mission to Denmark to free Hrothgar from the ravages of Grendel; and certain locutions strikingly resembling those in *Beowulf* seem awkward, out-of-place, and even ungrammatical in their contexts in *Andreas*, suggesting direct and ill-advised copying: for example, the temple in Jerusalem (*And.*, l. 668) is called *heah and horngeap* 'high and gabled,' an expression found elsewhere only in *Beowulf*, line 82, where it more fittingly describes the royal Heorot; the floodwaters destroying the Mermedonians in *Andreas*, line 1526, are referred to as *meoduscerwen* 'a serving of mead' (cf. *Bwf.*,

1. See review of Brooks's edition (n. 2) by R. Woolf, *MÆ*, xxxii (1963), 134–136.
2. Edited in *ASPR*, ii; G. P. Krapp, *Andreas and the Fates of the Apostles* (Boston, 1906); K. R. Brooks, *Andreas and The Fates of the Apostles* (Oxford, 1961). For poetic translation, see C. W. Kennedy, *Early English Christian Poetry* (London and New York, 1952), from which the translations of *Andreas* in this chapter are quoted.

l. 769: *ealuscerwen*), a much debated term;[3] and in line 303, Andreas, replying that he has no money to pay for his voyage, says that he not only has no gold or treasure but neither *landes ne locenra beaga* 'of land nor of linked rings' (cf. *Bwf.*, l. 2995), his reference to land being absurd and the genitives ungrammatical.[4] But the journey of Andrew to Mermedonia *is* in the Greek and Latin accounts, and its resemblance to Beowulf's to Heorot may be completely fortuitous (although we cannot altogether discount the possibility that the *Andreas* poet knew the *Beowulf* and was attracted to the story of Andrew because of the resemblance); and the nature of composition by theme and formula is such that the *Andreas* poet, an inferior to the *Beowulf* poet, may, under the influence of his poetic heritage, simply have chosen his formulas on occasion neither wisely nor too well.[5] But even in lines 405–414, a poignant passage in which Andrew's followers refuse to be put ashore despite the rigors of the ocean voyage, a passage reflecting so much of the Anglo-Saxon *comitatus* arrangement:

> "If we desert you   whither shall we wander
> Lordless and lonely,   lacking all good?
> We shall be loathed   in every land,
> Hated of all men   where valiant heroes
> Sit in assembly   holding debate
> Who best has bolstered   his lord in battle
> When hand and buckler   were bearing the brunt,
> Hacked with swords,   on the field of fate,"

—even here, Miss Woolf reminds us, the opening elegiac question, though characteristically Old English in its turn of phrase ("Hwider hweorfað we hlafordlease . . .") is nevertheless based upon its Latin-Greek original (see n. 1). And what is most noteworthy about Andrew's martial prowess in the Old

3. See R. M. Lumiansky, "The Contexts of O.E. 'Ealuscerwen' and 'Meoduscerwen'," *JEGP*, XLVIII (1949), 116–126.

4. Brooks, pp. xxiv–xxv.

5. See L. J. Peters, "The Relationship of the Old English *Andreas* to *Beowulf*," *PMLA*, LXVI (1951), 844–863, and a review of Brooks's edition by J. J. Campbell, *JEGP*, LXII (1963), 678–680. On the *Andreas* poet's handling of theme, see L. H. Frey, "Exile and Elegy in Anglo-Saxon Christian Epic Poetry," *JEGP*, LXII (1963), 293–302.

English poem is his *patience* in adversity; bold he is but in patience, a quality more eminently suited to a saint than to a Germanic hero, though the latter, too, had to learn to bear the slings and arrows of outrageous fortune.

That *Andreas* is not equal to *Beowulf* as poetry should not be taken as damning—very little in *all* of English literature approaches the literary power of that Old English epic. *Andreas* has its virtues. The epic-formulaic opening sets the heroic mood and then narrows its focus sharply to Matthew:

> Lo! we have heard   of twelve mighty heroes
> Honoured under heaven   in days of old,
> Thanes of God.   Their glory failed not
> In the clash of banners,   the brunt of war,
> After they were scattered   and spread abroad
> As their lots were cast   by the Lord of heaven.
> Famous those heroes,   foremost on earth,
> Brave-hearted leaders   and bold in strife
> When hand and buckler   defended the helm
> On the plain of war,   on the field of fate.
>   One was Matthew. . . .

With Matthew's incarceration and imminent death in Mermedonia established (l. 160), the poet continues with God's promised rescue by shifting the scene to Achaia where He calls upon Andrew to undertake that task. Andrew's dismayed reply is a tissue of Anglo-Saxon formulas and kennings appropriate to the themes of exile and sea voyaging, replete with the common technique of variation:

> "Hu mæg ic, dryhten min,   ofer deop gelad
> fore gefremman   on feorne weg
> swa hrædlice,   heofona scyppend,
> wuldres waldend,   swa ðu worde becwist?
> Ðaet mæg engel þin   eað geferan,
> <halig> of heofenum;   con him holma begang,
> sealte sæstreamas   ond swanrade,
> waroðfaruða gewinn   ond wæterbrogan,
> wegas ofer widland.   Ne synt me winas cuðe,
> eorlas elþeodige,   ne þær æniges wat
> hæleða gehygdo,   ne me herestræta
> ofer cald wæter   cuðe sindon."

("O God of heaven   and Lord of glory
How can I fare   on so far a course
Over the deep ocean   so soon as Thou sayest?
But this Thine angel   may easily do.
From heaven he sees   the ocean-stretches,
All the swan-road   and the salt sea-streams,
The tumult of waves,   the water-terror,
The ways that lengthen   across wide lands.
I have no friends   in that foreign folk,
I know not the mind   of any man there,
And the ocean-ways   across the cold water
To me are unknown.")

There is excess here to be sure, but the passage strikes me in context as not without merit. Its very excess suggests the enormity of the task, from Andrew's point of view, which God imposes upon the apostle, and his all-too-human reaction. And it prepares ironically for the later recounting by Andrew to the Helmsman (God) of the miracles Christ performed on earth, as well as for God's still later reminder to Andrew of the sin involved in that initial refusal when, on the coast of Mermedonia, the apostle finally recognizes his Shepherd-Helmsman. Further, in structure and syntax the passage moves logically and poetically from "How can I . . ." to "That can your angel easily do . . ." to "Friends to me are unknown . . ." (Kennedy's translation obscures this syntactic movement from the subject *I* to the indirect object *me*); and the formulaic terms for the sea move and vary from emphasis on the "depths" to a climactic attention to the "cold" water.

This history is not the place to explore further the poetic possibilities in individual passages of *Andreas*; but there are many. Lines 1253–65 paint a vivid picture of winter as Andrew sits bloody and broken in prison after the first day's tortures— a scene that may be out of keeping with the literal situation in Mermedonia but is nevertheless a fitting *metaphoric* depiction of mood and atmosphere. And the description of the flood engulfing the Mermedonians contains, among other notable features, the ironic "serving of mead" metaphor mentioned above (see n. 3). In addition, though the syntax is loose and important ideas receive grammatical subordination (these have been seen as weaknesses in the poem's style), these practices are not uncommon in the best speech and writing of even our own day, as some modern linguists have pointed out.[6] The narrative pace may jerk along, but it does so in accord with its subject matter, and there are many fine episodes, highlighted by the miracle God performs through Andrew whereby the Merme-donians, as they set upon Andrew to eat him, are beset by the watery flood issuing from the stone column and by the fire spread by God's angel (ll. 1521 ff.). Structurally the poem has virtues too, however much some of them may inhere in the original *Acts*. For example, the first part of the poem focuses on Andrew's talk with the Helmsman, in which the saint answers the Pilot's questions about Christ's life on earth while the rough seas act as counterpoint to the calmness of this discourse; the second part balances the first by pitting Andrew against Satan and his cohorts where Andrew's patience and calm under the three-days-plus tortures is counterpointed by the furious raging of the Mermedonians and the devils. In the first part Andrew relates how God commanded the stone image in the Temple to speak and convert the Jews, and failing in this conversion to travel to Canaan to bring people elsewhere to see the Light; in the second part it is by the gushing forth from the stone column that the Mermedonians are at last converted. *Andreas* is indeed not without literary merit.

Not as much can be said for the little poem that is always coupled with it in editions and commentaries—and shouldn't be: the *Fates of the Apostles*. Though this piece follows *Andreas* in the Vercelli Book and was long thought by some to be part of that Christian epic, there is no doubt now in scholarly quarters that stylistically and otherwise the poems are quite different. The *Fates*, in fact, bears the runic signature of Cynewulf; and

6. See Rynell, *Parataxis and Hypotaxis* (IV, 16), pp. 12–18. Cf. James Sledd, "Coordination (Faulty) and Subordination (Upside-Down)," *College Composition and Communication*, VII (1956), 181–187; reprted, *Readings in Applied English Linguistics*, ed. H. B. Allen (New York, 1958), pp. 354–362.

it is to the poems of this one Anglo-Saxon poet who left his imprimatur on four works that we now turn.

Cynewulf's name, spelled this way, appears near the ends of the poems known as *Juliana* and *Elene*; spelled without the *e*, it is woven into the conclusions of *Christ II* and the *Fates of the Apostles*. Although other poems were for long also considered part of the Cynewulf canon, the stylistic studies of such scholars as S. K. Das and Claes Schaar have convincingly demonstrated that only the four signed poems can be so assigned.[7] The *Dream of the Rood, Guthlac B*, and *Christ I* bear certain stylistic resemblances, but also enough differences to suggest that their authors may have been influenced by Cynewulf but could not have *been* Cynewulf; *Christ III, Phoenix, Guthlac A*, and *Andreas*, other poems considered Cynewulfian by earlier scholars, are definitely outside the canonical pale. Of the signed poems, three are martyrological in nature; the fourth, *Christ II*, is a special exposition of a devotional subject, the Ascension of Christ, and as such will be treated in Chapter VII.

But who was Cynewulf? Apart from the signatures and the content and style of his four poems, we know nothing. Although it was once fashionable to think that the "autobiographical" lines toward the end of *Elene*, in which the poet professes to speak of himself as having led a sinful life until God through His grace had enlightened him and conferred upon him the gift of song, might be taken as a literal confession, we now recognize the conventionality of the *topoi*, or motifs, therein and discount any element of personal revelation. Attempts to identify the poet with Cenwulf, Abbot of Peterborough (d. 1006), Cynewulf, Bishop of Lindisfarne (d. about 782), and Cynwulf, a priest of Dunwich (fl. 803), have proved abortive or inconclusive. Nevertheless, from the subject matter that he chose to write about, from his style, from the dialect that rhymes in *Elene* reveal as underlying the late West Saxon dialect in which the poems are transcribed, and from the two spellings of his

7. S. K. Das, *Cynewulf and the Cynewulf Canon* (Calcutta, 1942); C. Schaar, *Critical Studies in the Cynewulf Group* (Lund, 1949).

name in runic characters, certain deductions can be and have been made. Cynewulf was undoubtedly a literate man, a cleric, whose native dialect was Anglian (and probably West Mercian at that), who lived in the first half of the ninth century. Not a great scholar, he nevertheless knew Latin well; he had a knowledge of the liturgy and of ecclesiastical literature, of doctrine and dogma; and he modeled his Old English poetry upon the Latin sources that contributed his hagiographic and homiletic subject matter.[8]

Unlike the poet of *Andreas*, Cynewulf was not dominated by the traditional heroic conception, though he certainly utilized it, particularly in the *Elene*; nor did he have the taste for violence and the fantastic which that author had. Further, though he composed the famous sea-voyage metaphor at the end of *Christ II* and elaborated upon Elene's sea voyage beyond his source, he was not much given to nature or scenery description such as delighted the *Andreas* and *Beowulf* poets. Whereas the *Beowulf* poet deals with narrative facts and their immediate development, Cynewulf muffles his *narratio* in abstractions, lingers through an abundance of clauses upon the impression of each separate idea, and is generally reflective in his reconsiderations of concepts. Martial vigor is subdued; the emphasis is upon the spiritual conflict between the forces of evil and good, eternally opposed to each other.[9]

The difference between the heroic mood of *Andreas* and the Cynewulfian reflective mode may be seen by comparing the epic-formulaic introduction of the former (see above) with that of the *Fates of the Apostles*:

> Lo, I this song   travel-sick wrought
> In sad spirit,   gathered widely
> How the princes   made known their valor
> Bright and glorious.   Twelve they were
> Illustrious in deeds,   chosen by the Lord

8. See Sisam (II, 6), pp. 1–28; P. O. E. Gradon, ed., *Cynewulf's Elene* (London, 1958), pp. 9–15, 21–23. For an earlier dating of Cynewulf's writing, see G. Storms, "The Weakening of O. E. Unstressed *i* to *e* and the Date of Cynewulf," *ES*, xxxvii (1956), 104–110.

9. See Das, Ch. II, and Schaar, pp. 323–326.

Beloved in life;   their praise sprang widely,
Their might and fame,   over the earth,
Not a little glory   of the thanes of the Prince.
Fate (lot) guided   this holy band
To where they should preach   the Lord's Gospel,
Expound it among men.

There is reference here, as in *Andreas*, to the *Sortes Aposto-lorum, or Lots of the Apostles*; but the first-person opening is elegiac in tone, and the emphasis is upon the fame, the praise, the glory in abstract terms rather than as the concomitants of the "clash of banners" and the defense of "the helm." The *Fates* proceeds to enumerate how each of the twelve met his death; then the poet returns to the elegiac mood, asking for prayers for himself when he must make his long journey. At this point, in riddle fashion, he says that a shrewd man can discover who wrote this poem; and he entwines his runic signature (in the order F,W,U,L,C,Y,N, with a pun on "Wealth [ᚠ 'feoh'] stands last" to indicate that the F is out of natural position) into a general reflection on the transitoriness of life. Then he again says that "Now you know who has been revealed to man in these words." Another solicitation of prayers for himself— undoubtedly this desire for personal salvation rather than a desire for literary fame dictated the runic signature here and in the other poems—and a final hymning of the everlasting glory and joy of heaven conclude this 122-line poem.

The apostles as saintly heroes thus receive no more than catalog treatment in the *Fates*. *Juliana* and *Elene*, on the other hand, go at length into the spiritual struggles of one saint each, and women, interestingly enough. The former is the least impressive as poetry of the Cynewulf group, and for this reason and others has usually been considered the earliest of the four, but its latest editor suggests that its "comparative lack of ingenuity" coupled with its general effect "of uninspired competence rather than . . . of technical hesitancy of a poet working towards his maturity" makes plausible the theory that it is the last of Cynewulf's poems.[10]

10. R. Woolf, ed., *Juliana* (London, 1955), p. 7; but contrast R. W. V. Elliott, "Cynewulf's Runes in *Juliana* and *Fates of the Apostles*,

Juliana, which is preserved in the Exeter Book, consists of 731 lines as it stands, but two passages are missing, between lines 288 and 289 and between 558 and 559. The poem is clearly based on a Latin prose life, perhaps the very one printed in the Bollandist *Acta Sanctorum* for the feast day of February 16. Before Cynewulf's time, Juliana had made her appearance in various martyrologies, notably Bede's. This saint's life and passion follow a typical hagiographical route: in the reign of Maximian (308–314), the young Juliana had been betrothed by her father Affricanus of Nicomedia to Eleusius, a senator and prefect. But the girl, having been converted to Christianity and wishing to preserve her chastity to be a bride of Christ, demanded that her suitor be baptized and forsake his false gods before she would marry him. For her temerity, her father turned her over to Eleusius, who had her scourged, hung by the hair from a tree and beaten for six hours, cast into prison, engulfed in flame, spitted on a sword wheel, and immersed in molten lead. Cheerfully and without harm the saint endured all, finally receiving the palm of martyrdom by beheading.

Cynewulf's treatment of his material deserves respect, if not admiration. Though the subject may to modern taste be a poor one, Cynewulf does a workmanlike job with it, changing, condensing, expanding to concentrate on the great spiritual struggle that is his theological and poetic concern. In the Latin *Vita,* for instance, Juliana at the beginning is somewhat deceitful, demanding first that Eleusius become a prefect before she will marry him, and then, when he gains the prefecture, changing her ground to demand conversion as a prerequisite to marriage. Cynewulf omits the first request, thus whitening Juliana's character. On the other hand, he blackens Eleusius' by transforming the *Vita* prefect's somewhat tolerant attitude toward Christianity mixed with an understandable fear of the emperor's displeasure if he were converted, to a zeal in the serv-

---

ES, xxxiv (1953), 193–204, who, on the basis of the runes being taken together and used in riddle fashion in *Juliana,* upholds the traditional view of its priority in composition. Other editions: ASPR, iii; W. Strunk, Jr., *Juliana* (Boston, 1904), which contains the Latin *Vita* from the *Acta Sanctorum.*

ice of devil-inspired idols—a zeal that matches Juliana's fervid Christianity. Thus Cynewulf sets the stage for the conflict. Again, he expands considerably the role of the devil who, in the guise of an angel, visits Juliana in prison in an attempt to make her forsake her God. The devil is the spiritual counterpart of Eleusius; in the last part of the poem (ll. 514b ff.) he even suddenly rematerializes in the *narratio* before the pagan host to urge punishment on the girl who had so misused him. In the prison scene, the angel-devil pretends that God has sent him to tell Juliana to forsake her God and thus avoid the prepared tortures; but when Juliana appeals to God to reveal the true identity and nature of the visitor, she is told to seize him and demand what she would know. The devil capitulates. In his long "recitative," the torments and persecutions he admits having inflicted upon mankind can be seen as a parallel on a mass scale to those the human antagonist is inflicting upon Juliana. As a structural feature, the devil's quick collapse once Juliana has seized him and his betrayal of his lord Satan act as a contrast to the saint's steadfastness in her faith under much greater duress. And the devil's depressed feelings and lamentations of his lot in the fashion of an elegiac exile also contrast with the tone and spirit of the patient and exultant Juliana. Cynewulf's expansion upon his source in this exilic fashion and in his use of a subdued but nevertheless potent martial imagery (perhaps suggested by Ephesians vi.11–17) may best be seen in lines 382–405, crystallizing the conflict between good and evil that is the poem's dominant theme:

> "When I meet a brave man,   bold in the battle,
> A champion of God   unflinching in the fray,
> Who, heedful of heart,   lifts up against me
> His spiritual armor,   buckler and shield;
> Who deserts not God   but standing at bay
> In prayer is faithful;   then must I flee
> Abased and humbled,   with joyless heart
> In the grip of gledes   bewailing my sorrow
> That I could not conquer   by strength in the strife.
> Then must I sadly   seek out a weaker one,
> Less bold under banner,   whom I may ensnare,

Entice with temptation   and hinder in battle.
Even though in beginning   he purpose some good,
I am quick to spy out   his secretest thought,
How his heart is strengthened,   his resistance wrought.
Through corruption I weaken   the gate in the wall;
When the tower is pierced   and an entrance opened,
Then into his soul   in a storm of darts
I loose the arrows   of evil thought."[11]

The last part of this passage reminds us of Hrothgar's homily on pride in *Beowulf* (ll. 1740 ff.) :

"And then pride grows in his heart, planted
Quietly but flourishing. And while the keeper of his soul
Sleeps on, while conscience rests and the world
Turns faster a murderer creeps closer, comes carrying
A tight-strung bow with terrible arrows.
And those sharp points strike home, are shot
In his breast, under his helmet. He's helpless.
And so the Devil's dark urgings wound him. . . ."
                                                    [Raffel trans.]

After Eleusius and his thanes are drowned on the "swan-road" and sent to hell, where they are ever to be deprived of beer-drinking and the receiving of treasures, the poet ends on the note of his own salvation, weaving his signature into a generalized reflection on man's destiny which, unlike the similar passage in *Fates*, utilizes the letters of his name in groups: the first two groups are the equivalent of Old English words: CYN 'human race' and EWU 'sheep'; the last, LF, are probably to be taken as 'flood' and 'wealth,' the equivalent of the runic names.[12] Unlike the *Fates* epilogue, too, Cynewulf here emphasizes the Judgment Day requital of deeds rather than the ephemerality of life, an emphasis that seems fitting for the theme of *Juliana*. But once again Cynewulf concludes by asking for prayers for his soul's grace.

The 1321-line *Elene*, preserved in the Vercelli Book, is the most epic of Cynewulf's poems in its tone and imagery. The first part of the subject matter, the vision of the Cross that

11. Quoted from C. W. Kennedy, *The Earliest English Poetry* (Int., 5), pp. 211–212.
12. I follow the interpretation of Elliott, n. 10.

came to Constantine as his small force lay encamped waiting for battle against the Huns, lent itself naturally to epic-formulaic dilatation, as did the subsequent sea voyage of his mother Elene to discover the Cross. This search for the Cross and its recovery (on May 3), the *inventio crucis*, occupies the bulk of the poem.

Elene's source is ultimately the *Acta Cyriaci*, a version of which may be found in the *Acta Sanctorum* for May 4. The legend combines the story of the finding of the true Cross with the story of the anti-Christian Jew Judas who ultimately became converted and renamed Cyriacus. Cynewulf's model was undoubtedly a Latin prose recension, the closest parallels in an extant text being in the St. Gall MS 225. There is no valid reason to believe, as some scholars have proposed, that Cynewulf's Latin text was of Irish provenience.[13]

As a saint's life, *Elene* is somewhat unusual, treating not of a passion and death but of a series of revelations, outward miracles being matched by inner illuminations. One may see, in fact, the struggle between good and evil that preoccupied Cynewulf here presented thematically as a contrast between darkness and light, both on a physical and a spiritual level. The narrative opens in the sixth year of Constantine's reign—the poem kaleidoscopes the events of three years: 306, when the Franks threatened the empire; 312, when Constantine received the vision of the Cross; and 322, when he achieved his martial victory—and almost immediately we find ourselves in an epic environment, with Constantine presented in the guise of a Germanic chieftain and with the traditional beasts of battle, the wolf, eagle, and raven, clamoring for their wonted prey. The pagan emperor's vision appears at this literal and figurative darkest hour, dispelling the veil of darkness with its radiance (ll. 69–98). Rejoicing, Constantine has a replica of the visionary Cross made and carried into the thick of the fight, described, not without poetic force, in the conventional formulas

13. Gradon (n. 8), pp. 15–20. For other editions, see *ASPR*, ii, and A. S. Cook, *Elene, Phoenix and Physiologus* (New Haven, Conn., 1919). The poetic translations quoted in this chapter are from Kennedy, *EECP*.

of the attack on the shield wall. The beasts of battle are closer now, and the Romans exultantly triumph, pursuing their foes in a manner not dissimilar to the rout of the enemy depicted in the *Battle of Brunanburh*:

> Loud o'er the legions   the trumpets sang.
> The raven rejoiced;   the wet-winged eagle
> Gazed on the struggle,   the cruel strife;
> The wolf, woodland comrade,   lifted his wail.
> Battle-terror was come.   Then was crashing of shields,
> Crush of heroes   and hard hand-swing,
> The slaughter of many,   when first they met
> The flying darts.   . . . .
> Then headlong fled   the Hunnish folk
> When the Roman war-lord   waging the fight
> Bade lift on high   the Holy Tree.
> Heroes were scattered;   some war took;
> Some barely survived   in the bitter fight;
> Some half-alive   fled to a fastness,
> Sheltered themselves   in the stony cliffs,
> Beside the Danube   defended a stronghold;
> And some at life's end drowned   in the river-depths.
> Then the heroes exulted   pursuing the heathen
> Until evening came   from the dawn of day;
> Ash-spears flew,   their battle adders.
> The host was cut down,   the hated horde;
> Of the Hunnish troops   but few returned home.

After Constantine's conversion to Christianity, he sends Elene to search out the Cross. The famous elaboration of the sea voyage follows, from which I quote a few lines:

> Sea-horses stood ready   at the ocean's rim,
> Bridled sea-stallions   breasting the waves.
> . . . .   O'er the sea-monsters' home
> They drove their foaming   deep-flanked ships.
> Oft on the waves   the stout wood stood
> The blows of the billows.   . . . .
> There might he see   who beheld that sailing
> Sea-wood scud   under swelling sails,
> Sea-steeds plunge   and break through the billows,
> Wave-ships skim.

Lines 276–708 (Secs. 4–8 of the MS), in which Elene tries to ferret out from the Jews the location of the buried Cross, are usually slighted in criticism as a "rather tedious dialectic"

(Kennedy, *EECP*, p. 176), but they have a distinct literary if not necessarily poetic power. Elene's first speech to an assembled 3,000 Jews calls attention to the darkness-light dichotomy:

> "But lo! all wisdom   unwisely you spurned
> Reviling Him   Who with radiant might
> Thought to free you   from fiery torture,
> From burning damnation   and the bonds of hell.
> Upon His face   you spat your filth
> Who created anew   the light of the eye
> Healing your blindness   by His blessed spittle,
> . . . .
> With darkened minds   you thought to mingle
> Light with darkness,   lies with truth,
> Hatred with honour.   . . . .
> With darkened minds   you dared to judge,
> You dared condemn,   that radiant Power;
> You have lived in error   unto this day."

The mourning, fearful Jews select 1,000 of the most learned of their number to confront the queen; this time Elene asks for information by invoking learning herself, by citing David, Isaiah, and Moses. Of the thousand, 500 are now chosen, whom the queen excoriates in a short, pithy speech. In council by themselves, the Jews focus upon one man, Judas, who knows through his father's teaching the answer to Elene's seeking. As a character, Judas is the most interesting person in the poem. Psychologically divided, he knows the truth about the Cross and Christianity: pictured unhistorically as the brother of the protomartyr Stephen, he is yet unwilling to embrace that truth or to satisfy Elene's questioning lest the might of the Hebrews dwindle ever after, as his father had predicted. In informing the council of Jews about the Cross, Judas contrasts the darkness of Christ in the grave for three-days duration and His resurrection as "Light of all light, . . . apparelled in splendour,/ Shining in light, the Triumphant Lord!" He also mentions Saul's stoning of Stephen and his conversion to St. Paul, a foreshadowing of Judas's own hardheartedness toward Elene and his subsequent conversion to Bishop Cyriacus. At the end of the council, the Jews offer up this Judas to Elene, perhaps with some irony praising his wit. But he will not yield to her heart's desire for knowledge of the Cross, and Elene has him cast into a pit to starve until he repents and relents.

In lines 708 and following, Judas takes Elene's men to Calvary, where he prays for a miracle to reveal the exact spot where the Cross lies buried. Smoke rises, Judas digs, and twenty feet deep finds three crosses. Another miracle, the raising of one from the dead, identifies the true Cross. At this point, all else having failed to keep the true Light in darkness, the devil dramatically appears, prophesying the martyrdom of Judas under, presumably, Julian the Apostate. But Judas bests the devil in this "flyting," promising that the devil himself will be cast down by the "brightest of beacons" into eternal damnation. Of interest in the remainder of the poem is the search for and discovery of the nails from the Cross, and Elene's being advised to shape them into a bridle for her son's horse. The wise counselor reintroduces the martial note of the "vision" scene, providing some thematic and structural balance, when he suggests that thereby Constantine

> "shall have strength
> In all his battles,　　success in strife,
> Everywhere peace　　and rest after war
> Who reins his white steed　　with this best of bridles
> When the stout in strife　　in the storm of darts,
> Battle-bold heroes,　　bear shield and spear."

With Elene's departure, the poem proper ends. There follows the "autobiographical" passage mentioned above, and then the runic signature:

> Until then the man had always been buffeted with surging cares, (he was like) a drowsing torch [C], although he had received treasures in the mead-hall, apple-shaped gold. The (disused) bow [Y], his companion in need [N], mourned, suffered oppressive sorrow, an anxious secret, where formerly the horse [E] had measured for him the mile-paths, galloped proudly, decked with wire ornaments. Joy [W] is diminished, and pleasure, after the passing of years; youth is gone, the glory of old. Manly strength [U] was once the pleasure of

youth. Now the former days have departed after the passage of time, the joys of life gone, just as the flood [L] ebbs away, the rushing tides. Wealth [F] is transitory to every man beneath the heaven.

Elliott, whose translation I have cited and whose interpretation I have accepted, comments that by using rune names in this fashion, Cynewulf presented "a coherent picture of the day of judgment with its inherent contrast between man's earlier state and the elemental upheaval of doomsday itself, while at the same time weaving into the narrative the runes that spell his name, so that prayers might be offered for his salvation."[14] The appropriateness of *this* runic passage to the poem as a whole should be observed: the heroic imagery of the mead hall and the battle horse recall the Constantine episode, the "flood" hints at the sea voyage of Elene, and the suggestion of the Day of Judgment reflects various references to eternal punishments made by speakers throughout the poem. And it is on the note of the Judgment Day—in a passage based perhaps on Alcuin but more likely on Ambrose[15]—that the poem fittingly ends, with a threefold division of the adjudged souls into the faithful, the sinful, and the accursed transgressors: the third group will be cast down from the fierce fire in whose depths they shall burn into the depths of hell, while the first two groups, in the upper and middle reaches of the purgatorial flame, will be cleansed and come into everlasting bliss.

The struggle between good and evil that we have seen in the three Cynewulfian poems, *Fates*, *Juliana*, and *Elene*, is presented at a much more elemental and unsophisticated level in *Guthlac A*, the first of the two poems in the Exeter Book on the English saint.[16] For here the narrative is focused on the conflict between devils and the hero rather than upon heroes and heroines and primarily human adversaries. The body of the

14. "Cynewulf's Runes in *Christ II* and *Elene*," ES, xxxiv (1953), 56.

15. Gradon, p. 22.

16. Both are edited in ASPR, iii; no recent editions exist, but several are reported in progress as of this writing.

poem concerns itself with the attempts of the devils in the Crowland wastes, whom Guthlac has dispossessed in his anchoritic zeal, to regain their unblissful seats, and Guthlac's defiance thereof, aided and abetted by God's angels. There are many generalized threats by the demons, but attention is narrowed to one temptation (to despair), in which the devils show Guthlac the corruption of youth in the monasteries (ll. 412 ff.), and one specific threat of torture and damnation, when they carry Guthlac to the gates of hell and show him the horrors therein (ll. 557 ff.). The saint resists the first by pointing out, in effect, that even in monasteries youth will be served and is not necessarily unsalvageable; and he counters the second by placing his trust in God, reminding the devils of their own rebellion against Him and their falseness, and declaring their permanent damnation. God's messenger, St. Bartholomew, then orders the devils to return Guthlac unharmed to his *beorg* in the fens, and in something of an idyllic passage (ll. 733b ff.), he is welcomed home by the birds and beasts of the forest wasteland:

> Many a creature
> With fervent voices   blessed him,
> Woodland birds   made known by signs
> The saint's return;   often had he
> Held out food to them   when they flew hungry
> About his hand,   eager and desirous
> Rejoiced in his aid.   . . . .
> Peaceful was that victory-plain,   and home [re]newed,
> Fair the bird-song,   new-blown the earth;
> Cuckoos announced the time of year.

The 818-line versified saint's life comes to end quickly thereafter, describing how Guthlac's soul on his death day was led by angels into the eternal joys of heaven.

Guthlac A receives scant notice in most literary histories, but despite its primitivism it has a unity and focus that suggest the craftsman at work to good effect. From beginning to end there is emphasis upon the virtuous individual vs. the sinful crowd, upon earthly transience vs. heavenly permanence, upon ineffectual words vs. significant deeds. In addition, angelologydemonology is a dominant theological theme in the poem, with the conflict of the good and bad angel over Guthlac's earthly course of conduct and the routing of the fiend by God's command (ll. 108 ff.) foreshadowing the major conflict and resolution. Most important is the centrality of the *beorg* upon which Guthlac established his anchorite cell—the word is usually translated as "hill" or "mountain," but it more likely means "barrow" or "tumulus" in this context: not only is it the geographic center of conflict between the saint and the devils but in the course of the poem it comes to symbolize the spiritual life of the good Christian.[17] The *beorg* appears progressively more desirable, less and less fearful and treacherous, as a place of abode as the *bytla* 'builder' (ll. 148, 733, at the beginning and the completion of Guthlac's task) conquers threat and temptation, culminating in the pacific scene of home welcoming by the forest denizens. The dedicated and sanctified barrow thus prefigures the New Jerusalem, to which all blissful souls shall wend after their going hence (ll. 811–end), an ending that is nicely foreshadowed in the prologue (ll. 1–29), where we are shown an angel greeting a departed good soul and assuring it of a smooth journey to the Heavenly City.[18]

If we are to believe the testimony of the poem itself, *Guthlac A* was composed within the living memory of the English saint, who died in 714 or 715. The question of its basis in oral tradition or upon a written life focuses upon its relation to Felix of Crowland's prose *Vita* of about 740 (see I, 14), a much disputed point.[19] But there is no doubt as to the dependence of

17. See L. K. Shook, "The Burial Mound in *Guthlac A*," *MP*, LVIII (1960), 1–10.

18. See L. K. Shook, "The Prologue of the Old English 'Guthlac A'," *MS*, XXIII (1961), 294–304. Earlier scholars either assigned the prologue to the end of *Christ III*, which precedes it in the MS, or made a separate poem of it, neither procedure being sanctioned by the scribal recording. Father Shook believes that the soul in the prologue is Guthlac's, but such a reading runs counter to the generalizing of both the prologue and the ending of the poem.

19. Father Shook, for instance, accepts Gerould's arguments in *MLN*, XXXII (1917), 77–89, in favor of dependence; Schaar, pp. 39–41, does not.

the poem following it in the Exeter Book, the 561-line *Guthlac B*, upon that *Vita*. This second Guthlac poem, quickly mentioning the saint's life and reputation, the succor he gave to beasts and humans, launches almost immediately into its main concern, Guthlac's holy dying and death. It follows the *Vita* (V, 35 and 36) closely in its narrative sequence, describing the saint's last illness and the sorrow of his faithful servant, Guthlac's comforting speeches and his request that the servant inform his sister of his demise, the servant's questioning about Guthlac's mysterious visitor and the saint's climactic revelation of his guardian angel's role in his own miracles, the sweet smell and the heavenly light at night, the flight of Guthlac's soul to heaven, and finally the servant's flight to Guthlac's sister. The emphasis, as can be seen in this epitome, is twofold, and unlike that in *Guthlac A*: upon the death theme and upon the relationship between Guthlac and his "thane." The former receives attention from the very beginning, in the prologue which recounts the coming of death to mankind through the transgressions of Adam and Eve in Paradise, a passage resembling in many respects *Phoenix*, lines 393–423 (see Ch. IX). This Christian death theme is developed in Anglo-Saxon poetic fashion, as death is presented in a series of sharp vignettes as it advances upon the saint: first as the deliverer of a bitter drink, then as doorkeeper to the shades below, then as a greedy warrior stalking his prey:

> No man ever   of the sons of men,
> No mortal on earth,   from the first beginning
> Could shun the draught   of the bitter drink
> In Death's deep cup.   When the dark hour comes,
> Sudden the latch lifts,   and the entrance opens.
> No mortal ever,   mantled in flesh,
> Lofty or lowly,   has escaped with life,
> But Death rushes on him   with greedy grasp.
> So the Lone-Stalker   in the shadows of night,
> Gauntest of warriors,   greedy for slaughter,
> Drew nigh unto Guthlac.[20]

20. This passage and the next are quoted from Kennedy, *EEP*, pp. 256, 258.

(The last part of this passage greatly resembles Grendel's stalking of Heorot in *Beowulf*.) The lord-thane relationship—at heart a Germanic concept—is developed gradually as the poem proceeds, culminating in the end (though the last few lines are missing in the manuscript) as the servant flees to his ship to seek the saint's sister and reports to her in exile-elegiac fashion (see Ch. XI):

> "Courage is best   for the heart that must bear
> Many bitter evils,   and darkly brood
> On the loss of his lord,   when the dread hour nears,
> Fixed by Fate's weaving.   That he knows well
> Who with grieving heart wanders   knowing his gold-lord
> Rests under earth.   Wretchedly he departs
> With sorrowful spirit.   All joy is spent
> For one who heavy-hearted   endures such hardships."

We can perhaps see something of the difference in tone and style between *Guthlac* A and B, even in translation, by comparing the two poems' treatments of the departure of Guthlac's soul to its heavenly reward:

> Thus was Guthlac's   spirit led
> In the embraces of angels   to heaven aloft;
> In the sight   of the Eternal Judge
> They led him lovingly;   to him reward was given,
> A seat in heaven,   where he ever might
> To all eternity   be resident,
> Dwell joyfully.
>
> [*Glc*. A, ll. 781–787]

> Thus was Guthlac's   soul led
> Blessed in ascent;   angels bore him
> To that lasting joy.   His body grew cold,
> Lifeless beneath the sky.   Then there light shone,
> Brightest of beams.   Completely that beacon was
> About that holy house,   the heavenly gleam,
> From the earth rising   like a fiery tower
> Reared upright   unto the heavens' roof,
> Viewed beneath the sky   brighter than the sun,
> Than the splendor of noble stars.   Bands of angels
> Sang a victory-song;   music was in the air
> Heard beneath the heavens,   the rejoicing of saints.
> Thus the house was   filled with bliss,

With sweet fragrances   and heavenly wonders.

[*Glc. B*, ll. 1305 ff.][21]

Though *Guthlac A*, as I have suggested, has a unity and coherence that are pleasing, and though it reveals a knowledge of apocryphal literature and possibly of Felix, it possesses a strictly repetitive quality and an absence of poetic elaboration that might well, along with its comments on "living tradition," imply oral composition. *Guthlac B*, on the other hand, with its Cynewulfian elaborations and poetic power, its undeniable dependence upon the *Vita* (both of which suggest a ninth-century dating), certainly implies written composition. If this oral-written difference (see IV, 12) is valid for the provenience of composition, it contains an interesting paradox, for *A*, though oral, is in its poetic conception and formulation less in the vernacular tradition than *B*.

The mixture of the heroic vernacular tradition and the saint's life in Anglo-Saxon poetry, whether the heroes were of native or Mediterranean origin, has been seen in this chapter as varying in its proportions and in the quality of its poetic manifestations. We shall see something similar in the next chapter, in our discussion of the poetry in which Christ, rather than His saints, is hero, though we shall find there a greater lyrical than narrative orientation in the poets' treatments of their subject.

21. Present editions continue line numbering from *Glc. A* instead of starting anew, as they should.

VII

Christ as Poetic Hero

THE MOST PURELY LYRICAL of the Old English poems which deal specifically with Christ as the major figure is the ninth-century *Christ I*, or the *Advent Lyrics*. The 439 lines which comprise this series of twelve poems begin the Exeter Book collection of poetry. Often taken as only the first part of a three-part *Christ*, since they are followed in the manuscript by a poem on the Ascension which bears Cynewulf's signature (*Christ II*), and that by one on the Judgment Day (*Christ III*), there is nevertheless little reason to believe they form anything but an entity by themselves.[1] Though primarily lyrical, the twelve little poems possess a tonal and thematic coherence, and even a minor narrative unity.

The tonal quality of the *Advent Lyrics* is a complementation, in varying degrees, of the sorrowful and the joyful, imparted by the double mood of the liturgical Advent antiphons upon which the lyrics are based. These antiphons, or O's— so-called because they begin with the apostrophic O (OE

1. A. S. Cook, ed., *The Christ of Cynewulf* (Boston, 1900), believed the three parts composed one poem; Krapp and Dobbie, eds., *ASPR*, III (1936), were inconclusive in their introduction, but used consecutive line numbering throughout the three poems; Brother A. Philip, "The Exeter Scribe and the Unity of *Christ*," *PMLA*, L (1940), 903–909, argued against their unity, as did S. K. Das and C. Schaar (VI, 7) in 1942 and 1949. The latest editor of *Christ I*, J. J. Campbell, *The Advent Lyrics of the Exeter Book* (Princeton, N. J., 1959), is quite definite in his belief in the separateness of the three poems, as are most modern scholars.

Eala)—are the sources for the thematic improvisations of most of the twelve sections.[2] But whereas the Greater and the Monastic O's are binary in form, consisting of an invocation and a petition, the Old English lyrics are ternary, composed of an invocation or address, an elaboration upon a doctrinal concept, and a petition. The emotional attitude in both the antiphons and the lyrics results from the early Church's emphasis upon the dogmatic character of Advent, Christ being viewed not so much as infant but as Redeemer.[3]

Although the first poem is decapitated in the manuscript, it is clearly based on the *O Rex gentium et desideratum earum, lapisque angularis . . .* antiphon: 'O King of the people and their desire, the cornerstone who makes two one, come and save man whom you formed from clay.' The *lapis angularis* obviously contributed the unifying image to the poet, his view of Christ as the "wall-stone":

> Thou art the wall-stone   the workers rejected
> Of old from the work.   It befits Thee well
> That Thou shouldst be Head   of the glorious hall
> Locking together   the lengthy walls,
> The flint unbroken,   in a firm embrace,
> That ever on earth   the eyes of all
> May look with wonder   on the Lord of glory.
>   With cunning skill   display Thy craft
> Triumphant, Righteous;   and quickly raise
> Wall against wall.   The work hath need
> That the Craftsman come,   the King Himself;
> That He then rebuild   what now is broken,
> The house under its roof.   He wrought the body,
> The limbs, of clay;   now the Lord of life
> Must rescue from devils   the droves of the wretched,
> The damned from their terrors   as He oft hath done.
>   [Kennedy, *EECP*, p. 85]

We notice that the poet has elaborated upon the "who makes two one" of the antiphon in terms of the cornerstone image

2. In addition to Cook and Campbell, see E. Burgert, *The Dependence of Part I of Cynewulf's Christ upon the Antiphonary* (Washington, D. C., 1921).

3. See an important review of Campbell by R. Woolf, *MÆ*, xxix (1960), 125–129.

which links the "lengthy walls" and the "flint unbroken"; and
the "man whom you have formed of clay" becomes part of and
indeed the whole of the original house that is now decayed, a
reference to man individually and to the Church, perhaps, as
collective mankind. The Old English is worth quoting here:

Nu is þam weorce þearf
þæt se cræftga cume   ond se cyning sylfa,
ond þonne gebete—   nu gebrosnad is—
hus under hrofe.   He þæt hra gescop,
leomo læmena.

[ll. 11b–15a, Campbell text]

The reference to the 'craftsman' *and* the 'king' (the Kennedy
translation obscures the coordination) suggests the Son-Father
identity which manifests itself elsewhere in the *Advent Lyrics;*[4]
the 'then rebuilding' and the 'now ruined' can be seen as al-
literatively balanced in its line; and the use of alliteration to
cement semantic identification across a syntactic break—the
hra 'body' *is* the *hus under hrofe* 'house under roof'—reveals
the poet's fine use of an Old English stylistic practice (see IV,
14, 15).

Poem 2 begins:

You, O Lord and true King,
who govern the locks, you open and reveal Life.
The exalted paths to another you deny,
the glorious journey, if his acts are not worthy.

[Campbell trans.]

It is based upon the *O Clavis David* antiphon: "O key of
David, and scepter of the house of Israel, who opens and none
shuts, who closes and none opens: come and lead forth the
captives from the house of bondage, sitting in the darkness and
shadow of death." Moving from the key image to the prison
image, the Old English poet elaborates thereon, weaving together the concepts of life and lord and light with the idea of
unlocking. The first half of this poem ends with an historical
reference to the expulsion from Eden: "make us worthy whom

4. See J. E. Cross, "The 'Coeternal Beam' in the O. E. Advent Poem
(Christ I) ll. 104–129," *Neophil,* XLVIII (1964), 72–81.

He hath admitted unto the heavenly glory [i.e., through the Redemption] when we abjectly had to turn unto the Earth, deprived of our homeland [the Garden of Eden and heavenly heritage]." This reference in turn leads into a poetic exaltation of the virgin birth as the means by which the promised Redemption was fulfilled and by which the light of knowledge opened the prison of spiritual ignorance.

I cannot here expatiate on each of the individual lyrics that make up *Christ I*,[5] but Poem 7 calls for special attention, the section Cook called the *Passus* and Campbell prefers to call simply *Eala ioseph min* 'O my Joseph.' Often referred to as the first "drama" in English literature, this poem consists of five brief speeches, a dialogue between Joseph and Mary. Mary first lovingly and somewhat pathetically questions Joseph as he has confronted her with his decision to reject her, though she knows not why. Joseph's answer is beautifully nonexplicit: he says,

> "I suddenly am
> deeply disturbed, despoiled of honor,
> for I have for you heard many words,
> many great sorrows and hurtful speeches,
> much harm, and to me they speak insult,
> many hostile words. Tears I must
> shed, sad in mind. God easily may
> relieve the inner pain of my heart,
> comfort the wretched one. O young girl,
> Mary the virgin!"

> [Campbell trans.]

In her simplicity, Mary misunderstands, replying that she has never found fault in Joseph that he should reproach *himself*. At this, Joseph makes explicit his problem: her "virgin" pregnancy; but he is not simply accusing: he is a man torn, hurt in his pride, and also in a moral dilemma as to whether he must deliver Mary, whom he loves, to a death by stoning for her supposed infraction of the law, or, by concealing the crime, live

5. See Kennedy, *EECP*, pp. 75–78, the Introduction to Campbell's edition, and J. J. Campbell, "Structural Patterns in the Old English Advent Lyrics," *ELH*, XXIII (1956), 239–255, for further analyses.

himself forever perjured. Mary's final speech, of course, sets matters straight about the mystery of the virgin birth and her eternal virginity: "Prophecy had to be/ in Himself truly fulfilled," she concludes. The origin of this poem is not known; it is not based upon an antiphon, yet its dramatic quality, its psychological realism, and its style, so unlike other Anglo-Saxon poems, suggest some specific source as inspiration for the poet.

Binding the twelve poems together are the various motifs which can be found in the three lyrics discussed above: the co-existence of Father and Son, the purity of Mary and the mystery of the virgin birth, man's inability to understand God's mysteries, man's misery and need of grace, and the call to praise God. In addition, there is a narrative substructure in the recurrence of exile images, which we tend to associate with the elegies. These images take us chronologically from the expulsion from the Garden of Eden in Poem 2 (see above) through a time between that loss and the Incarnation in Poem 5 (based on the *O Oriens* antiphon): ". . . that you may come yourself, that you may bring light to those who for long already, covered with darkness and here in shadows, have sat the long night; shrouded in sins, they have had to endure the dark shadow of death," to in Poem 6 (based upon the *O Emmanuel* antiphon) a time shortly before the first Advent, when the souls in Limbo petition for the Redeemer's coming. Then follows the *Eala ioseph min*, chronologically apt. In Poem 8 (based upon *O Rex pacifice*), the petition refers to the exile of the scattered flock subsequent to the Crucifixion, and in the most elaborate of all the exile images, Poem 10's petition brings us down to the poet's own time of man's spiritual exile and need for grace.[6] *Christ I*, clearly, shows a beautiful confluence of Christian doctrine and feeling and Old English poetic feeling and tradition.

The lyrical quality found in *Christ I* is also present in *Christ II*, a poem superficially connected with the preceding

6. S. B. Greenfield, "The Theme of Spiritual Exile in *Christ I*," *PQ*, xxxii (1953), 321–328.

one by reference to the Advent in its opening lines. But this homiletic poem by Cynewulf incorporates some narrative material in its account of the actual Ascension of Christ, and it employs the lord-thane relationship in its account of the sorrowing disciples whose spirits burn hot within them when they watch their Lord ascend and when they depart from Bethany to Jerusalem.

The *Ascension* (*Christ*, ll. 440–866 in present editions; see n. 1) is essentially a poetic redaction of Gregory the Great's Homily xxix (*P.L.*, LXXVI, 1218–19). Like that homily, it begins with a question about why the angels who attended the Nativity did not wear white, whereas they came thus arrayed at the Ascension. Gregory proceeds to answer this question directly, in terms of the humbling of Divinity on the former occasion and the exaltation of humanity on the latter; but Cynewulf, addressing his poem to an "illustrious man," asks him to meditate on this question, and never does give an explicit answer, though he hints at it in lines 550–554 and 755. Here lies part of the tension of the poem. Cynewulf describes the Ascension and the song of the angelic hosts attending it. An interesting passage is one in which the poet elaborates on God's gifts to men, taking off from Gregory's quoting of Ephesians IV.8: *dedit dona hominibus*. This *sum* series in the Old English poem (the rhetorical device of *anaphora*, or *repetitio*)[7] includes the indigenous skills of harp-playing, shield-defense, and seamanship:

> He sowed and set
> Manifold skills.   He sends to one
> Wisdom of speech   in word and thought,
> Excellent insight;   he may sing and say
> All things well   who has wisdom's power
> Locked in his heart.   Loud before men
> One stirs with fingers   the sounding harp,
> Strikes sweetly the glee-wood.   Godly law
> One may interpret.   One tells aright
> The stars in their courses,   the spacious sky.

7. See J. E. Cross, "The Old English Poetic Theme of 'The Gifts of Men'," *Neophil*, XLIV (1962), 66–70.

One fashions well   the eloquent word.
To one He awards   war-might in battle
When the archers send a shower of darts,
A flickering arrow-flight   o'er the shield's defense.
One may with boldness drive his bark
Over the salt wave,   stirring the foam.
[Kennedy, EECP, p. 104]

Perhaps most interesting of all in the body of the poem is the symbolization, based on Gregory, of the phases of Christ's ministry as six "leaps." Gregory mentions only five leaps: the Incarnation, the Nativity, the Crucifixion, the Deposition and Burial, and the Ascension, to which Cynewulf has added, between the last two, the Harrowing of Hell. The *Ascension* suggests that we have no need to be sorrowing as the disciples did on the occasion of the sixth leap, for God's gifts now include not only the physical ones of this transient life but also the spiritual salvation of those who had been bound in Hell and our own redemption if we have the wisdom to meditate and understand. The patron addressed at the beginning of the poem thus becomes in effect "each of [my] beloved ones" whom the poet exhorts in lines 814 and following to think of his soul's welfare.

In the midst of his concluding peroration, Cynewulf, as he does most particularly in *Elene*, waxes eloquent on the Judgment Day motif, with his runic signature emphasizing God's righteous punishment of sinners and the transitoriness of the time-tide-bound wealth of this world (see VI, 14). The end of the poem contains the great sea-voyage metaphor, a spiritual enlargement upon the stock poetic metaphor:

Now is it most like   as if on ocean
Across cold water   we sail in our keels,
Over the wide sea   in our ocean steeds,
Faring on in our flood-wood.   Fearful the stream,
The tumult of waters,   whereon we toss
In this feeble world.   Fierce are the surges
On the ocean lanes.   Hard was our life
Before we made harbour   o'er the foaming seas.
Then help was vouchsafed us   when God's Spirit-Son
Guided us to the harbour of salvation   and granted us grace

```
That we may understand        over the ship's side
Where to moor our sea-steeds,        our ocean stallions,
Fast at anchor.        Let us fix our hope
Upon that haven        which the Lord of heaven,
In holiness on high        has opened by His Ascension.
```
                              [Kennedy, *EECP*, p. 109]

One may well compare and contrast this extended image with the pithy prose image of the sparrow in Bede's account of the conversion of Edwin (see Ch. I).

Christ III (ninth century?), related thematically to the ending of *Christ II*, is a longish poem of 798 lines on the Judgment Day. As a unified structure it is much less satisfying than the *Advent Lyrics* or the *Ascension:* the poet's apocalyptic fervor led him into repetitions and inconsistencies. What structure he has seems in the main to follow the sequence of ideas in the alphabetic poem *Apparebit repentina dies magna Domini,* quoted by Bede in his *De Arte Metrica.*[8] But the piece, with its many hypermetric lines, is a tissue of poeticized material from Gregory, Augustine, Caesarius of Arles, and other Christian writers on the great theme of Judgment. Nevertheless, it does reveal bursts of poetic energy, and it does move from a swift opening terror:

```
        Suddenly in the midnight        on mortal men
    The Great Day of the Lord God        shall come with might,
    Filling with fear        the fair Creation,
    Like a wily thief        who walks in darkness,
    A robber bold        in the black night
    Who suddenly assails        men fast in slumber,
    Lying in wait for the unwary        and the unprepared,
```
                              [Kennedy, *EECP*, p. 268]

to the calm of the blessed in heaven:

```
    There is glory of the saints;        day without darkness
    Bright with blessing;        bliss without sorrow;
    Accord among friends        without envy for ever
    For the happy in heaven        love without hate
    In that holy throng.        No hunger there nor thirst,
    Nor sleep nor sickness        nor burning sun,
```

8. Cook, pp. 171–177; Schaar, p. 37. On flaws in the poem, see Cook (n. 1), pp. xci–xciii.

> Nor cold nor care.   But the band of the blessed,
> Most shining of legions,   shall delight for ever
> In the grace of the King   and glory with God.
> [Kennedy, *EECP*, p. 289]

In its progress, it describes the trumpeting call of the angels to Judgment in a passage that calls to mind Donne's "From the round earth's imagin'd corners, blow/ Your trumpets, Angels, and arise, arise . . . ," it shows the coming of the Judge and the devastation of the universe, and it comments on the reinvestment in flesh of mankind as the souls rise to Judgment (through l. 1080). A long passage on the Cross follows (through l. 1214) in which Christ as hero has His darkest hour, the dumb universe sympathizing but sinners remaining unmoved. A description of the rewards of the virtuous and the punishments of transgressors leads to an exhortation (ll. 1300 ff.) to repentance, to a searching out of evil by the eyes within, since the "gems of the head" are useless for discovering inner evil. Then comes Christ's finest hour, in which He welcomes the blessed to heaven, then reminds the wicked of His love and Incarnation and Crucifixion. In a poignant passage Christ rebukes the sinners for their willful neglect of His Passion:

> "Why did you hang Me   on a Cross of your hands
> Where I hung more heavily   than that once of old?
> Lo! this seems the harder.   More bitter to Me
> The Cross of your sins   I unwillingly suffered
> Than was that other   I ascended of old
> Of My own will   . . . . ."
> [Kennedy, *EECP*, p. 284]

After Christ dooms the wicked to hell, the poet details some of hell's horrors which, interestingly enough, contain both fire and ice. The poem concludes on the rhapsodic note mentioned above.

On the same theme as *Christ III* are two other Old English poems, known as *Judgment Day I* and *II* (or *Doomsday B* and *A*, respectively, as Malone, Int., 5, calls them). Although these do not picture Christ as hero to any extent, except in brief mention of Him as Savior amidst the holocaust of Doomsday, it is convenient to consider them here.

By far the finer of the two is *Judgment Day II* (*Be Domes Dæge*), preserved in the eleventh-century MS CCCC 201—an important record of minor poetical texts of the later Anglo-Saxon period, the manuscript which also contains the Old English *Apollonius of Tyre* and a nucleus of Wulfstan homilies (see Ch. III). The poem is a close though expanded translation (306 lines to 157) of the Latin hexametrical *De Die Judicii*, attributed by the rubrics in the manuscript to Bede, though felt by some scholars to be by Alcuin.[9] It is a late work, probably late tenth century, which substitutes end rhyme for alliteration in a few places and even combines the two poetic techniques in a couple of lines; it also reveals the influence of Soul and Body poems (see Ch. IX) in its speaker's penitential exhortations to his flesh to forsake its geocentrism:

> Why grovelest thou in dust,   O guilty flesh,
> Filled with crime?   Why dost thou not cleanse
> With gushing tears   thy grievous sins?
> Why dost thou not pray   for plasters and lotions,
> For gentle leechdoms,   from the Lord of Life?
>   [Kennedy, *EECP*, p. 261, ll. 77–81]

Or:

> What doest thou, O flesh,   what performest thou here?
> What pangs in that hour   shalt thou deplore?
> Woe to thee now   that servest this world,
> That livest here gladly   in wanton delights
> Goading thyself   with sensual spurs?
>   [ll. 176–180]

These lines may well remind us of one of the greatest poetic expressions of this Christian theme, Shakespeare's sonnet "Poor soul, the centre of my sinful earth . . ."

The first of the above passages contains two of the dominant images of the first part of the poem: those of flowing

---

9. The Latin text, as well as the OE, is printed in H. Löhe, ed., *Be Domes Dæge*, Bonner Beiträge zur Anglistik, xxii (Bonn, 1907), and in J. R. Lumby, *Be Domes Dæge*, EETS 65 (London, 1876); the OE text alone in ASPR, vi. On OE eschatological poetry as a whole, see W. Deering, *The Anglo-Saxon Poems on the Judgment Day* (Halle, 1890). For more recent commentary, see n. 10.

water and of medical leechcraft. The flowing water is first enunciated in the opening lines of the poem, in a notable expansion on the Latin source:

Lat. Among the blossoming plants of fecund earth
       With the wind's blasts everywhere in echoing branches
       Under cover of a shady tree, sad and solitary
       As I sat, perturbed by a sudden bitter complaint,
       These sad lines I sang on account of [my] sad mind . . .

OE   Lo! I sat alone   in a leafy bower
       Deep in a wood   and sheltered in shade
       Where welling waters   wandered and murmured
       In the midst of a meadow,   all as I tell.
       There pleasant plants   were budding and blooming
       In a throng together   in that gay expanse;
       The trees of the wood   were tossing and sighing
       In a storm of wind;   the heavens were stirred,
       And my sad spirit   was sorely troubled.
              Then all suddenly,   fearful and sad,
       I commenced to sing   those mournful verses,
       All as you said.   . . . .

                                        [Kennedy trans.]

Huppé has plausibly suggested that the nature expansion of the Old English is symbolic in the light of Patristic exegesis, that the poet was amplifying for his latter-day lay audience, by more specifying symbols, meanings which would have been immediately obvious to the clerical readers of Bede's or Alcuin's days. The associations are with the Garden of Eden, with original sin, with the consequent need for repentance that is occasioned by thoughts of the Last Judgment, the subject proper of the poem. The fountain image not only helps conjure up Paradise, but also fuses with lines shortly following, wherein the speaker of the *carmina* calls upon his veins to open and flood his face with tears.[10] The appeal to the veins leads the Old English poet to his view of God as his "Heavenly

10. B. F. Huppé, *Doctrine and Poetry* (Albany, N.Y., 1959), pp. 80–94. Without resorting to the exegetical tradition, sense can still be made of these opening lines: the speaker's solitude even amidst nature's bounty and beauty is intensified by the bursts of wind, leading to a sudden inner dissatisfaction that expresses itself in the *planctus*.

Leech, who alone may heal/ Blundering spirits and free the bound"; and so forth, to the passage with medical imagery cited above.

Like *Christ III, Judgment Day II* emphasizes the need for inner probing of sin and for repentance, since on Judgment Day *all* is revealed. The terrors of the damned in hell on that occasion are even more powerfully portrayed in this poem than in the former, and an interesting passage shows vice abstractions, like those in the later morality plays, gliding away at the end of the world:

> Drunkenness and Feasting   shall take flight,
> Laughter and Play   shall depart together;
> Lust shall go hence,   and Greed fare far;
> Vice shall vanish   and every excess
> Guiltily hastening   into the gloom.
> And Sleep shall fly   careworn and feeble,
> Torpid with slumber,   slinking away.
>
> [ll. 234–240]

The poem ends on the usual thematic note of eschatological poetry, with the bliss of the blessed in heaven, but it has the unusual feature of the Virgin Mary leading that white-clothed band "through the lovely bright kingdom/ Of the Glorious Father."

Judgment Day II is a good poem on all counts. Not as much can be said for the homiletic-oriented *Judgment Day I*, a poem of 119 lines recorded in the Exeter Book and reproduced in editions thereof. This poem depicts the end of the world and the suffering of the damned repetitively, as if to exemplify the poet's statement: "Therefore ever shall I/ Teach the people that they glorify on high the praise of God/ . . ." (ll. 46b ff.). Suggestive of the elegies, the *Seafarer* in particular, are lines 77b and following:

>   Little does he think,
> Who joyous over wine   enjoys his pleasures,
> (Who) sits proud at the feast   (and) is not anxious about
>   his journey (hence),
> How it may befall him   after this world.

There is no particular source for this poem; it draws heavily upon the Anglo-Saxon homiletic tradition we have earlier observed.

If Christ is not prominent in either of the two Doomsday poems just discussed, He is, by the nature of His Passion, eminently central to the *Dream of the Rood*, the finest expression of the Passion in Old English poetry.[11] This 156-line narrative-lyrical adoration of the Cross survives in the Vercelli Book, and part of it appears in Northumbrian runic inscription in the margins of the east and west faces of the eighth-century Ruthwell [rivl] Cross in Dumfriesshire, Scotland. Two lines reminiscent of the poem also appear on the late tenth-century Brussels Cross. The relation between the Ruthwell inscription and the Vercelli text is not clear: is the former a condensation of an original Anglian poem of about A.D. 700, preserved in its West Saxon tenth-century form in the Vercelli MS, or is the manuscript poem, even in its earliest shape, an expansion of the Cross inscription? There is also a problem with the longer poem itself: lines 79 and following seem to be in a different style from the Crucifixion segment that precedes, and are possibly an addition by a later redactor. Even so, the *Dream of the Rood* is a coherent and unified poem as it stands, compact and intense in its emotional effect.

> Listen! I'll tell the sweetest dream,
> That dropped to me from midnight, in the quiet
> Time of silence and restful sleep.
>   I seemed to see a tree of miracles
> Rising in the sky, a shining cross
> Wrapped in light. . . .
>   It was a tree of victory and splendor, and I tainted,
> Ulcered with sin. And yet I saw it—
> Shining with joy, clothed, adorned,
> Covered with gold, the tree of the Lord

11. Ed. in *ASPR*, II; separately by B. Dickins and A. S. C. Ross, *The Dream of the Rood*, 4th ed. (London, 1954). For recent critical commentaries, see J. A. Burrow, "An Approach to the Dream of the Rood," *Neophil*, XLIII (1959), 123–133, and esp. R. Woolf, "Doctrinal Influences on *The Dream of the Rood*," *MÆ*, XXVII (1958), 137–153, to which the following discussion is greatly indebted.

Gloriously wrapped in gleaming stones.
And through the gold I saw the stains
Of its ancient agony when blood spilled out
On its right-hand side. I was troubled and afraid
Of the shining sight. Then its garments changed,
And its color; for a moment it was moist with blood,
Dripping and stained; then it shone like silver.

[ll. 1–23][12]

This beginning not only sets the mood and tone of wonder and sinful remorse but its image of the double-visaged cross, gemmed on the one hand and stained with blood on the other, functions as a symbolic prelude to the triumph and suffering that are doctrinally and poetically at the poem's core. In the body of the poem, the Cross itself is made to speak and to describe from its particular point of view the Crucifixion, a rhetorical device known as *prosopopoeia*.[13] The Cross's speech begins in riddle fashion (see Ch. X), describing quickly and succinctly its origins as a tree, its felling and shaping into a rood, and its "planting" in the hillside. Then:

"I saw the Lord of the world
Boldly rushing to climb me
And I could neither bend, nor break
The word of God. I saw the ground

12. The translation in this section is from B. Raffel, *Poems from the Old English* (V, 37).
13. See M. Schlauch, *"The Dream of the Rood* as Prosopopoeia," *Essays and Studies in Honor of Carleton Brown* (New York, 1940), pp. 23–34. See Woolf's n. 32 for suggestion of a more direct source in a Pseudo-Augustinian sermon. Miss Woolf compares the style of this passage with that of the Crucifixion scene in *Christ III*. In the latter, antitheses occur pointed by the alliteration:

"*Ic wæs on worulde wædla,   þæt þu wurde welig on heofonum,
earm wæs ic on eðle þinum,   þæt þu wurde eadig on minum.*"

('Poor was I in the world   that you might become wealthy
in heaven,

Wretched was I in your homeland,   that you might become
blessed in mine.')

Both the antithetical device and the *communicatio idiomatum*, though different, are not native Anglo-Saxon. I would also call attention to another stylistic peculiarity of *Dream*: many of its verses begin with active verbs, a feature contributing significantly to its emotional pitch.

> Trembling. I could have crushed them all,
> And yet I kept myself erect."
>
> [ll. 33b–38]

This advance of Christ upon the Cross is not, of course, the usual picture of Christ carrying the Cross to Calvary, but it has traditional sanction. More important, it shows Christ the hero freely willing His own Crucifixion, heightening this "leap's" heroic and voluntary nature. Stripping Himself for battle— again an action within Patristic tradition, and again emphasizing Christ's heroism and voluntarism—Christ climactically mounts the Cross, an admirable symbol of the Divinity of Christ and of the earlier Middle Ages' conception of the Redemption:

> "I trembled as His arms went round me. And still I could not bend,
> Crash to the earth, but had to bear the body of God.
> I was reared as a cross. I raised the mighty
> King of Heaven and could not bend.
> They pierced me with vicious nails. I bear the scars
> Of malicious gashes. But I dared not injure any of them.
> We were both reviled, we two together. I was drenched with the blood that gushed
> From that hero's side as His holy spirit swept to Heaven.
>   Cruel things came to me there
> On that hill. I saw the God of Hosts
> Stretched on the rack. Clouds rolled
> From the darkness to cover the corpse,
> The shining splendor; a livid shadow
> Dropped from Heaven. The creation wept,
> Bewailed His death. Christ was on the cross."
>
> [ll. 42–56]

Crist wæs on rode: the breathtaking account of the Crucifixion ends on this simplistic yet highly emotional note. But we may observe in this passage two things at least. First, the Cross's presentation of itself as a loyal retainer in the epic mode, with the ironic reversal that it must acquiesce and even assist in the death of its Lord, and cannot aid or avenge Him. Second, the Cross's trembling and suffering, taking upon itself the Passion of Christ. By its passive endurance it becomes a surrogate for

Christ, representing that other aspect of the Crucifixion which was to predominate in the later Middle Ages, the humanity of Christ. Its suffering as a "thane" also foreshadows the Dreamer's own reflections toward the end of the poem where, after the vision has ended, he describes himself as an exile in this world, deprived of friends, longing for a new "patron" (God, of course) in a manner similar to the speaker's of *The Wanderer*.

The Cross of the poem continues its speech describing the Deposition and Burial:

> "They carried away almighty God,
> Raised Him out of His torment. I was abandoned of men,
> Standing bespattered with blood, driven through with spikes.
> They laid down the weary-limbed God, stood and watched at
>   His head,
> Beholding Heaven's King as He lay in quiet sleep,
> Exhausted with hardship and pain. And they started to carve
>   a sepulchre,
> With His slayer watching. They chiselled the tomb of the
>   brightest stone
> And laid the Lord of victories there."
>
> [ll. 60b–67a]

Christ's death is pictured here as a sleep, a catharsis of exhaustion, release, and temporary rest—a depiction probably not original with the poet, yet exquisitely handled by him. (The concept of death as a sleep has become a commonplace in speech and literature, but its use in the *Dream of the Rood* is as effective as is Donne's later handling of it in his sonnet "Death be not proud.") This passage stylistically fuses the human and divine doctrinal aspects of the Crucifixion by its use of the paradoxical *communicatio idiomatum:* "*They carried* away *almighty God*," "*They laid* down the *weary-limbed God* . . . *beholding Heaven's King*," "*And laid* the *Lord of victories* there." Miss Woolf's comment on this device and its doctrinal-esthetic result is worth quoting:

> In the thirty lines of dramatic description of the Crucifixion . . . there are ten examples of the *communicatio idiomatum*, and each one stimulates a shock at the paradox, a shock which grows in intensity as the poem progresses.

. . . The habit of variation in Anglo-Saxon poetic style and the richness of synonym in Anglo-Saxon poetic diction, assist the poet in each instance to use a fresh word or phrase to emphasize some attribute of God, His Rule, majesty, omnipotence. . . . The theological point that the Christ who endured the Crucifixion is fully God and fully man is thus perfectly made, and with it the imaginative effect which is the natural result of the *communicatio idiomatum* is attained, the astonishment at the great paradox of Christianity that God should endure such things.[14]

No known source has been found for the *Dream of the Rood*. Some liturgical influence there may have been,[15] but the fine tensions of the poem between the Divinity and triumph of Christ on the Cross on the one hand and His humanity and suffering on the other, probably owe their inspiration to the poet's awareness of the Christological disputes of the seventh-eighth centuries about the human-divine nature of the Savior, and from the doctrine of the Redemption as taught at this time. The poem's double stress on the triumphant and suffering Christ argues that the poet knew well the difficult theological line he was treading and, *mirabile dictu*, succeeded in keeping his balance in the brilliant fusion he effected in his use of the Cross as narrator within the dream vision. As an emotional sequence of words and ideas, the *Dream of the Rood* also moves brilliantly from the fear and sorrow of the Dreamer at the beginning to the hope he visualizes at the end:

> He broke our bonds and gave us life
> And a home in Heaven. And hope was renewed
> In bliss for those who'd burned in Hell.
> The Son triumphed on that journey to darkness,
> Smashing Hell's doors. Many men's souls
> Rose with Him then, the Ruler of all,
> Rising to Heaven and the angels' bliss
> And the joy of the saints already enthroned
> And dwelling in glory, welcoming almighty
> God returning to His shining home.

14. Woolf, pp. 151–152.
15. See H. R. Patch, "The Liturgical Influence in the *Dream of the Rood*," *PMLA*, XXXIV (1919), 233–251.

In the later Middle Ages the Crucifixion was pictured predominantly in terms of Christ's human suffering, and His divine triumph was reserved for the Harrowing of Hell motif, which we see here at the conclusion of the *Dream of the Rood.* Christ as the hero in this episode of His "life" finds independent expression, however, in the *Descent into Hell* of the Exeter Book. The *Descent* (called the *Harrowing of Hell* in some editions, though the poem does not cover the release of the patriarchs) is a 137-line poem of uncertain date whose major portion is ultimately traceable to the Apocryphal Gospel of Nicodemus (see III, 30). Lines 1–23a recount the visit of the Marys to the open tomb. Then the scene switches to hell, where John the Baptist predicts Christ's coming, the souls who await Him are briefly listed, and John (or Adam?) greets Christ, with several apostrophes to Gabriel, Mary, Jerusalem, and the River Jordan in a manner similar to the invocations of the antiphon-based lyrics of *Christ I.* The poem ends with the speaker (John?) pleading for baptism for the rescued souls.[16]

The most interesting aspect of this poem is its heroic-Christian mode of presentation of Christ's conquest of hell:

> The Lord of mankind   hastened on His journey;
> The Protector of the heavens   would break down
> and lay low
> The walls of hell,   the Sternest of all Kings
> Begin to dismantle   the might of that fortress.
> He did not require at that strife   helmet-bearers,
> Nor did He wish to lead   to the fortress gates
> Armed warriors;   but the locks fell open,
> The bars from that stronghold;   the King rode in.
> [ll. 33–40]

In the disdaining of armed help, there is perhaps a suggestion of Beowulf's magnanimity in rejecting the use of swords in his fight with Grendel; but the emphasis here is certainly not upon

16. See G. Crotty, "The Exeter *Harrowing of Hell*: A Re-interpretation," *PMLA*, LIV (1939), 349–358, for the problem of the speaker and various solutions offered for the last three lines. Malone (Int., 5), p. 80, suggests the scribe omitted an uncertain number of lines between 134 and 135, wherein a change of speaker occurred.

character in the old heroic sense, but upon the ease with which, without shield or spear, Christ is able to overcome the enemy in spiritual battle. When John perceives the victory, it is in Christian terms of light conquering darkness:

> He saw the doors of Hell   brightly shining,
> Which formerly long   had been locked,
> Shrouded in darkness.

[ll. 53–55a]

The Harrowing of Hell motif receives fuller expression in the last piece to be considered in this chapter, the 729-line poem at the end of the Junius MS known as *Christ and Satan*.[17] Lines 1–365 consist in the main of a series of plaints by Satan after his unsuccessful revolt; lines 366–662 are concerned chiefly with the Harrowing of Hell, though this episode is buttressed by accounts of the Resurrection, Ascension, and Last Judgment; the remainder of the poem centers on Satan's Temptation of Christ in the wilderness. The different contents of the various sections and the unchronological placing of the Temptation led earlier scholars to believe that separate poems had been here conjoined without proper forethought, but Clubb and Krapp, the poem's most recent editors, have argued for the unity of the whole, as have more recent commentators. The theme that binds is "the incommensurate might of God," statements to this effect reappearing again and again throughout: lines 32–33, 193–201, 282–300, 348–352, 582–584, 642–669. The Temptation scene is not out of place in this thematic scheme: it is properly climactic in the poet's indication to his audience that they should be like Christ, not Satan; for though God's might was surely revealed in the Creation and in the fall of the rebellious angels, and in His Harrowing of Hell, Christ's example of temptation withstood is the closest parallel to man's own pos-

17. Edited in *ASPR*, I (whose line numbering I follow herein). A separate edition is by M. D. Clubb, *Christ and Satan*, Yale Studies in English, LXX (New Haven, Conn., 1925). The first part is translated in verse in Kennedy, *EECP*; for a translation of the whole (in prose), one must turn to C. W. Kennedy, *The Cædmon Poems* (London and New York, 1916).

sible flesh-bound experience in imitating God—and in the humility of his humanity Christ-God paradoxically achieved his most profound triumph.[18]

The Satan of the plaints, or Part I of *Christ and Satan*, is a wretched figure taunted by his own followers. His negative capability is a fitting beginning for the great theme of the poem. He laments his folly and the torments of his fiery, windy, dragon-guarded abode like an exiled thane: "Here is no glory of the blessed,/ Wine-hall of the proud, nor joy of the world,/ Nor troop of angels . . ." (ll. 92b–94a); "Wherefore I must dejected and wretched turn the wider,/ Move in the paths of exile, deprived of glory,/ Parted from joys . . ." (ll. 119–121a);

> *Eala drihtnes þrym!*   *Eala duguða helm!*
> *Eala meotodes miht!*   *Eala middangeard!*
> *Eala dæg leohta!*   *Eala dream godes!*
> *Eala engla þreat!*   *Eala upheofen!*
>
> [ll. 163–166]

> (O Lord's power!   O the hosts' guardian!
> O Creator's might!   O earth!
> O day of lights!   O joy of God!
> O angels' throng!   O heavens above!)[19]

Like the sins of man, he cannot be hid even in the wide hall of hell with its mingled heat and cold, so large is Satan of limb. But the full extent of his powerless misery is dramatically reserved for the third section of the poem, after Christ's delivery of the souls from hell, where the poet briefly but magnificently, however unchronologically, takes us back to Christ's rejection of the tempter's offer of the kingdoms of the world:

> "Depart now, accursed one,   into that house of torment,
> Thou very Satan;   for thee is torture prepared,
> Held in readiness,   not at all the Kingdom of God.
> . . .   Get thee behind me!
> Know thou also, accursed,   how wide and broad
> Is the dreary pit of hell,   and measure it with thy hands.
> Take hold against its abyss;   go then so

18. Huppé, pp. 227–231; cf. Malone, p. 69.
19. Cf. *Wan.* 92–96.

Until thou its circumference   all knowst
And measure it first   from the top to the bottom,
And how wide may be   the black vapor.
Then shalt thou know more readily   that thou strovst
                                             against God,
When thou then hast   measured with hands
How high and deep   hell within may be,
The grim grave-house."

[ll. 690–707a]

And Satan sinks into hell to commence his measuring, and "it then seemed to him that thence [from the pit] to the doors of Hell were 100,000 miles. . . ." With the curse of his own fiends on his head, "Lo, thus be now in evil! Formerly thou didst not wish for good," the poem abruptly ends.

Genesis, the Apocrypha, the Gospels, homilies—such were probably the sources of this early ninth-century (?) poem. In the previous chapter and in this, I have discussed Old English poems of the ninth and tenth centuries dealing with Christ and His saints as the heroes of narrative and lyric. We have observed the fusion or overlapping of secular heroic concepts and Christian tradition in a poetic style that is sometimes native Anglo-Saxon and sometimes borrowed from and fused with Latin rhetorical practices. Cynewulf figured prominently as the one Anglo-Saxon poet whose name we have to conjure with, and though only four poems bear his runic signature, several others considered here have been described by stylistic critics (Das, Schaar) as Cynewulfian in manner: Dream of the Rood, Guthlac B, and Christ I. Although no thoroughgoing stylistic study has been made of Christ and Satan in the light of recent scholarship, it has been felt by critics and literary historians to partake of the Cynewulfian manner because of certain resemblances to poems long associated with Cynewulf, notably Guthlac A; but Guthlac A is now clearly recognized as un-Cynewulfian, and studies of formulas show we can place no confidence in verbal parallels as an indicator of borrowing or even of stylistic influence. Christ and Satan, therefore, may be viewed tentatively as standing between the Cynewulfian and the earlier so-called Cædmonian poems in the rest of the Junius MS. It is to this earlier "school" of poetry (*Genesis B* being exceptional) that we now turn, along with the later *Judith*, to poems which have Old Testament figures as their heroes and heroines.

VIII

Old Testament Narrative Poetry

Christ and Satan, recorded by three different scribes, occupies the second part of the Junius MS; the two poems that constitute *Genesis,* as well as the *Exodus* and the *Daniel,* all in the hand of one scribe, make up the first part of the same manuscript. Forty-eight somewhat crude eleventh-century illustrations in the first ninety-six pages depict scenes from *Genesis.*[1] This manuscript was for long felt to contain poems written by the famed and fabled Cædmon himself, since Bede's account (*HE,* IV. xxiv) tells how, after his receiving miraculously the gift of song, the humble cowherd composed pious verses:

> He sang first about the creation and about the origin of mankind, and all that story of Genesis . . .; in turn about the exodus of the Israelites from the land of the Egyptians and about the entrance into the promised land; and about many other stories of the Holy Scripture. . . .

Since Bede also tells us that Cædmon's monastic teachers under the Abbess Hild (657–680) acted as amanuenses for the oral compositions of this unlettered scop, we would seem to have some evidence in these poems of a bridge between oral and written composition.[2] But scholarship now firmly rejects attribution of any extant poems to Cædmon save for the *Hymn*

1. For reproductions of the illustrations, see Kennedy, *CP* (VII, 17), which contains a translation of the whole Junius 11 MS.
2. See IV, 10, 11, 12.

(see Ch. IX), and the cowherd's oral improvisations on Old and New Testament material are not, alas, available for our scrutiny. The poems we do have, however, whatever their provenience, undoubtedly found high favor in the refectory and helped to satisfy the narrative desires of the monastic inhabitants, though even over a century later, as indicated in the opening pages of this history, stories of pagan heroes were still vying with Biblical narrative for the clerics' attention.

The first of the "Cædmonian" poems in the Junius MS runs to 2935 lines, divided by the scribe into 41 fits, but lines 235–851 are in origin and style a separate poem on the Fall of Man. Lines 1–234 and 852–2935 are usually taken together as *The Earlier Genesis*, or *Genesis A*, and dated around 700; and the inserted portion, fitted chronologically into sequence, is known as *The Later Genesis*, or *Genesis B*, and dated midninth century.[3] The former follows the Biblical account of the First Book of Moses through xxii.13, the sacrifice of Isaac, with expansions, omissions, and changes of various kinds, perhaps most notably the addition of the Apocryphal Fall of the Angels near the beginning of the poem. There is evidently a lacuna in the manuscript after the creation of the sea on the third day, at which point the text jumps to the creation of Eve.

The nature, quality, and meaning of *Genesis A* have been chiefly considered by commentators in terms of the Teutonicizing of the Biblical story by the addition of poetic formulas for heroic concepts. Recently, however, the poem has been approached in the spirit of Christian charity. B. F. Huppé has devoted a long chapter of his *Doctrine and Poetry* (VII, 10) to interpreting *Genesis A* in the light of what he calls, a bit too simplicistically, "the Christian theory of poetry," based upon ex-

3. Editions: see *ASPR*, I; Gollancz, *The Cædmon Manuscript* (IV, 18); *Genesis A* is edited separately by F. Holthausen, *Die ältere Genesis* (Heidelberg, 1914), and *Genesis B* by Fr. Klaeber, *The Later Genesis* (Heidelberg, 1913), and by B. J. Timmer, *The Later Genesis* (Oxford, 1948; rev. ed., 1954). On the whole question of "three poems or one?" and of the dating of the poems, see E. B. Irving, Jr., "On the Dating of the Old English Poems *Genesis* and *Exodus*," *Anglia*, LXXVII (1959), 1–11, which refers to earlier scholarship.

egetical method developed in St. Augustine's *De doctrina Christiana*. Huppé's fundamental thesis is that the Christian poet of the seventh century, and his clerical audience, were always aware of the possibilities of spiritual-symbolic meanings in the literal accounts of literary productions; indeed, it was the purpose and duty of the Christian to find therein such meanings, the overall intent of which was to conduce man to *caritas*, to love of God and his fellow-man. For the modern explicator or critic, the key to the spiritual *significatio* of medieval literature lies in the complex of meanings that Patristic exegetes—Ambrose, Augustine, Gregory, Isidore of Seville, Bede, and so on—expounded in their writings. By referring particularly to Bede's comments in his *Hexaemeron* and by examining the additions to and changes from the Vulgate text made by the Old English poet, Huppé finds a unity in *Genesis* A that embraces its use of the Fall of the Angels and its rather strange ending with the sacrifice of Isaac:

> *Genesis* A seems not to be a mere paraphrase. It follows a plan in developing the related concepts of the Fall and the Redemption, as they are prefigured in Genesis, in order to enforce the basic theme announced at the beginning of the poem—the praise of God. Beginning with this theme, the poet shows the angels blissful in their praise of the Creator and, in contrast, the bitter fate of the fallen angels, who would not praise Him. He then speaks of the creation of the world, which in God's intention will be populated by a race that may prove itself worthy through obedience to inherit the empty thrones of heaven. The interpolated *Genesis* B tells of the Fall of Man. In the remaining portion of *Genesis* A are developed those portions of the biblical story which trace figuratively the salvation and damnation of mankind, first symbolized in the actions of expelling Adam and Eve from Paradise. . . . It is on Abraham, as a figurative character, that the poet chiefly concentrates. . . . The sacrifice of Isaac represents the fulfillment of God's promise to Abraham of the birth of Christ and the Redemption of mankind. The poem ends, as it began, in thanksgiving. The theme is the need for man to praise God, so that he may regain the heaven which was lost in disobedience and so that, God willing, he may not suffer the punishments of the damned.[4]

4. Huppé, pp. 206–207.

I would comment on the above that the thematic pattern perceived in *Genesis* A seems quite a lucid account of that poem's coherence, but also that many of the "spiritual" meanings need no specific exegetical knowledge to fathom, but are rather naturally inherent in the narrative material: Cain's slaying of Abel, for example, as symbolizing "the results of the Fall—man's self-willed sinning," or the fall of Sodom and Gomorrah as symbolizing "both salvation, in Lot's escape, and damnation, in the destruction of the city and in the fate of Lot's wife." I find myself hesitant, moreover, to accept Huppé's arguments over particulars, especially in his slighting of the secular heroic values that the poet *does* seem to build into his account of the battle between the northern kings who fought and defeated the southern kings of Sodom and Gomorrah, and into his description of Abraham's ensuing rescue of Lot, taken captive in that conflict. In the first battle scene, for example, the dewy-feathered raven sings in expectation of carnage, and

> There was hard battle-play,
> Exchange of slaughterous spears, great tumult of war,
> Loud battle-noise. With hands heroes
> Drew from sheaths the ring-mailed sword,
> Doughty in its edges;

[ll. 1989–93b]

in Abraham's rescue operation,

> In the dwellings was noise
> Of shields and spears, the fall of archers,
> The crash of battle-arrows; sharp spears
> Bit bitterly men beneath their armor,
> And the enemies' lives perished quickly
> Where laughing warriors and comrades
> Had borne away booty.

[ll. 2061b–67a]

It is at least doubtful that the poet or his audience, despite exegetical commentaries, would at this point be thinking of Abraham not as a pagan warrior but as "an ideal of Christian living."

The differences between "the Christian" approach to and

two other kinds of critical views of Old English poetry may be
neatly illustrated by reference to the passage in *Genesis* A
in which Noah first sends the raven to see whether the flood
waters have ebbed:

> Noah considered   that he [the raven] of necessity,
> If he on that sea   should find no land,
> Over the broad water   would seek him
> In the ark.   In turn his expectation deceived him,
> For the enemy perched   on floating corpses;
> The black-winged one   had no wish to return.
>
> [ll. 1443–48]

The earlier Germanic emphasis may be seen in Kennedy's comment that even in this watery scene the poet is utilizing the
traditional association with the beasts of battle; a modern folk-
loristic view appears in Utley's wry comment on Kennedy that
the raven must feel lonely without "his Anglo-Saxon companion, the wolf," and that the raven here is pictured, rather,
as a traditional feeder on carrion corpses, "a commonplace of
medieval flood-stories"; while Huppé, referring to Bede, seizes
upon the reference to the raven as "the enemy" (l. 1147—a
reference which Kennedy altogether ignores in his translation
by substituting the word "raven" for "enemy"), suggesting that
it "represents those who dwell in Babylon, the enemies of God,
and those who refuse the way of Redemption, which leads to
Jerusalem. Bede calls them 'men most abominable in the shame-
lessness of their cupidity, devoted to the world.' "[5]

Genesis A, on the whole, is universally regarded as inferior
to the poem inserted in its midst on the temptation and fall of
Adam and Eve, a poem that in conception and poetic power
has often been compared with *Paradise Lost*. There has even
been some speculation that Milton may have seen the manuscript through his acquaintance with Junius, who had the
manuscript in London before Milton went blind. As early as
1875, Sievers advanced the notion that this portion of *Genesis*
was a translation of an Old Saxon (Low German) poem; and
his theory was triumphantly vindicated in 1894 with the dis-

5. Kennedy, *EEP*, p. 173; F. L. Utley, "The Flood Narrative in the
Junius Manuscript and in Baltic Literature," *AGB*, p. 214; Huppé, p. 175.

covery of an Old Saxon fragment in the Vatican Library corresponding to lines 791–817a.[6] Since the Saxon poem clearly dates
from the midninth century, the Old English translation cannot
be placed any earlier.

Genesis B opens in the middle of a speech by God to Adam
and Eve, in which he is telling them to enjoy the fruits of
Paradise, but not to taste those of the forbidden tree. A long
flashback follows, recounting the Creation and the Fall of the
Angels. Satan here is the same proud rebellious tyrant-hero as
he is in *Paradise Lost,* a conception of character that both the
Old English poet and Milton may owe to the fifth-century
Avitus' *Poematum de Mosaicae Historiae Gestis Libri Quinque.*[7]
In raising his standard of defiance, Satan says,

> "I have strength to rear
> A goodlier throne,   a higher in heaven.
> Why must I yield   or fawn for His favour
> Or bow in submission?   I may be God
> As well as He.   Brave comrades stand by me,
> Stout-hearted heroes   unfailing in strife.
> These fighters fierce   have made me their leader;
> With such may one plan   and muster support.
> They are loyal friends   and faithful of heart;
> I may be their lord   and rule this realm.
> So it seems not good   that I grovel before God
> For any boon.   I will obey Him no longer."
> [Kennedy, *EECP,* p. 53]

Even in defeat he is the undaunted Germanic warrior, not the
lamenting exile of *Christ and Satan;*[8] bound in iron bands in
hell as he is, he yet hurls defiance at the Almighty:

> "Woe! Alas!   Could I lift my hands
> And feel their strength,   be free for an hour,
> One winter hour,   with this host I would—

6. E. Sievers, *Der Heliand und die angelsächsische Genesis* (Halle,
1875). For his later views on the structure of *Genesis,* see his "Cædmon
und Genesis," *Britannica, Max Förster Festschrift* (Leipzig, 1929), pp. 57–
84; but see Irving, further, n. 3.

7. *P. L.,* LIX; verse translation in W. Kirkconnell, *The Celestial Cycle*
(Toronto, 1952), pp. 3–19.

8. On the figure of Satan as a combination of Germanic and first-
phase Patristic account of the devil, see R. E. Woolf, "The Devil in Old
English Poetry," *RES,* N. S. IV (1953), 1–12.

> But bands of iron   bind me about,
> Sorely the rings   of my bondage ride me!"
> [Kennedy, *EECP*, p. 55]

Ironically, he urges the *comitatus*-thane bond as reason for one of his fallen comrades to succor him by escaping into the world to deceive Adam and Eve, that thereby they may be thwarted in receiving the fallen angels' now-lost heavenly heritage:

> "If to any thane ever   in days of old
> When we dwelt in that good kingdom   and happily held
>   our thrones
> I dealt out princely treasure,   at no dearer time
> Could he give me requital,   repayment for gifts,
> If some thane would be my helper   and outward hence
> Break through these bolted gates, . . .
> [Kennedy, *EECP*, p. 56]

It is with the acceptance of this task by an unnamed subordinate that the Old Saxon poet and his Old English translator move from Aprocryphal story into the Biblical account, but there are several modifications apart from the initial substitution of the devil's disciple as tempter that are unusual and of significance for the meaning of *Genesis B*. For one thing, the tempter tries Adam first, telling him that it is God's command that he eat of the proffered fruit from the forbidden tree, here pictured as evil and ugly, a tree of death, not of knowledge. Adam rejects the temptation, saying he does not understand the message and the messenger is unlike any angel he has ever seen and furthermore bears no token of God's faith in him. Angered, the devil turns to Eve with the story that Adam has forfeited God's favor in his rejection of His command to eat, that Eve can regain that favor by playing the better part and eating, that he is indeed God's messenger, and, he concludes ironically, "I am not like a devil." Eve succumbs, eats, and sees a vision of heaven the devil grants her, which she takes for a token of the truth. Thereupon, with the devil's prompting, she urges Adam "all the long day/ Driving Adam to that dark deed." The deed done, the apple eaten, the devil gloats and returns to hell, Adam and Eve recognize their deception, repent, and pray for punishment; there is no hint that they refuse to acknowledge their guilt, with Adam blaming Eve and Eve in turn the serpent, as in Biblical and Augustinian versions of the Fall, nor do they seek to blame God.

One further modification in the Biblical story that is mentioned by critics is the disguise of the fiend as an angel of light in his appearance to Adam and Eve, despite the fact that he is said to assume a *wyrm*'s shape to get the apple from the tree, and that the poet comments that the *wyrmes gepeaht* 'the serpent's counsel' worked within Eve (l. 590).[9] This disguise—the eleventh-century illuminator of the manuscript pictures the devil as an angel in the temptation scenes—as well as the description of Eve as innocent (ll. 625–627, 699–701, 820–822) and loyal (ll. 585, 653, 707), and the regard both Adam and Eve display for a "sign" (ll. 539–540, 652, 712–713, 772–773), seems to lead to the conclusion that the Old Saxon poet endeavored to depict the Fall not to show man's moral disobedience but to stress the deception of innocence by malevolence and fraud, to remind us of the forces of destruction that lurk behind human choices of action, however good our motivations. On the other hand, one recent critic boldly suggests that the view of Eve as morally innocent is "Victorian," that the poet meant us to see that the devil's disguise was penetrable (as Adam's rejection of him indicates), and that Eve, unlike her counterpart Juliana, who quickly recognized the nature of the seeming-angel in her prison cell (see Ch. VI), was culpable in listening to the devil "with a willful credulity springing from nascent vanity." The poet's *extenuation* of her behavior—her "innocence," her weak-mindedness, her loyalty—is not a *denial* of her evil conduct. This view of *Genesis B*'s core of meaning and its poetic presentation is summed up by the same scholar in a comparison of the poem with *Troilus and Criseyde*:

> The poet's treatment of Eve cuts across the Anglo-Saxon—and presumably Old Saxon—kind of characterization according to ideals, the noble to be admired and the wicked

9. I believe the fiend remains as a serpent (winged) throughout the temptations, giving added ironic thrust to Eve's failure to penetrate his deception (see below) and to her calling him "this beautiful messenger" *after* she has eaten of the fruit.

abhorred, by presenting a character sinful but sympathetic; and in his guidance to a sympathy for Eve which her conduct alone would not have provoked, he comes nearer to the attitude of Chaucer in *Troilus and Criseyde* than does any writer in the intervening period.[10]

The more "orthodox" interpretation may be seen in another recent critic's statement that *Genesis B* is good tragedy but bad Catholic theology, since motives are irrelevant in the poem's denouement, and in his comparison of the poem with *Oedipus*, to the effect that "Their [Adam and Eve's] errors are errors of judgment, not sins, and the nemesis which overtakes them is determined by a causal rather than a moral law."[11]

The difference of opinion about *Genesis B*'s theological-esthetic orientation has a counterpart in consideration of the poem's sources: Evans believes them to be literary, that is, Christian poems like Avitus', the *Vita Adæ et Evæ*, Victor's *Alethia*, and others; Miss Woolf would stress rather the theological tradition of the Jewish Apocrypha and Christian exegesis (e.g., Gregory's *Moralia*) as the sources of the poet's inspiration. A similar difference of opinion, which also involves the literal-allegorical question raised about *Genesis A*, exists over the sources and the interpretation of the poem following *Genesis* in the manuscript, the *Exodus*. This is in many ways the most difficult of the Cædmonian poems, and of all Old English poems: unlike *Genesis A*, it adds a great deal to its Biblical source, Exodus XIII.17 to the end of 14; its style is rather spasmodic; the poet uses many unusual metaphors; lacunae exist in the manuscript; unrealistic details appear in the midst of the realistically portrayed scenes; there is a questionable flashback to Noah and Abraham in the midst of the Red Sea crossing; the last part of the poem, lines 549–590, seems structurally faulty; and many individual words offer interpretative problems. Further, there is the over-all "strategy" of the poet to consider:

10. R. Woolf, "The Fall of Man in *Genesis B* and the *Mystère d'Adam*," AGB, p. 197 (total pp. 187–199).
11. J. M. Evans, "*Genesis B* and its Background," RES, N. S. XIV (1963), 115 (total pp. 1–16; 113–123); cf. Kennedy, EECP, pp. 27–32.

but whether we view him as primarily interested in facts and in re-creating historical events as accurately and pictorially as possible, or as writing in the Christian allegorical tradition which visualized the historical Exodus as spiritually signifying man's progress toward salvation through Christ,[12] *Exodus* is one of the most stirring and exciting of Old English poems.

It begins with praise of Moses as lawgiver and of the laws themselves, quickly summarizes Moses' career, stressing his *sapientia et fortitudo*,[13] and by line 53 has recorded the tenth plague (omitting the first nine) and the release of the Israelites by the Egyptians. Moses leads his people forward under the protection of a pillar of cloud that shields them from the hot Ethiopian sun and of a pillar of fire that staves off the terrors of the night—the passage, in its deviation from the Vulgate, poses some technical problems we cannot go into here (see Irving's edition, pp. 4–6). With the Israelites encamped by the Red Sea on the fourth night and the news of the pursuing Egyptian host reaching them, there is a gap in the manuscript (after l. 141); with the resumption of the narrative, the Egyptians are approaching the encampment. In the following passage (ll. 154–204), the poet shows considerable scenic skill in his use of a cinematographic technique of shifting back and forth between the opposed forces as they converge.[14] First he shows the terrified Hebrews as they watch the approach of the "shining troop of horsemen," with the dewy-feathered birds of battle circling over dead bodies and with fated souls fleeing—a literally awkward use of the traditional themes and formulas, to be sure, since no battle has yet occurred, but certainly creative of at-

12. See E. B. Irving, Jr., ed., *The Old English Exodus*, Yale Studies in English, 122 (New Haven, Conn., 1953), pp. 20, 29. For allegorical interpretations in particular, see J. E. Cross and S. I. Tucker, "Allegorical Tradition and the Old English *Exodus*," *Neophil*, XLIV (1960), 122–127, and Huppé, pp. 217–223. Besides Irving's edition, see ASPR and Gollancz (n. 3). The latest complete translation is Kennedy's in CP.

13. For this heroic theme in *Beowulf*, see R. E. Kaske, "*Sapientia et Fortitudo* as the Controlling Theme of *Beowulf*," *SP*, LV (1958), 423–456.

14. Cf. A. Renoir, "*Judith* and the Limits of Poetry," *ES*, XLIII (1962), 145–155.

mosphere, especially in its ambiguous applicability to the fearful Israelites who will not die and to the exulting Egyptians who will. The poet then views the scene from the side of the advancing cavalry, with its king bright in his armor. A brief parenthetical glance back to the entrapped Hebrews (ll. 178b–179), and then a long description of the number, organization, and determination of the Egyptians to gain vengence on the tribes of Israel for the slaying of their brothers. Again the "camera" swings back to the Israelites, as their fear rises to a crescendo in the sound of wailing; the enemy is resolute as the gap narrows between the forces; till suddenly God's angel intervenes and scatters the foe in the night.

At dawn Moses summons his people together, bids them organize their armies, and also to take heart and trust in the Lord; he describes the miracle he performs as he strikes the waters of the Red Sea with his wand and the waves part in ramparts on each side of the now-revealed ancient sea bottom. As the tribes cross, the poet turns briefly to the story of Noah and the flood and at greater length to Abraham and the sacrifice of Isaac. At the end of God's covenant with Abraham after the latter has proved his loyalty, there is another large gap in the manuscript, and the narrative begins again with the already trapped Egyptians trying in vain to flee the closing walls of water. At the end of this passage, line 515, in which the drowning of the host is emphasized reiteratively in a somewhat confused fashion that consciously or unconsciously reflects the Egyptians' panic, the manuscript lines briefly touch on Moses' preaching to the Israelites on the shore of the sea, then move to a conventional homiletic passage on the contrast between transitory earthly joys and the bliss of heaven, then back to Moses' address to his people and the despoiling of the dead Egyptians of the wealth of Joseph. In his edition, Irving, in the interest of structural unity, puts the address and despoiling section first— that is, lines 548–590 before lines 516–548—so that the story will first proceed to its logical conclusion and the poem then end on a typical homiletic note; but this, as Wrenn points out, is perhaps assuming an architectonic skill that the poet did not actually possess.[15]

Whatever the structure of its final portion, *Exodus* still possesses a thematic unity embracing its opening celebration of Moses, the narrative of the flight and crossing, the flood and sacrifice passage, and the homiletic section. Bright, followed by Kennedy, suggested that the liturgy for Holy Saturday (the Saturday before Easter Sunday dedicated to the baptism of the catechumens), which included in its reading of twelve "prophecies" from the Old Testament the Red Sea crossing, the flood, and the sacrifice of Isaac, provided a symbolic structure for *Exodus* as a kind of *carmen paschale*.[16] Huppé accepts the symbolic theory, though he prefers to believe that the written commentaries rather than the liturgy provide the best clues for interpreting the poem. Irving reads the poem more literally, finding theme and unity in the opening emphasis on God's laws and Moses as lawgiver: the necessity of obeying God. As the poem develops, we see that it is difficult always to obey and trust in Him, but also that those who keep their covenant with God, like Noah, Abraham, and Moses, are rewarded for their fidelity and trust. Because the Israelites ultimately kept the faith and hearkened to Moses, they too were saved.

That the crossing of the Red Sea held allegorical meaning for the commentators is well known; we saw in Chapter III that Ælfric in the early tenth century reproduced an exegetical treatment of it. Even Irving, who so strenuously denies allegorical intention on the part of the early eighth-century poet, admits that he does show familiarity with the tradition, though he specifically excludes Bede's exegetical works as one of the poet's sources. Of some interest, if we accept the allegorical possibility, is the depth given to the apparently naïve nautical imagery applied to the Israelites as they *march* toward the Promised

---

15. See C. L. Wrenn's important review of Irving's edition, *RES*, N. S. VI (1955), 184–189.

16. J. W. Bright, "The Relation of the Cædmonian *Exodus* to the Liturgy," *MLN*, XXVII (1912), 97–103; Kennedy, *EEP*, pp. 177–180.

Land and along the road bottom of the Red Sea. While the metaphors may indeed be part of the native Anglo-Saxon heroic apparatus with which the poem is liberally furbished, they can also point to a standard Christian interpretation of the sea voyage as a representation of man's journey as an exile in this life to his spiritual home in heaven[17] (cf. Cynewulf's extended simile at the end of *Christ II* and interpretations of *The Seafarer*; see Chs. VII and XI). It is perhaps another matter to see an unrealistic detail like the sons of Judah fighting in the van of the crossing when the enemy is in the rear as signifying a type of baptism because Augustine and Gregory spoke of baptism as a battle.[18]

Allegorical or not, *Exodus* exhibits an epic tone and quality almost everywhere in its exposition of the Flight as a battle between armies. Even the overwhelming of the Egyptians by the closing walls of water is depicted in martial imagery:

> . . . *flod blod gewod.*[19]
> *Randbyrig wæron rofene,* *rodor swipode*
> *meredeaða mæst;* *modige swulton,*
> *cyningas on corðre* . . .
>
> [ll. 463b–466a]
>
> (blood stained the sea.
> Shield-walls [of water] were shattered, the greatest of
>   sea deaths
> Lashed the heavens; the proud ones died,
> The kings amidst their troop.)

Or:

> The waters foamed, the fated ones fell,
> The sea fell on the land, the air was agitated;
> The defending walls (of water) gave way, the waves broke,
> The sea-towers melted, when the Almighty slew

17. See Cross-Tucker, n. 12.

18. See Cross-Tucker, n. 12. Irving comments: "No sane reader would be likely to call *Exodus* a poem about baptism" (p. 15); Cross-Tucker seem to agree with this verdict as regards the poem *as a whole*.

19. This half-line is a good example of the poet's awareness of sound possibilities, of word play (the sea is bloody because it is the *Red* Sea), and of his use of anticipation, since at this moment the Egyptians are not yet dead to incarnadine the multitudinous waters.

With His holy hand,   the God of heaven,
The Warden of the warrior,   that proud nation.

[ll. 482–487]

Inevitably, *Exodus* has been compared with *Beowulf*, certain parallels of phrasing between the two poems—notably the line *enge anpaðas, uncuð gelad* 'narrow lonely-paths, unknown ways' (*Exo.* l. 58, *Bwf.* l. 1410)—having become *causes célèbres* in critical controversy over who borrowed from whom. But as we have seen earlier in general and in the cases of *Andreas* and *Christ and Satan* in particular, such similarities, in the light of recent formulaic studies, no longer constitute sufficient evidence to establish borrowings in a stylistically conventional poetry like Old English; and we had best regard such parallels as coincidences springing from poets with similar subject matters, or wishing to create the same mood and atmosphere and finding the answers to their poetic needs in the common stock of traditional formulas they were heir to.

Following *Exodus*, and the last piece of Book 1 of MS Junius 11, is the poem called *Daniel*.[20] But though based upon the Vulgate Daniel i–v, the Old English poem seems to concentrate, at least to line 485, on the three youths Hannaniah, Azariah, and Mishael and their miraculous salvation in the fiery furnace. Daniel as seer and prophet is not even mentioned when Nebuchadnezzar seeks out young scholars from among the now-enslaved Jews for training as his counselors; he appears only after the king's first dream, when the Chaldean wise men have failed (l. 149b). It should be noted, moreover, that this dream is not related in its literal details nor in Daniel's explanation, unlike its unfolding in the Bible; so that it is quickly passed over, with a transition indicating the untouchability of Nebuchadnezzar's heart, to get to the building of the idol on the plain of Dura, the prelude to the furnace miracle. It is only after the king's temporary conversion to goodness as a result of the three-youths episode, and his backsliding into insolence,

20. For editions, see *ASPR*, 1; Gollancz; F. A. Blackburn, *Exodus and Daniel* (Boston and London, 1907). The latest complete translation is Kennedy's, *CP*.

that Daniel comes into his own as hero, with Nebuchadnezzar's second dream. This dream, about the wondrous tree, is told in detail, as is the prophet's interpretation of it. The poem here follows the Vulgate fairly closely, recounting the king's exile and return, Belshazzar's ultimate inheritance of the kingdom, his feast, and the writing on the wall. The incomplete 764-line poem ends in the midst of Daniel's denunciatory explication of the writing.

It would almost seem that two poems are involved here, though both can be viewed as unified in terms of the general theme set forth in the opening lines, which describe the flourishing of the Jews while they obeyed God's laws and their downfall and Babylonian captivity when they lost "lasting wisdom" and turned to the "devil's craft": the theme of the way of righteousness *vs.* the way of the world.[21] But the text offers an even greater complication in that the scribe has inserted a passage (ll. 279–361) in the first part of the poem that differs in style from the rest—a passage Malone (Int., 5, pp. 66–67) distinguishes as *Daniel B*. Moreover, an almost identical text is preserved in the Exeter Book in the poem known as *Azarias*.[22] This 191-line poem consists of Azariah's prayer (ll. 1–48), an account of the dispersal of the flame (ll. 48–72), and the song of the three youths in the flames blessing the Lord (ll. 73–179b), concluding briefly with Nebuchadnezzar's bidding the youths to come forth and the poet's comment that they triumphed over sin and the fire by their hearts' love and wisdoms' prudence. The great similarity of *Daniel* to *Azarias* lies in the prayer section and in the protection of the youths from the flame (*Dan.* ll. 279–332; 333–361 = *Aza.*, ll. 1–48; 49–72). The passage is awkward in *Daniel*, repeating the already described rescue of the three by the angel (*Dan.* ll. 268 ff.)—which is

21. See Huppé, pp. 223–227, who comments really on only the beginning of the poem, including some stylistic features. For Bright's view of *Daniel* as a symbolic structure based on the liturgy of Holy Saturday, see n. 16.

22. See Exeter Book editions; also, W. Schmidt, *Die altenglischen Dichtungen Daniel und Azarias*, Bonner Beiträge zur Anglistik, xxiii (Bonn, 1907), 1–84.

awkward enough, since there is a still earlier account of that miracle in lines 234b and following. The passage even repeats in varied form the simile describing that miracle:

> But it was within there   most like
> To when in summer   the sun shines
> And the dew-fall   comes at dawn
> Sown by the wind . . .

[ll. 274–277a]

> Then it was in that oven,   where the angel walked,
> Windy and winsome,   most like to the weather
> When in summer time   happens to be sent
> The fall of rain   during the day time,
> Warm shower from the clouds.   As it is the choicest of
>   seasons,
> So was it in that fire . . .

[ll. 345–350a]

We may observe that the *Azarias* counterpart of the second passage above omits the equivalent of line 349. Other differences between the two poems, which include further omissions (e.g., ll. 343–344 of *Dan.* have no equivalent in *Aza.*), additions (*Aza.*, ll. 57–58, for example, have no equivalent in *Dan.*), and even reversal of lines (*Dan.*, ll. 331–332 = *Aza.*, ll. 48–47); dictional displacements; grammatical variations—such differences preclude the possibility that the scribe of *Daniel* merely copied the *Azarias* passage to fill in a portion of the text omitted by the original poet. The exact relationship between the two texts remains uncertain, especially since the versions of the song of the three youths in the two poems diverge even more radically.[23] As to date, *Daniel* A is probably Cædmonian, about 700, while *Daniel* B and *Azarias* are later, possibly ninth century.

Later still is *Judith*, preserved as the last poem of MS Cotton Vitellius A.xv and written in the same hand as that of the second scribe (ll. 1939b ff.) of *Beowulf*. Earlier attributed to Cædmon by some scholars, to Cynewulf or a later ninth-century poet by others, and likewise considered of Anglian

23. The basis of the song is a canticle version of the Benedicite of the Vulgate, a text of which is preserved in the *Vespasian Psalter*.

provenience, *Judith* is now more confidently placed in the tenth
century by its latest editors, and said to be of West-Saxon
origin.[24] This 349-line poem, though based in the main on the
Old Testament Apocryphal story in Judith xii.10 to xv.1,[25]
seems influenced by Patristic tradition and by Latin and English
saints' lives. Judith is a martial Christian saint, like Juliana and
Elene before her, and even prays for guidance and aid to the
Trinity (l. 86a). Her faith in God's grace is stressed in the
beginning and throughout the poem; and at the end the poet
moralizes on her conquest over Holofernes and the earthly
reward given her by her nation—Holofernes' sword, helmet,
armor, and treasures—treating this recompense as but a prelude
to the greater reward the heroine will receive in heaven.

Judith is not a straightforward paraphrase of the Apocryphal text. Its beginning is missing in the manuscript, and when
the narrative commences, at line 7b with the epic formula
Gefrægen ic 'I heard,' we are in the midst of Holofernes' feast,
a riotous occasion, unlike the more decorous beer feasts of
Beowulf:

> Shining bowls
> Were carried back and forth along the benches, and cups
> Were filled to the rim; . . .
> . . .   When the wine
> Rose in him their chieftain roared and shouted
> With triumph, bellowed so loud that his fierce
> Voice carried far beyond
> His tent, his wild pleasure was heard
> Everywhere. And he demanded, over and over,
> That his men empty their cups, drink deep.
>   Thus the evil prince, haughty
> Giver of rings, soaked his soldiers

24. E. V. K. Dobbie, *ASPR*, iv, who locates the poem in the last
half of the tenth century, and B. J. Timmer, *Judith*, 2nd ed. (London,
1961), who locates it about 930, definitely before 937 (*Brunanburh*); the
connection with *Brunanburh* by Timmer, by appearance of the word
"horned-beaked" in the two poems, is tenuous. For facsimile, see *EEMSF*,
xii (III, 42). For translations, see Gordon (Int., 5) and Raffel (V, 37);
quotations in this section are from the latter.

25. The Vulgate text is conveniently reproduced in Timmer, pp. 14–
16. See Dobbie, p. lix, on the Vulgate vs. the Septuagint texts.

In wine, the whole day through, drenched them till their heads
    swam
And they fell on the ground, all drunk, lay as though death
    had struck them
Down, drained of their senses.

[ll. 17a–32a]

After Judith decapitates the lecher-tyrant—a very realistic
account, in which the heroine draws him by the hair into a position suitable for her bloody vengeance and takes two strokes to
cut through the neck so that the head rolls on the floor—she
and her servant return to Bethulia with the head and announce
to the people her triumph. She bids the army make haste to
attack the now-leaderless Assyrians. The ensuing battle is a
vigorous epic expansion over its Biblical counterpart. In fact,
there is *no* such battle in the Vulgate, since there the Assyrians
find Holofernes dead and flee before the Hebrews leave their
city in pursuit of them; but in the Old English poem, the discovery of the dead leader is made the climax of the military
engagement that had begun at dawn and proceeded apace all
morning long.

This reorganization of the narrative helps to glorify the
Jews, who do not wait for the flight of their enemy before
leaving their stronghold. It also indicates something of the
poet's dramatic and structural sense. Renoir has recently analyzed for us the visual impact the battle scene makes in the
poet's cinematographic handling of the action.[26] Beginning
behind the marching Jews, with the traditional beasts of battle
eager for their prey, we are swiftly moved to the main body of
troops, then to its front ranks:

Now the Jews

Were approaching the Assyrian camp, carrying
Jewish flags, and fighting would more
Than repay gentile taunts. The Hebrew
Archers bent their horn-tipped bows
And a stream of poisoned arrows dropped

26. See n. 14.

> From the sky, a bold hail-storm of bitter
> Darts. The angry Jews shouted
> With a roar, and sent spears and javelins
> Flying through the air.

In the next "shot" we are in the center of the action, the drink-exhausted front-line Assyrians stumbling awake, the Bethulians drawing their swords for close-in fighting. Then the scene focuses on the fleeing enemy, and then beyond them on the warriors running to their chief thanes with the news of the assault, they in turn pressing to Holofernes' tent, where they ironically dare not disturb him, thinking he lies with the Jewish maid (to l. 261a). A sudden shift of scene to the battlefield once again (ll. 261b–267a), as a suggestion of what is on the anguished Assyrians' minds as they mill about the tent gnashing their teeth and shouting. And then the one warrior who enters, discovers the beheaded torso, and laments their ruination; the utter rout of the Assyrians, and once again the beasts of battle, this time taking their prey. The victorious Jews despoil the bodies of their armor and treasure: the Christian poet makes symbolic use of this treasure trove as he concludes on the note mentioned above, extolling the greater treasure of heaven.

The main current of critical opinion runs that *Judith* is but a fragment of a religious epic originally about 1300–1400 lines in length. The bases of this opinion are twofold: 1) there is more in the Book of Judith than the Old English poem preserves; 2) fit or section numbers in the margins of the manuscript begin with x, at line 15, indicating the loss of eight-plus fits of the poem before its decapitated opening. R. E. Woolf suggests, however, plausibly to me, that the latter point is no indication of *authorial* numbering, since the poems of the first book of the Junius MS (*Genesis, Exodus, Daniel*), though clearly by different poets, have consecutive fit markings from I to LV. Further and significantly, there is a modification of the Vulgate source to give a thematic emphasis in the preserved episodes of the Anglo-Saxon *Judith* that argues for the poem's unity and coherence as it stands, with perhaps a slight loss at the beginning which included a brief account of the loss of Judith's husband; even thus did Aldhelm utilize the life of Judith as one of his exempla in the *De Laudibus Virginitatis*. For the Old English poet carefully omits proper names previously introduced in the Vulgate that reappear in the sections he is poeticizing (for example, Ozias, one of the two rulers of Bethulia, greets Judith on her return in the Vulgate, but in the poem, there is only the splendid welcoming crowd; and the episode involving the renegade Achior, summoned by the Biblical heroine, is altogether omitted by the Old English poet). More important, he has not given the same emphasis the Biblical account gives to the Jewish nation's triumph over the enemy of Jehovah; his poem is, rather, almost a hymn to the virtuous maiden who conquered the dissolute Holofernes. *Judith*, therefore, should properly be regarded as a religious lay, akin to the secular *Finn Fragment* or *Maldon*, and not as a fragment of a larger religious epic.[27]

Some aspects of style and technique have been indicated in the foregoing discussion. Mention may also be made of the high proportion of end-rimes in the poem—higher than in any other Old English poem save for the *tour de force* of the *Riming Poem*—and of expanded or hypermetric lines, that is, of verses with three major stresses instead of the usual two. The use of the latter especially calls for comment, the poet reserving them for the most part for reflective or psychological passages, as a contrast to his use of the regular line for rapid narrative action.[28] Two extended passages of hypermetric verses illustrate this well: lines 54–68, in which Holofernes anticipates his night with Judith, and lines 88–99, in which Judith prays for God's grace to help her take vengeance on the besotted Holofernes who lies before her. I cite the former; even in translation, the shift in stress can be observed at beginning and end, the movement

27. R. E. Woolf, "The Lost Opening to the 'Judith,'" *MLR*, L (1955), 168–172.
28. Cf. Kennedy, *EEP*, p. 288.

into the short line at the end beautifully coinciding with the
quickening of the narrative pace:

> but none of the sons of men
> Could know he was staring [through the fly-net] except
> when he called
> Some brave lieutenant, proven in battle,
> 54   To come close, and whispered secret words. They came,
> hurrying
> The wise virgin to his bed, then went where their lord
> awaited them
> And announced that his will had been done, the holy
> woman led
> To his couch. The famous conqueror of cities and towns
> smiled
> And laughed, hearing them, his heart joyful, thinking how
> Judith
> Could be smeared with his filth, stained with dishonor.
> But our Glorious Saviour,
> Guardian of the world, Lord and Master of men, refused
> him,
> Kept her safe from such sin. . . .
> . . .   He entered, their great general,
> 68   And fell across his bed, so full of wine that his brain
> Was numb. Quickly, his followers left
> His chamber. . . .

In its concentration on a single event and its consequences,
Judith resembles *Exodus* rather than *Genesis* A or *Daniel* (if we
accept the last as all one poem). Like the earlier *Exodus*, too,
it expands upon Germanic heroic motifs, though it is noticeable
that here, despite the references to Holofernes as a ring-giver
and to his warriors as bench-sitters, and so on, there is no
suggestion of *comitatus* loyalty. Perhaps the poem was written,
as some critics have theorized, as an encouragement to the
harassed English people during the Danish invasions. Speculation on the occasion of the poem leads nowhere, really,[29] but
observation of the virtuosity of the poet assuredly does lead
us to the comment that Old English poetry, even as its prose,
was not decadent toward the end of the Anglo-Saxon period. As

29. For example, that the poem was written to honor Æthelflæd,
daughter of Alfred, Queen of Mercia—see editions.

the late tenth-century *Maldon* reflects the earlier Old English secular ethos in a brilliant use of the conventional poetic techniques, so the tenth-century *Judith*, with perhaps a greater experimentation in its use of verse, reflects the earlier glorification of religious heroism of both the Cædmonian and the Cynewulfian schools.

IX

Miscellaneous Religious and Secular Poetry

IN THE COURSE of the present chapter, we shall consider poems that do not fall into the categories of the following two chapters, "Lore and Wisdom" and "Elegiac Poetry." Many short poems as well as the longer *Phoenix* will come under our scrutiny, most of them of historical rather than intrinsic interest. But one of the shortest poems combines literary power and historical significance; and it lies at the heart of the fusion of the native Anglo-Saxon and the Latin-Christian heritages in the Old English period. The poem is, of course, the nine-line *Hymn* of Cædmon; and it is with this only authentic work of the first English Christian poet that I should like to begin.

Heretofore I have alluded on several occasions to Bede's account of the miracle of poetic composition granted to the unlettered cowherd; it is appropriate now to give the fuller narrative:

> In the monastery of this abbess there was a certain brother specially distinguished by the divine grace, in that he used to compose songs suited to religion and piety. . . . By his songs the minds of many were often fired with contempt of the world and with desire for the heavenly life. . . . he did not learn that art of singing from men, nor taught by man, but he received freely by divine aid the gift of singing. . . . he had lived in the secular habit until he was well advanced in years, and had never learnt anything of versifying; and for this reason sometimes at an entertainment,

when it was resolved for the sake of merriment that all should sing in turn, if he saw the harp approaching him, he would rise from the feast and go out and return home.

When he did this on one occasion, and having left the house where the entertainment was, had gone to the stable of the cattle which had been committed to his charge that night, and there at the proper time had composed himself to rest, there appeared to him someone in his sleep, and greeting him and calling him by his name, he said: "Cædmon, sing me something." But he replied: "I cannot sing; and for this reason I left the entertainment and came away here, because I could not sing." Then he who was speaking to him replied: "Nevertheless, you must sing to me." "What," he said, "must I sing?" And the other said: "Sing me of the beginning of creation." On receiving this answer, he at once began to sing in praise of God the Creator, verses which he had never heard, of which this is the sense: [Bede here gives a Latin paraphrase of the poem, for which see below, and apologizes for the loss of beauty and grandeur in his translation.] Awaking from his sleep, he remembered all that he had sung when sleeping, and soon added more words in the same manner in song worthy of God. [Having recounted his gift to the reeve the next morning, Cædmon was brought before the abbess; and after proving his new-found powers by turning a passage of Scripture or doctrine recited to him into poetry, he was joined to the brethren.] And remembering all that he could learn by listening, and like, as it were, a clean animal chewing the cud, he turned it into most harmonious song, and, sweetly singing it, he made his teachers in their turn his hearers.[1]

In the Latin text, as the above translation indicates, Bede says that he is giving only the *sensus* of Cædmon's Old English *Hymn*. But the Old English poem must quickly have become popular in the houses of religion, for versions of it are preserved in seventeen manuscripts: four in the Northumbrian dialect native to Cædmon, in manuscripts of the Latin text of the *HE*; eight in the West Saxon dialect in manuscripts of the Latin text; and five in West Saxon in texts of the late ninth-century Old English translation of the *HE*. These manuscripts date from the early Moore MS of 737 to the late fifteenth-century

1. Quoted from *EHD*, pp. 663–665.

Paris MS.[2] To give some notion of dialectal differences, I cite below both the Moore MS version (Northumbrian) and the Tanner 10 MS (West Saxon),[3] followed by a literal translation and then by the poetic re-creation of Burton Raffel (V, 37):

> Nu scylun hergan   hefaenricaes uard
> metudæs maecti   end his modgidanc
> uerc uuldurfadur   sue he uundra gihuaes
> eci dryctin   or astelidæ
> he aerist scop   aelda barnū
> heben til hrofe   haleg scepen.
> tha middungeard   moncynnæs uard
> eci dryctin   æfter tiadæ
> firum fold^v   frea allmectig
> primo cantauit caedmon istud carmen.

> Nu sculon herigean   heofonrices weard
> meotodes meahte   his modgeþanc
> weorc wuldorfæder   swa he wundra gehwæs
> ece drihten   or onstealde.
> he ærest sceop   eorðan bearnū
> heofon to hrofe   halig scyppend.
> þa middangeard   moncynnes weard
> éce drihten   æfter teode
> firum foldan   frea ælmihtig.

(Now let us praise the Keeper of the Heavenly Kingdom, the Might of the Creator and His Thought, the Work of the glorious Father, how He each of wonders, Eternal Lord, established the beginning. He first created for the sons of men [Nthn.] / for the children of earth [WS] heaven as a roof, the Holy Shaper; then middle-earth the Keeper of Mankind, Eternal Lord, afterwards made for men, [made] earth, the Lord Almighty.)

Now sing the glory of God, the King
Of heaven, our Father's power and His perfect
Labor, the world's conception, worked
In miracles as eternity's Lord made
The beginning. First the heavens were formed as a roof
For men, and then the holy Creator,
Eternal Lord and protector of souls,

2. See E. V. K. Dobbie, *The Manuscripts of Cædmon's Hymn and Bede's Death Song* (New York, 1937); also A. H. Smith, ed., *Three Northumbrian Poems* (London, 1933).

3. From Dobbie, *Manuscripts*, pp. 13, 24; see also Dobbie, *ASPR*, VI, pp. 105, 106.

Shaped our earth, prepared our home,
The almighty Master, our Prince, our God.

We may consider here a few of the major problems this apparently simple poem of praise has occasioned. First, what is the nature of the miracle that Bede felt to be present in Cædmon's song? Shepherd sees it in the light of *prophetism's* connection with song, calling the *Hymn* "the first of a long line of English writings in the prophetic tradition"; Huppé thinks that the miracle to Bede lay "in the concrete, empirical truth . . . that a man unlearned in Scripture, with its great intellectual demands, had the insight to proclaim what he never formally learned"; most critics feel it resided in the linguistic feat which enabled Christian thought to be expressed for the first time in the native alliterative meter.[4] In connection with all these views, we should remember that Cædmon composed about 670, and his *Hymn* is the earliest extant poem, secular or religious (apart possibly from some Charms, segments of *Widsith*, etc.), that we possess; further, that it was composed less than one hundred years after Augustine's Christianizing mission landed in England and only about fifty years after the conversion of the Northumbrian King Edwin at York (see Ch. I). A second problem concerns the nature of Cædmon's linguistic accomplishments. Recently Magoun has challenged the older view that Cædmon was responsible in his following of native tradition for the coining of new vocabulary and formulas necessary for his Christian purposes, claiming that oral formulas develop slowly and that those in the poem must have had prior existence and simply lain in solution in Cædmon's mind from his having heard them recited many times.[5] Even more recently

4. G. Shepherd, "The Prophetic Cædmon," *RES*, N. S. v (1954), 113–122; Huppé (VII, 10), p. 122; C. L. Wrenn, "The Poetry of Cædmon," *PBA*, 1946, xxxii (1947), 277–295, and Malone, "Cædmon and English Poetry," *MLN*, lxxvi (1961), 193–195.
5. F. P. Magoun, Jr., "Bede's Story of Cædman: The Case History of an Anglo-Saxon Oral Singer," *Speculum*, xxx (1955), 49–63; Magoun rationalizes the miracle as possibly the removal of a psychological block to speaking in public. For objection to this theory, see Malone, n. 4; Huppé also continues to think of Cædmon himself as building upon the earlier heroic vocabulary—pp. 117 ff.

the cowherd's source of inspiration in vocabulary as well as in content and form has been seen in the Psalms rather than in native tradition at all.[6]

The *Hymn* would seem to pose few critical problems as such, yet one scholar has felt it incumbent to provide a lengthy interpretation in terms of Patristic exegesis, a view of the poem as Trinitarian in doctrine, structure, and stylistic development; and a further theological explication of *modgeþanc* (l. 2b) as God's design, an externalizing in the Son of His internal eternal thought, has continued the doctrinal-literary school of criticism.[7] That the untutored cowherd could bear in mind such subtle doctrinal notions may be explained, if not by the miracle Bede thought it was, by his having absorbed some of the intellectual discussions current in the monastery; that he could express these ideas in such felicitous poetic form I prefer to leave unexplained, as part of the miraculous stream from which all true poetic compositions flow.

Since Cædmon's *Hymn* does bear some resemblance, though I think slight, to various of the Psalms invoking the praise of the Lord, it is appropriate that we consider next in our review of the nonhomiletic religious verse the Old English metrical translations of the Psalms. A translation of all the canticles into Old English survives in the beautiful but mutilated mideleventh-century *Paris Psalter*.[8] The Latin text is on the left, the Anglo-Saxon on the right, the first fifty Psalms

6. N. F. Blake, "Cædmon's Hymn," *N & Q*, N. S. ix (1962), 243–246; Blake goes so far as to suggest that it was the later poets who borrowed what we regard as heroic diction from Cædmon's *Hymn*.

7. Huppé, pp. 99–130; M. W. Bloomfield, "Patristics and Old English Literature," *AGB*, pp. 41–43. Among the stylistic features Huppé calls to our attention is the parallel in movement between epithets for "God" and the structural development of the poem: God is called first the "Ward of Heaven" as the poem opens on the call to praise, and later is called the "Ward of mankind" as His creation is described chronologically in terms of "first," "then," and "afterwards." A balance is maintained by the repetition of "Eternal Lord" in both parts, and the poem reaches an *O altitudo* at the same time that it returns to its beginning in the epithet "Almighty Lord."

8. See the facsimile edition by B. Colgrave et al. (II, 18). Ten to twelve color illustrations have been cut out of the MS.

being in West Saxon prose and often attributed to Alfred (see Ch. II), Psalms 51–150 being in verse.[9] The metrical translation was probably made in the tenth century as part of the Benedictine Reform (see Ch. III). These verses are not very distinguished as poetry: meter and alliteration, however regular, are mechanical and uninspired, common adjectives and adverbs as well as unusual words are overworked as verse fillers, and the traditional poetic vocabulary finds little place. As an example of adverbs overused and emptied of meaning, we may glance at the translation of Psalm 90: 12–14 (Psalm 91 in the Authorized Version):

> 12 *And þe on folmum   feredan swylce,*
> *þe læs þu fræcne on stan   fote spurne.*
> 13 *þu ofer aspide miht   eaðe gangan,*
> *and bealde nu   basiliscan tredan,*
> *and leon and dracan   liste gebygean.*
> 14 *Forðon he hyhte to me,   ic hine hraðe lyse,*
> *niode hine scylde,   nu he cuðe naman minne.*

(And in their hands they shall bear you up *likewise,* lest you *rashly* dash your foot on a stone. You may *easily* pass over an adder, and tread *boldly* now upon a basilisk, and lion and dragon *skillfully* subdue. Because he trusted in me, I will *readily* deliver him, *necessarily* protect him, now that he has known my name.)

Obviously the italicized adverbs do not have the literal meanings the translation suggests: they are padding, nothing more.[10]

Fragments of the metrical psalter, undoubtedly transcribed from the original of the Paris MS, also appear in MS Junius 121, and a lengthy paraphrase of Psalm 50 (Vulgate)—which appears as prose in the *Paris Psalter*—in MS Cotton Vespasian

9. For edition of prose Psalms, see II, 18; the metrical Psalms are edited in *ASPR*, v.

10. Cf. K. and C. Sisam in Colgrave, *Facsimile,* p. 17; text cited from *ASPR*, v, p. 62. See, however, R. E. Diamond, *The Diction of the Anglo-Saxon Metrical Psalms* (The Hague, 1963), Introduction, who feels that the poet makes capital of "empty" words and phrases to fulfill metrical requirements without deviating from or adding to the sense of the Latin original. Diamond also shows the diction to be as formulaic as that of the older poetry.

D.vi.[11] *Psalm 50*, a 157-line poem in a mixed West Saxon and Kentish dialect, is probably also to be connected with the tenth-century monastic revival; but its translator was more of a poet than the *Psalter* versifier. His paraphrase, in about a six-to-one ratio of Old English to Latin original, employs many of the conventional formulas and the technique of variation to good if not startling effect. He has a thirty-line introduction, following the line of Patristic exegesis of the Psalm as David's repentance for his affair with Bathsheba, then expands upon each verse, which he quotes, usually only in part, in Latin, and concludes with a brief epilogue praying that he and others, like David, may receive God's forgiveness. In the same manuscript is the forty-three-line *Kentish Hymn*, a conflation and paraphrase of passages of the *Te Deum* and *Gloria*, presenting rather an exposition on the Trinity than a prayer for intercession and a confession of faith.[12]

The *Fragments of Psalms* are part of the *Benedictine Office*, compiled by Wulfstan (see Ch. III). In addition to these poems, embedded in the *Office* are the *Gloria I*, the *Lord's Prayer III*, and the *Creed*.[13] Like *Psalm 50*, the *Gloria I* quotes each phrase of its Latin text, here the *Gloria patri*, and then poetically expands upon its original; the opening extended paraphrase of the simple word *Gloria* will illustrate:

Let Thy glory and praise   be widely declared
Among all nations,   Thy grace and love,
Thy might and mercy   and all Thy heart's love,
Thy peace for the righteous,   and Thine own judgment
(Be) glorified in the world,   as Thou hast power to rule
All earthly might   and heavenly,
The wind and the clouds.   Thou rulest all in right.

11. See *ASPR*, vi, pp. 80–86, 88–94. A further fragment, in the *Eadwine Psalter* (EETS 92, London, 1889) is overlooked by this volume —see n. 3 of Whitbread, "O.E. Poems of *Benedictine Office*," in n. 15, below.

12. See G. Shepherd, "The Sources of the OE 'Kentish Hymn'," *MLN*, lxvii (1952), 395–397. The poem is edited in *ASPR*, vi, pp. 87–88.

13. Pp. 74–80 of *ASPR*, vi. Texts and discussion also in Ure, *Benedictine Office* (III, 26).

The *Lord's Prayer III* follows the same pattern as the *Gloria I*, but is much less expansive in its versifying of the *Pater noster*. For example, the opening *Pater noster qui es in cælis* becomes the two lines "Father of mankind, I pray Thee for comfort, / Holy Lord, Thou who art in heaven." Dobbie comments that the *Lord's Prayer III* "is a clear, straightforward paraphrase, and is probably to be regarded as the best of all the Anglo-Saxon verse translations of Latin liturgical texts."[14] The *Creed* resembles the *Gloria I* in its lengthy paraphrase of the *Credo*. It is almost stanzaic in form: of the first five sections, four are of eight lines each, and the second, which expatiates upon the only Son and gives prominence to the Annunciation, is exactly twice as long: the remaining ten lines translate five Latin phrases. Like the other poems of the *Office*, the *Creed* seems to have been already in circulation when Wulfstan drew upon it for his compilation.[15]

Another text of the *Gloria I*, substantially the same, appears in MS CCCC 201, which is preceded there by another version of the Lord's Prayer known as *Lord's Prayer II*.[16] The latter is similar to the former in technique, building up its expansion of the Latin text phrase-by-phrase, bearing touches of the liturgy and Scriptural matter, owing little to earlier verse vocabulary but being comfortable in its use of earlier metrical patterns. Both poems are almost surely by the same author, but the *Lord's Prayer II* differs enough in style, length, and subject matter to warrant our considering it an independent poem from its namesake in the *Office*.[17]

The two poems preceding the *Lord's Prayer II* in the Corpus Christi MS are known as *An Exhortation to Christian*

14. ASPR, vi, p. lxxvii.
15. Cf. Bethurum, *Homilies* (III, 17); L. Whitbread, "The Old English Poems of the *Benedictine Office* and Some Related Questions," *Anglia*, lxxx (1962), 363–378.
16. ASPR, vi, pp. 70–74, and Appendix A of Ure.
17. So Whitbread, n. 15. Ure argues for *LPr II* and *LPr III* as variants of the same poem. There is also a still briefer, workmanlike metrical translation, *LPr I*, in the Exeter Book, and a three-line *Gloria II* preserved in MS Cotton Titus D.xxvii—see ASPR, iii and vi.

Living and *A Summons to Prayer*.[18] Though the former should properly be considered in the chapter on "Lore and Wisdom," I take it up here for a reason that will become obvious in a moment. *Exhortation* is an eighty-two-line poem, homiletic in tone, urging the reader or listener to abstain from sin and to perform good deeds, especially alms-giving, so that his soul may be secured against the coming Judgment Day. It is not a very distinguished piece of poetry, being a loose collocation of urgings, and using some of the conventional formulas rather mechanically: for example, *wis on wordum* 'wise in words,' line 4a; *bliðemode* 'with joyful heart,' line 6a; the exilic *frofre bedæled* 'deprived of comfort,' line 27b; the epic *har hilderinc* 'gray-haired battle-warrior,' line 57a.[19] Two prose adaptations of the poem exist, one in the Pseudo-Wulfstan Homily xxx (Napier's numbering) and the other in Homily xxi of the Vercelli Book. The *Summons to Prayer* is a thirty-one-line macaronic poem, the first half-line of each full verse being in Old English, the second in Latin (cf. the ending of *Phoenix*). It is a call to repentance through prayer to God the Creator, to His Son, to Mary (who receives the greatest attention), and finally to all the saints that they intercede for mercy for "thy soul" from the "great Judge." Whitbread, following Förster, finds the *Summons* as belonging to the *Confiteor* genre of literature, and suggests that it is interrelated in a pattern of penance with the other four poems of the Corpus Christi MS, the five being transcribed in the following order: *Judgment Day II (Be Domes Dæge)*—see Chapter VII—*Exhortation, Summons, Lord's Prayer II,* and *Gloria I.* He sees the second and third poems as having been added by the compiler to the Judgment Day poem in a conventional pattern of confession (*Judgment Day II*), and final absolution (*Summons*), with the two last poems (*LPr II* and *Gloria I*) as part of the imposition

18. ASPR, vi, pp. 67–70.
19. Whitbread comments, however, that there is little trace of the older vocabulary in the poem—see "Notes on the Old English 'Exhortation to Christian Living'," SN, xxiii (1951), 96–102.

on the penitent of the reciting of prayers and the performing of devotional exercises.[20]

I mentioned above that the Junius MS 121 *Creed* was almost stanzaic in form. In this respect and in several others it resembles the *Seasons for Fasting*, a poetic calendar of sorts on the observance of fasts.[21] *Seasons* was discovered only rather recently, in 1934, by Robin Flower in the sixteenth-century transcript made by Laurence Nowell from the now-destroyed MS Cotton Otho B.xi. It consists of some 230 lines divided into stanzas of eight lines each, save for the fourth, which has six lines, the fifteenth, which has nine, and the incomplete last stanza. The first few stanzas are concerned with the Jews, their observance of the Laws of Moses and their fasts, after which the poet discusses the four Ember day fasts, urging his readers to follow the custom established by Gregory and not Continental recommendations; that is, they should observe the Ember fasts in March in the first week of Lent, in June in the week after Pentecost Sunday, in September in the week before the equinox, and in the week before Christmas. Several stanzas are then devoted to the forty-days fast of Lent. The age-old problem of the sinful priests—we recall Bede's, *Guthlac A's*, and Ælfric's wrestling with it—crops up in stanzas 25 and following. The last three stanzas present a vigorous portrait of the sinful priests who, instead of observing the fast, hurry after mass to the tapster and persuade him that it is no sin to serve oysters and wine before noon, rationalizing as they sit and tipple that it is permissible to refresh oneself after mass. Although not very remarkable as poetry, this probably late-tenth-century piece is notable for its experimentation with the alliterative meter in

20. M. Förster, "Zur Liturgik der angelsächsischen Kirche," *Anglia*, LXVI (1942), 1–52; L. Whitbread, "Notes on Two Minor Old English Poems," *SN*, XXIX (1957), 123–129. See further L. Whitbread, "The Old English 'Exhortation to Christian Living': Some Textual Problems," *MLR*, XLIV (1949), 178–183.

21. Edited in *ASPR*, VI, pp. 98–104; also F. Holthausen, in *Anglia*, LXXI (1953), 191–201. The most valuable commentary is in Sisam's *Studies* (II, 6), pp. 45–60. For comment on technical calendar matters, see H. Henel, *Studien zum altenglischen Computus* (Leipzig, 1934).

stanzaic form; and it does reveal a logical and orderly structure, a knowledge of its subject, and an emotional sensitivity in its depiction of the sacerdotal sinners.

Seasons for Fasting only impinges upon the concept of the calendar. More clearly in that genre is the poetic *Menologium*, which, like several Latin poetic martyrologies and like the prose *Menologium* which resembles it, gives a chronological account of the Christian year.[22] The 231-line poem is preserved in MS Cotton Tiberius B.I, one of the manuscripts recording the *Anglo-Saxon Chronicle*; it seems to have been viewed by the scribe as a prologue to the *Chronicle*, though it was clearly in origin an independent piece. The poet's object was presumably to give a detailed and exact account of the place and sequence of liturgical facts in the Christian year, at the same time putting them into the perspective of the natural year of months and seasons.[23] His sources were the ecclesiastical calendars in missals and other liturgical books; the date of his writing is uncertain, probably late tenth century.

Mention of three minor poems here will lead into a discussion of three more significant religious poems which will conclude our survey of miscellaneous nonhomiletic religious poetry. The three pieces are *A Prayer, Thureth*, and *Aldhelm*.[24] The last is unique in its irregularly macaronic composition and in its inclusion of Greek as well as Latin words; it is a seventeen-line poem in praise of the great Canterbury religious writer, preserved fittingly in a manuscript of his prose *De Virginitate*. *Thureth* is eleven lines long, preserved in MS Cotton Claudius A.III; it represents a *halgungboc*, or 'coronation liturgy,' as speaking in intercession for Thureth (Thored) who commissioned its making. *A Prayer*, extant in MS Cotton Julius A.II and in part in MS Lambeth Palace 427, is a seventy-nine-line poem in which the speaker rather tearfully and melodramatically

22. Edited in *ASPR*, VI, pp. 49–55; also R. Imelmann, *Das altenglisch Menelogium* (Berlin, 1902). The only English translation is in the early edition of S. Fox, *Menologium seu Calendarium poeticum* (London, 1830). On the prose *Menologium*, see Henel.

23. See J. Hennig, "The Irish Counterparts of the Anglo-Saxon *Menologium*," *MS*, XIV (1952), 98–106.

24. Edited in *ASPR*, VI, pp. 94–98.

beats his breast, acknowledging over and over his smallness as compared to the lord's greatness, and asking Him for grace for his soul.

Man's soul comes off much better *poetically* in the longer *Soul and Body I* and *II,* preserved in the Vercelli and Exeter Books respectively.[25] The former is the more complete poem, 166 lines, though its ending is missing. It presents first the speech of a damned soul to its decaying body and a description of that body's disintegration that is unparalleled in English literature; then, at line 127, it turns to the speech of a saved soul to its former earthly habitation. The Exeter Book poem contains only the first address, in 121 lines; it is substantially the same as its Vercelli counterpart, though with some omissions, one addition, and numerous small differences in diction and in arrangement of parts.

The soul and body *topos* runs throughout medieval literature, and it has certain obvious affinities with the Doomsday *topos*.[26] It takes two forms: the address and the debate. In the former, the dead body lies unansweringly by as the soul castigates or (more rarely) blesses it for its deeds while living; in the latter, a dialogue ensues. The Old English poem is an address. First the poet comments that a man had better ponder his soul's state before their separation by death; he then states that the soul must visit its body weekly for three hundred years, unless the end of the world comes sooner. When the damned soul speaks, it reproaches the body for making it suffer in its earthly housing as well as now, and foretells their further punishment on Judgment Day. With some grim satisfaction it vilifies the body in anaphoric parallels:

Now are you none the dearer   to any one living,
As a comrade to man,   neither to mother nor to father,
Nor to any kinsman,   than is the dark raven,
Since I alone from you   journeyed away
By that very hand [God's]   by which I was formerly sent.

25. Edited in *ASPR*, II and III; also R. Willard, "The Address of the Soul to the Body," *PMLA*, L (1935), 957–983.
26. For a discussion of the theme, see E. K. Heningham, *An Early Latin Debate of the Body and Soul* (New York, 1939).

> Nor can anyone from you hence take   the red ornaments,
> Neither gold nor silver   nor any of your goods,
> Nor your bride's ring   nor your wealth,
> Nor any of those possessions   you formerly held,
> But now must abide   your stripped bones,
> Despoiled by sins,   and I your soul must
> Against my will   often seek you out,
> Revile you with words,   as you did unto me.
>   [ll. 52–64 of Vercelli text]

When the soul departs, the poet graphically describes the body, helpless to answer: with cloven head, disjointed hands, distended jaws, severed palate, sucked sinews, gnawed-through neck, and slit tongue; and further shows the decomposing worms at work, with their leader Gifer[27] who first descends into the grave and

> . . . tears at the tongue   and bores through the teeth
> And eats through the eyes   up into the head,
> And to the feast   leads the way for others,
> For worms to the banquet,   when that wretched
> Body has become cold . . .
>   [ll. 119–123a]

Soul and Body is savage in its denunciation of the body, its vigor making living flesh creep. The portrayal of the righteous soul's words of consolation to its decaying body while it awaits resurrection is pallid by comparison. Nevertheless, the whole poem is quite effective in its presentation of the lesson that all is vanity, and that as we live on earth, so shall we reap after death. No specific source has been discovered for this undatable poem, but there is probably some connection with the Book of Job, at least, and with Doomsday homiletic material; one of the Vercelli homilies contains remarks on a similar theme.

Quite a different kind of poem is the Old English *Physiologus*, extant in the Exeter Book.[28] It, like the other religious poems, deals with the broad themes of salvation and damnation,

---

27. See B. P. Kurtz, "Gifer the Worm," *Univ. of California Pubs. in Eng.*, II (Berkeley, 1929), 235–261.
28. Edited in ASPR, III; see also A. S. Cook, *The Old English Elene, Phoenix, and Physiologus* (New Haven, Conn., 1919), esp. valuable for its Introduction, pp. lvii–lxxxv—the *Physiologus* is republished separately, with verse translation by J. H. Pitman (New Haven, Conn., 1921).

but allegorically; that is, it describes the traits and actions of animals or birds and then didactically explicates their signification in terms of God, Christ, mankind, or the devil. The characteristics attributed to the beasts do not necessarily bear any resemblance to natural history. The physiologus-bestiary genre has a long history, going back to Alexandria in pre-Christian times. Its great popularity in the Middle Ages is attested to by the many European and non-European translations in which it is preserved; that it still finds an audience today may be seen in the recent publication of T. H. White's *The Book of Beasts.*

The Old English poem consists of seventy-four lines on the Panther, eighty-nine lines on the Whale, and a fragmented sixteen lines on a bird whose identity has been questioned. The gap between the first line of the last section, which ends folio 97, and the remaining fifteen lines beginning folio 98, occasioned much critical controversy in the late nineteenth and early twentieth centuries. Was the poem a fragment of a large cycle (Continental versions of the *Physiologus* can amount to fifty "stories"), with several leaves missing from the manuscript, or was it a short-cycle type, in which the Panther, Whale, and Partridge were often associated? Krapp and Dobbie remove all doubt that this is a short-cycle physiologus, with only one leaf missing, which, containing about sixty-four lines, would have made the Partridge poem about eighty lines long, quite comparable to its predecessors in the mansucript.[29] Apart from the evidence of the manuscript gatherings that only one leaf is gone, the poem itself shows a unity: it begins with a generalizing introduction applicable to all beasts and birds, embracing earth, water, and air, before narrowing its focus to one representative of each category; it continues with transitions of "further" between sections; and the word *Finit* at the end of "Partridge" explicitly calls attention to the completion of the poem.[30]

The "Panther" characterizes that beast, rather surprisingly, as one gentle and kind to all save the dragon, with a wonderful

29. ASPR, III, pp. xi–xii, li.
30. See also F. Cordasco, "The Old English *Physiologus:* Its Problems," *MLQ,* x (1949), 351–355.

coat of many colors. It further considers his actions: after he has eaten his fill, he sleeps in a cave for three days and on the third arises with a wondrous-sounding roar, and with such a fragrance emanating from his mouth that men and beasts all hasten to it. Then follows the *significatio*: the Panther is God-Christ, gentle to all but Satan; and his sleep and waking are His Death and Resurrection. Those who hasten to the fragrance are the righteous, performing good deeds for their salvation. While the "Panther" may seem quaint to us today, the "Whale" seems more in the mainstream of our literary tradition. The Whale (or asp-turtle, as it originally was) is pictured as he appears to mariners: like a rough rock or a mass of sea weed on dunes near the shore. Sea-weary sailors are deceived into believing him an island and, mooring thereon, build a fire; when they are most secure and "rejoicing in fair weather," the crafty whale suddenly plunges to the depths, drowning them "in the halls of death." Significantly, this is the way of deception of the devil, luring men to pride and wicked deeds and then dragging them off to hell.[31] The Whale also has another trick: when hungry, he opens wide his jaws, from which issues a sweet smell that attracts little fish to their doom. Here is a parallel to the lure of fleshly joys whereby the devil ensnares men into hell.[32] The deliberate contrast in *Physiologus*, as in

31. The ME *Bestiary* contains a similar depiction of *Cethegrande*; Milton draws on the same tradition for his simile of Leviathan in his description of Satan, *Paradise Lost*, I, 200 ff.:

> or that Sea-beast
> *Leviathan*, which God of all his works
> Created hugest that swim th'Ocean stream:
> Him haply slumb'ring on the *Norway* foam
> The Pilot of some small night-founder'd Skiff,
> Deeming some Island,oft, as Seamen tell,
> With fixed Anchor in his scaly rind
> Moors by his side under the Lee, while Night
> Invests the Sea, and wished Morn delays:
> So stretcht out huge in length the Arch-fiend lay.

32. The open jaws of hell are common in medieval pictorial representations, as witness the illuminations of the Junius MS; see Kennedy, *EEP*, p. 307.

most bestiaries, between the sweet smell of Panther-Christ drawing men to good deeds and salvation and that of whale-devil luring men to fleshly lusts and damnation emphasizes the polarity of good and evil that is central to the poem.

We cannot tell much about the poetic representation of "Partridge" because in its fragmentary condition we have only one line on the physical bird; in fact, our identification of the bird as a partridge stems from the similarity in its allegorical representation of the parental relationship between God and man to the corresponding explication in the ninth-century Bern *Physiologus*, in which there is also the larger parallel of association of the Panther, the Whale, and the Partridge.

The allegorical nature of the Old English *Physiologus* is simple and its poetry, for the most part, mediocre; but Anglo-Saxon literature produced an outstanding example of the poetic possibilities in the allegorical genre in the more complex *Phoenix*, "perhaps the most graceful and finished of all the Old English religious poems that have survived to us."[33] Certainly it moves beyond the mere extended equation of story or fable with moral or spiritual truths that we are accustomed to in this kind of allegory: it achieves a symbolic density that only the best of its genre reveal.

The *Phoenix* is found on folios 55b–65b of the Exeter Book.[34] Though earlier attributed to Cynewulf, it is now no longer considered his, though there may be some trace of the Cynewulfian style as well as of the style of *Andreas* in it.[35] Its date of composition is uncertain, perhaps late ninth century. Of its 677 lines, the first 380 hew closely to the fourth-century Latin poem *De Ave Phoenice*, attributed to Lactantius. The remaining lines, which furnish an explicit allegory, would seem to be the poet's own, though there are obvious incorporations of Biblical material and probably of exegetical writings on the con-

33. Kennedy, *EECP*, p. 221.
34. Edited in *ASPR*, III; see also Cook, above; a recent separate edition is by N. F. Blake, *The Phoenix* (Manchester, 1964).
35. See Ch. VI and O. Hietsch, "On the Authorship of the Old English Phoenix," *Anglo-Americana* (Stuttgart, 1955), pp. 72–79.

cept of the resurrection. For this fable about the mythical bird
which renews its life through immolation—a motif of Oriental
origin and, in its handling by Lactantius, connected with worship of the sun—lent itself readily to the Christian idea of
resurrection through and after the flames of Judgment Day.

In the opening section of the eight parts into which the
manuscript divides the poem, we find a description of the
Earthly Paradise presented in negatives and positives; for instance:

> The gentle plain rolls to a distant
> Horizon, green with forests, and neither
> Rain or snow, nor the blast of frost,
> Nor blazing fire, nor hail falling,
> Nor the sun's glow, nor cold or warmth
> Or winter's showers can injure anything
> Where everything lies securely suspended
> In unharmed bliss. All that land
> Bursts into blossoms.

[ll.13–21][36]

The landscape is Lactantian, with echoes of Genesis, Ezekiel,
and Revelation. When the Phoenix is presented in the next
section, it is associated with the sun: it bathes twelve times
daily in the cold streams of Paradise before the sun rises, and
then it rises swiftly into the air, offering its adoration to God's
bright token in song and carol. This routine continues for 1000
years when the bird, grown old, flies westward to a wood in
Syria, attended for a while by a concourse of birds. But seeking seclusion, the Phoenix drives off his attendants and builds
his nest atop a lofty tree named after itself. There, in Section 3
of the poem, the bird's "solarium" is enkindled by the sun;
and nest, bird, and sweet herbs the lone dweller has gathered
are consumed together on the pyre. In the cooled ashes, however, an apple's likeness appears, and from thence a wondrously
fair worm emerges, which grows into a fledgling Phoenix that
eats naught but honeydew till (Sec. 4) it seeks again the terrestrial Eden whence it came, again attended by flocks of birds

36. B. Raffel translation (V, 37).

singing hosannahs unto this powerful leader. But the birds must once more retire when the Phoenix reaches its ideal land (Sec. 5); and the self-containment of the bird, and its lack of fear of death are praised, as the paraphrase of the Lactantian part of the poem runs its course.

The Anglo-Saxon poet's interpretation of the fable commences in the middle of Section 5, thus mitigating the division between "cortex" and "nucleus" of his poem:

> So is it
> With each of the blessed, bearing misery
> And choosing the darkness of death for themselves
> In order to find eternal life
> And the protection of God repaying pain
> On earth with endless glory and endless
> Joy.
>
> [ll. 380–386]

The complexity of the poet's allegory becomes apparent as he develops the equation of the Phoenix with the Elect, reverting to the loss of Eden and the source of all our woe when

> The arch-fiend's hatred followed them [Adam and
>   Eve], and his envy
> Poisoned them, suggested forbidden fruit
> And coaxed them down a foolish path
> Leading away from God to the taste
> Of an apple.
>
> [ll. 400–404]

He further equates the departure of the Phoenix from the Earthly Paradise with this Biblical exile. Among his other allegorical equations is the interpretation of the sweet herbs the old Phoenix gathers as the good deeds men do on earth (ll. 465 ff.) and, of course, the paralleling of the Phoenix's rebirth through fire with the resurrection of all good Christians. But the texture of the poem is enriched in many other ways. The poet compares the bird with Christ—explicitly in lines 646b–649, where the rebirth of the bird is equated with Christ's coming as a child, and imagistically in lines 591 and following, where Christ is described as attended by a flock of shining birds, symbolic of the souls of the blessed, a passage paralleling lines 335b–346a, which describe the Phoenix being adored as a "dear chieftain" by the race of birds. He uses, in lines 548b and following, the figure of Job who, like the Phoenix, is certain in his faith, knowing he will rise again to enjoy happiness with the Lord (Job xxix.8). Even more impressively, he incorporates an extended harvest and sowing image in Section 3 (ll. 243 ff.), which "appears as a figurative means for explaining and vivifying the rebirth of the bird which, in turn, functions as the major metaphoric framework for the doctrine of the resurrection, providing in each phase of its rebirth a typology for the good Christian and his Savior."[37] The metaphor suggests that resurrection is a natural phenomenon, a familiar process of nature, as well as a mysterious and unique event like the mythical Phoenix or a Biblical asseveration like Job's. The use of this extended simile in the Lactantian part of the poem also reveals the poet's attempt to unify fable and meaning, cortex and nucleus, artistically. Another way in which he fuses his material is in his choice of diction. For example, he anthropomorphises the Phoenix by applying to it terms from the heroic vocabulary, thus helping to identify the life of the bird and that of man, which it symbolizes in its life, death, and resurrection.[38] As a final critical comment I would note that the unsuppressed pagan sun worship of the fable, most prominent in Section 2, has a symbolic counterpart in the references to God's shining on the host of the saved in Sections 7 and 8 of the poem.

As I hope I have sufficiently indicated, the *Phoenix* is a splendid piece of literature in its entirety, though it is usually only the Lactantian fable that is called to our attention. Of the remaining poems to be surveyed in this chapter, not so much can be said. As something of a bridge between the religious poems so far surveyed and the few secular verses to be con-

37. J. S. Kantrowitz, "The Anglo-Saxon *Phoenix* and Tradition," *PQ*, XLIII (1964), 13.
38. See Blake edition, p. 29, and his article "Some Problems of Interpretation and Translation in the OE *Phoenix*," *Anglia*, LXXX (1962), 50–62.

sidered, we have the philosophical-religious *Meters of Boethius* and a few metrical prefaces and epilogues. In Chapter II, I discussed King Alfred's prose translation of Boethius's *Consolation of Philosophy*; here the versified *Meters* is my province. The *Meters* are preserved only in MS Cotton Otho A.vi, damaged in the Cottonian fire of 1731, and in a transcript made by Junius before the damage was incurred (MS Junius 12). They represent a poetic paraphrase of the earlier Old English translation, not of the original Latin; like the prose, they may on good grounds be attributed to the authorship of Alfred himself.[39] As poetry, they are not especially noteworthy, and a small sampling will suffice.[40] I quote the first part of the Old English *Meter 4*, Boethius's prayer to the Creator (Bk. 1, m. 5), with a translation of the Old English prose version of the same and of the Latin original in the R. H. Green translation (see II, 13):

O, Thou Creator   of the bright stars,
Of heaven and earth!   Thou on Thy throne
Eternal reignest,   and Thou quickly all
Heaven movest,   and through Thy holy might
The stars are constrained   that they obey Thee.
So also the sun   the shadows
Of dark nights dispels   through Thy might.
With its pale light   the moon tempers
The bright stars   through the power of Thy might,
Sometimes also deprives   the sun of its
Bright light,   when it may happen
That so near   they get by necessity.

O, Thou Creator of heaven and earth, Thou who rulest on thy eternal seat, Thou turnest the heaven on its swift course, and Thou makest the stars obedient to you, and Thou makest the sun to dispel the shadows of the dark night with her bright light. Likewise does the moon with her pale light that dims the bright stars in heaven, and sometimes deprives the sun of its light when it comes between us and it. . . .

[OE prose]

Creator of the star-filled universe, seated upon your eternal throne You move the heavens in their swift orbits.

39. The *Meters* are edited in *ASPR*, v. See Sisam, *Studies* (II, 6), pp. 293–297, for arguments for Alfred's authorship.
40. For an extended discussion, see Anderson (Int., 5), pp. 273–285.

You hold the stars in their assigned paths, so that sometimes the shining moon is full in the light of her brother sun and hides the lesser stars; sometimes, nearer the sun she wanes and loses her glory.

[Latin text]

One of the changes from the Latin to both Old English prose and verse is that the paling of the moon from its closeness to the sun becomes an eclipse. A greater transformation may be seen by comparing lines 1–8 of *Meter* 27 with the Latin text of its equivalent Book IV, meter 4:

Why must you ever   with unrighteous hate
Trouble your mind,   even as the sea-flood's
Waves stir up   the ice-cold sea,
Move before the wind?   Why blame you
Your fate   which has no power?
Why cannot you await   bitter death
Which the Lord shaped   for you by nature,
Towards which he hastens you   each day?

Why do you whip yourselves to frenzy, and ever seek your fate by self-destruction? If you look for death, she stands nearby of her own accord; she does not restrain her swift horses.

The sea image is Alfred's; and in his employment of the poetic vocabulary and formulas, as well as of the alliterative line, the king forged his *Meters* in the Old English poetic tradition, despite the intractability of much of the subject matter of the *Consolation*.

The metrical prefaces and epilogues may be more casually mentioned: a verse Preface and Epilogue to Alfred's translation of the *Pastoral Care* appear in the ninth-century MS Hatton 20, sent by Alfred's order to Wærferth, Bishop of Worcester, as well as in two or three other manuscripts. There is also a verse Preface to Wærferth's translation of Gregory's *Dialogues*, and a ten-line Epilogue to the Old English translation of Bede's *HE*.[41]

Six secular pieces remain for our brief consideration in this

41. Edited in *ASPR*, VI, pp. 110–113.

chapter.[42] Five of them are found in four of the manuscripts of the *Anglo-Saxon Chronicle* and hence, along with *Brunan-burh* (see Ch. V), are referred to as *Chronicle* poems. They are, like that heroic poem celebrating Æthelstan's victory of 937, concerned with national history, but none of the five compares in poetic quality with it. *The Capture of the Five Boroughs* commemorates King Edward's victory over the Norsemen in 942, by which he liberated the boroughs from Viking rule. *The Coronation of Edgar* (973) describes the ceremony performed by Dunstan and Oswald at Bath when, fourteen years after his accession, King Edgar decided to be officially anointed (see Ch. III). *The Death of Edgar*, rather than dealing with a single event, treats of five important happenings in 975. One of these, the expulsion of Oslac, Earl of Northumbria, illustrates the mechanical piling up of the older poetic formulas with little regard for specificity of meaning:

> And þa wearð eac adræfed   deormod hæleð,
> Oslac, of earde   ofer yða gewealc,
> ofer ganotes bæð,   gamolfeax hæleð,
> wis and wordsnotor,   ofer wætera geðring,
> ofer hwæles eðel,   hama bereafod.

[ll. 24–28]

> (And there was also driven   the brave-hearted warrior,
> Oslac, from his dwelling,   over the rolling of waves,
> Over the sea-mew's bath,   grey-haired warrior,
> Wise and clever with words,   over the concourse of waters,
> Over the whale's home,   deprived of [his] homes.)

Despite this overaccumulation, the last line is effective with its contrast of home and homeless-ness. *The Death of Alfred* (1036), only partially in verse, recounts the imprisonment and murder of Prince Alfred, Æthelred's son, at the hands of Earl Godwine; and *The Death of Edward* (1065) eulogizes Edward the Confessor for about thirty lines, ending with a brief mention of his alleged bequest of the crown to Harold.

The sixth poem, and last, is chronologically the latest of all extant Anglo-Saxon poems. It is a sample of the *encomium*

42. Edited in ASPR, VI, pp. 20–28.

urbis or 'praise of the city,' a standard rhetorical exercise of the Middle Ages, an example being the Latin poem of Alcuin's on York. This twenty-one-line "De situ Dunelmi," or *Durham*, begins with a description of the famous city, its stones, its fish-filled river and its animal-filled forest, and then relates the famous men whose bones rest in Durham: St. Cuthbert, Bishop Aidan, King Oswald, and others. The poem was composed in the early years of the twelfth century, but is surprisingly regular in its use of the older vocabulary and meter. Thus in *Durham*, a poem in praise of a city, composed more than five centuries after the illustrious Cædmon had uttered his hymn in praise of the Creator, the Anglo-Saxon poetic tradition found its last exponent, before it became transmogrified in the freer Middle English alliterative poems like Layamon's *Brut* and in the later fourteenth-century poems of the Alliterative Revival.

X

Lore and Wisdom

FROM POEMS celebrating God and His handiwork and man in his chronicle of years we turn to verse more didactic in purpose, to verse embodying secular and Christian lore and wisdom. In a largely unlettered society like the Anglo-Saxon, man's observations on man and of natural phenomena are apt to take a somewhat aphoristic form. It should occasion no surprise, therefore, that runes, charms, gnomes and proverbs, riddles, and some more pointedly homiletic Christian poems comprise the bulk of the material to be considered in this chapter.

Earlier I mentioned in passing the use of runes in Germanic, and particularly in Old English poetry: the inscription on the Golden Horn of Gallehus, the runic signatures in Cynewulf's poems, and the *Dream of the Rood* selection on the Ruthwell Cross are the most memorable. As these illustrations suggest, runes were employed to identify the maker (and sometimes the owner) of instruments of pleasure or warfare, to identify the maker of a poem who wished to have prayers said for the salvation of his soul, or to ornament a monument. They might also be used to convey a message, as in the *Riddles* and *The Husband's Message*, but their primary function was magico-religious. Even the word *rune* means "mystery" or "secret"; and from the time of its adoption by Germanic tribes, possibly from North Italic models (c. 250–150 B.C.?), the formalized non-cursive script of the *fuþark* (OE. *fuþorc*), or runic alphabet, served ritualistic purposes.[1]

The Germanic runic alphabet consisted of twenty-four letters, headed by those which give it its name. ᚠ (f) ᚢ (u) ᚦ (th) ᚨ (a) ᚱ (r) ᚲ (k). The Old English runic alphabet modified the forms of the letters somewhat—for example, ᚦ became þ, ᚨ became ᛗ, ᚲ became h—and ultimately added nine more letters for a total representing thirty-three phonetic sounds. The runes also had names, as we have seen in the Cynewulfian signatures, in large part taken from the Germanic world of gods and men, the world of natural powers and treasured possessions. Thus the first six Old English runes had the names *feoh* 'wealth,' *ur* 'ox,' *þorn* 'thorn' (replacing Gmc. *þurisaz* 'giant'? or from *þuranaz* 'thorn'?), *os* 'god' (see n. 4), *rad* 'riding,' and *cen* 'torch.'[2] The ninety-four-line *Rune Poem*, preserved in Hickes's *Thesaurus* transcript of 1705, the manuscript having been destroyed in the Cottonian fire,[3] furnishes us with a poeticized alphabet of twenty-nine characters. Each stanza, of from two to five lines, describes the thing named by the corresponding letter. Again, I will illustrate by citing in translation the verses for the first six runes:

> *Wealth* is a comfort   to each of men.
> Nevertheless, every man must   share it fully
> If he wishes before the Lord   to obtain glory.
> *Ox* is bold   and great-horned,
> A very dangerous animal   (who) fights with horns,
> Notorious moor-stepper;   that is a proud creature.
> *Thorn* is very sharp;   to each of thanes
> Seizing (it) is evil,   immeasurably rough

1. The origins of the Germanic runic alphabet are much debated; for a general discussion, see R. W. V. Elliott, *Runes* (Manchester and New York, 1959); for specifically English runes, see R. Derolez, *Runica Manuscripta: The English Tradition* (Brugge, 1954).

2. The most recent work on rune names is K. Schneider, *Die germanischen Runennamen* (Meisenheim am Glan, 1956); see also Elliott.

3. Edited in ASPR, VI, pp. 28–30; also B. Dickins, *Runic and Heroic Poems of the Old Teutonic Peoples* (Cambridge, 1915). For discussion, see T. Grienberger, "Das altenglische Runengedicht," *Anglia*, XLV (1921), 201–220, and W. Keller, "Zum altenglischen Rungedicht," *Anglia*, LX (1936), 141–149.

To each of men   who rests among them.
Mouth[4] is the source   of every speech,
Support of wisdom   and comfort of the wise man,
And to each of earls   ease and refuge.
Riding in the hall seems   to each of men
Soft, but very strenuous   for him who sits above
On the stout steed   over the roads.
Torch is to each of living men   known on fire,
Blazing and bright   it burns most often
When they, nobles,   rest within.

The informative and hortatory nature of the *Rune Poem* is evident in the above stanzas. As poetry the verse needs little comment, though one may observe the Christian emphasis in stanza 1, the use of formulas (e.g., *mære mearcstapa* 'nortorious moor-stepper,' l. 6a; cf. *Beo.*, l. 103a, *mære mearcstapa*, of Grendel), the humor in the stanza on *riding*, and a pervasive riddling quality that will become more apparent after a discussion of the *Riddles*. The poem is of eighth- or ninth-century composition.

Akin to the runes in their magical properties are the charms. The oldest relics of Anglo-Saxon and Germanic literature, despite their Christianization in their Old English forms, the charms are openly rather than secretively magic. Their magic stems from three elements: a source in *cræft* 'power, cunning, knowledge,' an operational power that is nonphysical, and a ritual whose threefold purpose is to secure the power, to transmit it to the desired site of operations, and to utilize it effectively. In Chapter III, I called attention to the presence of charms in the *Leechbook* and *Lacnunga*; these volumes, along with three others, contain the texts of the twelve extant metrical Old English charms: For Unfruitful Land, the Nine Herbs Charm, Against a Dwarf, For a Sudden Stitch, For Loss or Theft of Cattle (three charms), For Delayed Birth, For Water-

---

4. Most scholars interpret "mouth" here, seeing a replacement of *ōs* (Gmc. *ansuz*) 'god' by the Latin homonym *ōs* 'mouth'; but the context of the stanza also supports—perhaps even better supports—a reference to Oðinn (Odin), the god of eloquence and wisdom. Cf. Schneider, pp. 374, 615. Possibly there is *double entente* here.

elf Disease, For a Swarm of Bees, A Journey Charm, and Against a Wen.[5]

Something of the character and quality of the charms may be seen in a charm intended to keep a swarm of bees from flying away (Storms, 1; *ASPR*, vi, 8):

> Take earth, cast it with your right hand under your right foot and say:

> I catch it under foot,   I have found it.
> Lo, earth has power   against each of all creatures,
> And against ill-will   and against forgetfulness,
> And against [the charm] of the mighty   tongue
>   of man.

> Whereupon cast sand over them, when they swarm, and say:

> Settle ye, victorious women,   sink to earth,
> Never wild   fly to the woods.
> Be as mindful   of my prosperity,
> As is each of men   of food and native home.

The first part of the ritual states the speaker's knowledge of the power residing in earth and of his own power in controlling the earth he throws under foot and catches. The repetitive formula in the last two-and-a-half lines emphasizes the power in the words themselves. In the second part of the ritual, the speaker applies his power at the proper moment, when the bees swarm, casting sand which forms, as it were, a magic circle in the air, at the same time cajoling the bees with a "circle" of words. The image of the "victorious women" has sometimes been taken as a relic of the pagan valkyrie, but it more likely is a simple metaphor suggested, perhaps, by the analogy of the sting of the bee with the "sting" of a victorious sword.

In a longer and more complex charm, "For a Sudden Stitch," or "Against Rheumatism" (*ASPR*, vi, 4; Storms, 2), there is another reference to "mighty women," but here it *is* to

5. Edited in ASPR, vi, pp. 116–128; see also Storms (II, 23), which provides a facing translation and excellent commentary, and Grattan and Singer (III, 38). Further, see reviews of the last two by F. P. Magoun, Jr., in *Speculum*, xxviii (1953), 203–212, and xxix (1954), 564–569, who furnishes concordances to the numbering of the charms in the different editions.

female spirits that were thought to cause the disease. The whole charm is against evil spirits, whose secret of "shooting spears" into the sick person the conjurer, who will answer fire with fire, claims to have discovered. He repeats at intervals the incantation "Out little spear, if you be within here," and concludes:

> Whether you have been shot in the skin   or in the flesh
> Or shot in the blood   . . .
> Or shot in a limb,   let your life be never endangered.
> If it be the shot of Æsir,   or the shot of elves,
> Or the shot of hags,   I will help you now.
> This as your remedy for the shot of Æsir,   this for the shot of elves,
> This as remedy for the shot of hags,   I will help you.
> Fly there   to the mountain head.
> Hale be you.   May the Lord help you.

The reference to the Germanic gods, the Æsir, here shrunken in significance to evil sprites, is unique in Old English literature. Notice, too, the Christian ending.

The Christian-pagan fusion and confusion may perhaps best be seen in "For Unfruitful Land" or "Field Ceremonies" (*ASPR*, vi, 1; Storms, 8). The first part (ll. 1–48) consists of ceremonies honoring the sun; yet for all its turning to the east and bowing nine times, it includes saying a *Pater noster*, four masses, the names of the four Gospelers, a prayer to Mary, the litany, a *Sanctus*, and so on. The second part (ll. 49–87) is a ceremony in honor of Mother Earth, with an apostrophe to a mysterious *Erce*:

> Erce, Erce, Erce,   mother of earth,
> May the Almighty grant thee,   eternal Lord,
> Fields waxing   and fruitful,
> Flourishing   and sustaining,
> Bright shafts   of millet-crops,
> And of broad   barley-crops,
> And of white   wheat-crops,
> And of all   of the crops of the earth.

The above is to be said as the seeds are placed on the body of the plough; further incantation is indicated in the charm as one cuts the first furrow, and again when one places a baked loafof-many-flours under the first furrow. The charm ends with a *Pater noster* said thrice.

However little literary value the charms may have, they possess a certain magic in their occasional imagery, in their genuineness of sentiment, and in the suspense created by their ritualistic intention and structure. As for practical value, their wisdom was obviously very specialized, unlike that of the gnomes or maxims, which provided generalized reflections on the properties naturally inherent in creatures and objects or served as moral guides for large socioreligious areas of human endeavor. Like the charms, however, these sententious bits of wisdom have a long pedigree, and we may observe parallels in many different languages, from the Book of Proverbs of the Old Testament to the Greek Hesiod and to the Old Icelandic *Hǫvamǫl*. Strands of gnomic wisdom are found throughout Old English poetry encased in lyric or narrative form, in the elegies and in *Beowulf* in particular. But there are two distinctive heterogeneous collections of apothegms per se, one in the Exeter Book, *Maxims I*, and a shorter one in MS Cotton Tiberius B.i following the *Menologium*, *Maxims II*.[6] Although attempts have been made to find pagan and Christian strata in these collections, undoubtedly the author (ninth-tenth century?) was a cleric who fused, in however ill-made a way, ancient and more contemporaneous aphoristic lore.

The *Exeter Gnomes* (*Maxims I*) come to 206 lines, divided into three sections by the scribe. The first part begins as if it were to be a riddling match, the scop requesting the audience to question him with words; but this tack is soon dropped, and in line 4 the gnomes begin with the advice that it is fitting to praise God our Father, since he at the beginning established life and this transitory joy, and He will in the end reclaim those gifts. A group of verses contrasting man's ephemerality and God's eternality follows, then one on God's gifts to men. Cita-

6. Edited in *ASPR*, iii and vi; also B. C. Williams, *Gnomic Poetry in Anglo-Saxon* (New York, 1914), not only for the poems but for an excellent general discussion of gnomes and for a critical analysis of the OE poems.

tion of lines 18b and following will illustrate adequately the way the poem develops its aphorism:

```
                                  Meeting shall hold
Wise man with wise man;      their minds are similar;
They ever settle strife;      they teach peace,
Which evil men      have previously taken away.
Counsel shall accompany wisdom;        righteousness with
                                           the wise;
A good man with good men.      Two are mates:
Woman and man shall      bear in the world
Children through birth.      A tree shall on earth
Suffer in its leaves,      mourn its branches.
The ready man shall depart,      the doomed one perish
And every day struggle      about his parting
From the world.      The Creator alone knows
Whence death comes      which departs hence from the land.
He multiplies children      whom sickness takes soon . . .
Foolish is he who knows not his Lord,      since death often
                                          comes unexpected.
Wise men save their souls,      hold their truth righteously.
```

Are these loosely collocated maxims, or is there some sense of structure in the whole? A recent critic suggests that the several members are connected by association of ideas, through meaning and through sound.[7] The end of one gnome may suggest the next, or a central theme may run through several maxims, or both methods may be combined. In the above citation, we may see how the theme of the wise man runs through several verses and then leads, through the association of a good man with good men to the concept of another grouping of two, wife and husband, and this in turn to their children, and in turn to death. The tree gnome is perhaps a vivid image here for parents mourning the death of children, a theme followed up in succeeding verses. At the end of the passage, there is a gnomic generalization about wisdom and foolishness in the face of unexpected death, a philosophical aphorism we find also in *The Wanderer* and in *The Seafarer*.

7. R. M. Dawson, "The Structure of the Old English Gnomic Poems," *JEGP*, LXI (1962), 14–22; see also K. Malone, "Notes on Gnomic Poem B of *The Exeter Book*," *MÆ*, XII (1943), 65–67.

The beginning of Part B of *Maxims I* illustrates the combination of natural lore and Christian wisdom:

> Frost shall freeze,   fire consume wood,
> Earth flourish,   ice form a bridge,
> Water wear a helmet,   wondrously lock
> Earth's growths: One shall unbind
> The fetters of frost,   almighty God;
> Winter shall depart,   fair weather return,
> Summer brightly hot.

Though the second half of the first line above seems out of place in the series on winter-summer, it is not simply a survival "from an early stichometric arrangement of nature gnomes in which the freezing of frost and ravage of fire were brought into contrast in a single line by the *f* alliteration,"[8] because the fire motif re-emerges shortly and has its own small development.

One of the oft-quoted passages from *Maxims I* is the lyric section on the joyous welcome the Frisian wife gives her sailor husband; it leads into an admonition to women to keep faith with their husbands, not to betray them though they need take long journeys away from home. As part of the wisdom proffered in Part C, we find the philosophical-elegiac theme of man's aloneness in the world; yet he who can sing and play the harp is less lonely than others, and it is better for a man to have a brother to help him in the hunt, in battle, and in pastime hours over the chessboard. The *Exeter Gnomes* ends on an heroic note:

> Ready shall be the shield,   the dart on the shaft,
> The edge on the sword   and the point on the spear,
> Courage in a brave man.   Helmet shall be for the bold
> And ever for the faint-hearted   treasure most scarce.

The sixty-six lines of the *Cotton Gnomes* (*Maxims II*) are for the most part more concerned with natural properties than with codes of ethical behavior: the wild hawk shall abide on the glove, the wolf endure in the wood, the dragon dwell in a cave, water flow from a hill, salmon dart in the pool, and so on. But

8. Kennedy, *EEP*, p. 148.

again, good comrades shall urge a young nobleman to deeds of valor and the bestowal of rings, and so on. *Maxims II* ends on a semi-Christian note that no one returns here to tell what the Lord's decree is or to describe the place where the Creator dwells.

Another but smaller collection of popular wisdom appears in Durham Cathedral MS B.III.32. The *Durham Proverbs*[9] appear in Latin and Old English single lines. Most of the Old English lines are alliterative and approach verse form, though some do not. They employ some of the formulas of the *Cotton* and *Exeter Gnomes*, the *sceal* and *byþ* formulas in particular: "A man *shall* not be too soon afraid, nor too soon pleased"; "A friend avails whether far or near, but *is* the nearer more useful." There is more of a sense of humor in these few proverbs than in the gnomes: "Those do not quarrel who are not together," and, "It is far from well, said he who heard wailing in hell." In addition to the maxims and proverbs in this collection and the two larger collections, we may mention two Latin-English proverbs and A *Proverb from Winfrid's Time*, both edited in ASPR, VI.

Similar to the gnomes and proverbs in their exposition of wisdom through formulaic repetition are two more pointedly Christian poems of the Exeter Book, *The Gifts of Men* and *The Fortunes of Men*. Both employ the anaphoric *sum* 'one' formula and its grammatical variations to express the various crafts and destinies that God in His wisdom distributes to men. We have observed the use of this theme and formula in *Christ II*, lines 664–685; the source for the OE *repetitio* may well have been a key phrase in Gregory's *Homilia IX in Evangelia*: "Alius . . . tamen didicit artem qua pascitur," which Ælfric in his *In Natale Unius Confessoris* translated as "Sum . . . leornode swa-þeah sumne cræft þe hine afet" (One learned however a craft which fed him)—the concept lending itself to easy extension of the crafts that "feed" a man.[10] *The Gifts of Men*

9. O. Arngart, ed. *The Durham Proverbs* (Lund, 1956).
10. See Cross, "Gifts of Men," (VII, 7).

begins with an introduction in which the poet states that God gives some kind of natural endowment to every man lest he become depressed, and nevertheless will grant no man too much lest he become arrogant (ll. 1–29). The body of the poem enumerates some forty secular and ecclesiastical talents (ll. 30–85; 86–97): among the former are such diverse occupations as gem-working, carpentry, minstrelsy, scholarship, and soldiering, and such natural aptitudes and capacities as beauty of form, swiftness of foot, agility in swimming, and wittiness at wine-taking; among the latter are the discernment to choose the grace of God above worldly treasures, fondness for fighting the devil, capability as a Church functionary, and skill in the arts of the scriptorium. The poem concludes (ll. 97–113) with a reiteration of God's wisdom in not overendowing any one individual, and a call to praise of Him and His bounty.

Although *The Fortunes of Men* has the same structural outline as *Gifts*, it is a superior poem. It is more graphic and detailed in its enumeration of the evil fates and the good fortunes which overtake and are allotted to men. Even its introduction is more integral to the poem as a whole, setting forth succinctly the human ritual of the begetting, birth, and rearing of offspring, leading to the challenging remark that "God alone knows what the years will bring to the growing boy," this observation in turn being developed in the body of the poem. First the evil destinies of men are vividly portrayed: the wolf-devoured, the hunger-wasted, the storm-wrecked, the spear-slain, the sightless, the limb-injured. At greater length is described one who falls from a high tree in the forest, sailing through the air like a bird, yet featherless, to lose his life at the roots; one who swings on the gallows, where the raven plucks his eyes and he is powerless to ward off the outrage committed on his person; one who, becoming drunk, cannot hold his tongue and loses his life thereby. But another shall pass from adversity to prosperity; and here, about line 64 and following, the poet shifts gears, as it were, and in describing the good fortunes God distributes he picks up the theme of the gifts of men. An

example of the difference in treatment accorded the theme by
Gifts and *Fortunes* may be seen in their respective descriptions
of the aptitude for harping:

> One with his hands can   touch the harp,
> He possesses the cunning   of deft playing of the gleewood.
>   [*Gifts*, 11. 49–50]

> One shall with his harp   at his lord's
> Feet sit,   receive wealth,
> And ever rapidly   sweep the strings,
> Let the leaping plectrum   sound loudly,
> The nail sounding sweetly;   in him is great desire.
>   [*Fortunes*, 11. 80–84]

But though the poet of *Fortunes* has perhaps swerved from his
original intention of depicting the destinies of men, he draws
both the gifts and fates themes together in his conclusion (ll.
93–98):

> Thus wondrously   the Savior of hosts
> Throughout the world   the crafts of men
> Shaped and bestowed,   and ruled the destiny
> Of everyone on earth   of mankind.
> Wherefore to Him now thanks   let each man say
> For all that He in His mercy   ordains for men.

Gifts and *Fortunes* are concerned with the paths men follow in this world. The famous little poem known as *Bede's
Death Song* is more concerned with the preparation man makes
for his eternal destiny:

> Before the necessary journey [death]   no one becomes
> Wiser in thought   than there be need for him
> To ponder   before his going hence
> What to his soul   of good or evil
> After the day of death   will be adjudged.

There is an enigmatic quality to this one-sentence poem preserved in Northumbrian and West Saxon in some twenty-nine
manuscripts of the *Epistola Cuthberti de Obitu Bedæ*.[11] The
"day of death" seems to have reference both to the individual's dying and to the Day of Judgment. The acme of wis-

11. The authoritative discussion of the *Epistola* MSS, etc., is Dobbie
(IX, 2), see also ASPR, VI, pp. 107–108, and Smith (IX, 2).

dom, the poem suggests, is the renunciation of all wisdom save that which conduces to good, since one will be judged finally not by what he knows but by what he has done of good and evil in this world.[12] Whether Bede was simply quoting a poem he knew (Cædmon's?) or whether he composed the *Death Song* as he lay dying is not clear from Cuthbert's letter; but most critics accept the attribution to Bede himself. There is, from the modern point of view at least, a certain irony in the thought that the eighth-century scholar *par excellence* should at the end have so depreciated his own worldly wisdom; but the example is not unparalleled (for example, Chaucer) and indeed was something of a *topos* in the medieval period.

Wisdom of a more homiletic and less poetic sort appears in several other minor poems recorded in the Exeter Book. Preceding the *Gifts of Men* is a ninety-four-line verse piece called variously *Precepts* or *A Father's Counsel* or *A Father's Instructions to his Son*. In the course of this uninspired admonition to follow certain precepts in order to prosper, a father ten times delivers himself of platitudinous advice about not committing crimes, not associating with evil companions, guarding against the deadly sins, learning what is fitting to be learned and honoring traditional knowledge, and so on. Though a parallel with the Ten Commandments seems indicated, only the first injunction in the poem actually corresponds to any part of the Decalogue: honor thy father and mother. The Book of Proverbs may well have influenced the eighth- or ninth-century poet who wrote zealously but not too well.

The eighty-four-line *Vainglory*, or *Pride*, which is the second poem before the *Fortunes of Men*, concentrates on the one admonitory theme by which modern editors entitle it. It begins with an "autobiographical" introduction stating that the poet long ago was instructed by a book-learned sage how to distinguish a true child of God from a sinful man. This opening is not very firmly cemented to what follows, which deals with the combination of pride and drunkenness, leading to cheating and vicious speech. The source of man's vainglory is

12. See Huppé (VII, 10), pp. 78–79.

traced in lines 57 and following to the revolt of the angels, and the conclusion contrasts the humble and the proud, and their respective eternal rewards. A resemblance to the denunciatory passage in Isaiah xxviii.1–4 is too general to admit of specific borrowing.

The Order of the World or *Wonders of Creation*, a poem of 102 lines, follows the *Exeter Gnomes*. It is even more loosely structured than *Vainglory*, with a similar "autobiographical" introduction. The largest segment of the description of God's creation is devoted to a glorification of light, concluding with the comment that no man knows whither the sun goes when it drops beneath the waters, nor who may then enjoy its light. The fundamental stability of God's creation is then maintained, and a reference to the joy of those who see the King of Glory leads into the moralizing ending that is so typical of homiletic wisdom. A suggestion of Cynewulfian diction indicates a probable ninth-century date of composition.

Of the tenth century, in all probability, is the twenty-line *Homiletic Fragment II*, seemingly addressed by way of consolation to one in distress. The wisdom imparted is, that though the affairs of the world seem uncertain and man betrays man, there is one faith, one living God, one baptism, one Father everlasting, one Lord of the people, who created this earth, its blessings and joys. The addressee is gnomically adjured in the beginning to bind fast the thoughts of his heart, to guard his *hordlocan* 'treasure-chamber'; the end of the poem refers to the Nativity, to the dwelling of the Holy Spirit in the *hordfate* 'treasure chest' of the Virgin. Although the poem is considered fragmentary by most critics, the thematic linking of beginning and end suggests completion. (*Homiletic Fragment I* is, on the contrary, indeed fragmentary, since its beginning is missing. This poem is extant in the Vercelli Book: it, too, waxes wise on the uncertainties of the world, but concentrates most of its fire on the calumny of tongues. Near its beginning it paraphrases verse 3 of Psalm 28.) Mention of an eight-line poem on the size of Pharaoh's army and a nine-line poem on the virtue of almsgiving conclude this survey of the lesser religious wisdom and knowledge preserved in the Exeter Book.[12a]

Our discussion of gnomic wisdom has led us down a path to homiletic verse of no great distinction. But if we return to our starting point we can take another direction and come thereby to the Old English *Riddles:* the compressed observations of nature and characteristic behavior that constitute gnomic utterance are but a twist and a turn of presentation from the riddle genre. For there, too, we find representations of natural phenomena (storm, sun, fire, iceberg, etc.) and of the proprieties of civilized conduct (for example, some lines in the *Exeter Gnomes* about the lord's lady's duty to tender the mead cup first to her husband have a counterpart in the "Horn" riddle: "Sometimes a maiden fills my ring-adorned bosom"); but the riddles, of course, elaborate metaphorically upon their subjects with the deliberately designed ambiguities that are their generic essence.

Riddling is an ancient art, finding a place in many a narrative action. In Chapter III, I mentioned the incest riddle which became something of a plot-motivating force in the Greek-Latin-Old English romance of *Apollonius of Tyre*. Oedipus' solving of the riddle of the Sphinx, we recall, led ultimately to that Greek hero's tragedy. Samson's riddle to the Philistines: "Out of the eater came forth meat, and out of the strong came forth sweetness" (Judg. xɪv.12–14) played its role in the hostilities between Samson and his enemies. But the Old English riddles we are concerned with here exist in their own right for sheer intellectual stimulation and titillation in their imparting of wisdom. They are preserved in the Exeter Book in three groups: 1–59, a second version of number 30 and *Riddle* 60, and 61–95.[13] Many of the last group, occupying

12a. A hitherto unedited series of apothegms in MS I.i.I.33 of Univ. Lib., Cambridge, has just been edited by J. L. Rosier, " 'Instructions for Christians': A Poem in Old English," *Anglia,* ʟxxxɪɪ (1964), 4–22.

13. In addition to editions of the Exeter Book (and the *Riddle* numbers I use herein are those of ASPR, ɪɪɪ), see F. Tupper, Jr., *The Riddles of the Exeter Book* (Boston, 1910) and A. J. Wyatt, *Old English*

the latter part of the manuscript have unfortunately been seriously damaged by the action of some corrosive agent upon the last folios. Further, it is impossible to tell whether there were originally 100 riddles in imitation of the 100 three-line hexameter *Ænigmata* of Symphosius (an unknown Latin author of c. fifth century), the 100 *Ænigmata* of the seventh-century Aldhelm (which range in length from four to eighty-three hexameter lines), and the combined one hundred riddles of Tatwine (Archbishop of Canterbury in 731) and Eusebius (Hwætberht, Abbot of Wearmouth in 716, and friend of Bede?).[14] It is clear, however, that the Latin enigmas did exert some influence on the Old English vernacular collection, since *Riddles* 47, 60, and 85 ("Bookworm" and "Reed-pen" and "Fish and River") are indebted to Symphosius, and *Riddles* 35 and 40 ("Coat of Mail" and "Creation") are reworkings of the *lorica* and *creatura* enigmas of Aldhelm.[15]

The *Riddles* are a heterogeneous collection of verse on secular and Christian subjects, reflecting both oral or popular and literary or learned traditions. Although at one time the whole group was assigned to Cynewulf on the basis of a misreading of *Wulf and Eadwacer* as "The First Riddle" (see Ch. XI), the variety of technique, subject matter, and tone argues overwhelmingly for multiplicity of authorship and a range in date of composition (eighth to tenth centuries?). Among the subjects treated in no particular order in the *Riddles* —and it should be noted that the solutions in several cases are questionable, since the Old English manuscript does not identify the answers, unlike that containing the Latin enigmas

Riddles (Boston and London, 1912). Apart from the facing translation in Mackie's *Exeter Book* (IV, 18), the only translation of all the *Exeter Riddles* is that of P. F. Baum, *Anglo-Saxon Riddles of the Exeter Book* (Durham, N.C., 1963).

14. See R. T. Ohl, *The Enigmas of Symphosius* (Philadelphia, 1928); J. H. Pitman, *The Riddles of Aldhelm* (New Haven, Conn., 1925); A. Ebert, *Berichte über die Verhandlungen der k. sächsischen Gesellschaft . . . zu Leipzig*, Philol.-Hist. Klasse, xxix (1877), 20–56.

15. Aldhelm's *Lorica* riddle was also translated into the Northumbrian dialect sometime in the latter half of the eighth century—see the *Leiden Riddle*, ASPR, vi, p. 109, and Smith (IX, 2).

of Aldhelm—are domestic equipment like the loom and churn, agricultural implements like the rake and plow, various birds, animals, and natural phenomena, items of food and drink, artifacts connected with the pen, the sword, and the priestly cloth, and even such an anomaly as a one-eyed seller of garlic. At one extreme in manner of presentation is the lyric, which by its obviousness places greater emphasis upon its thematic development than upon any residual ambiguity. Foremost in this category are the "Storm" *Riddles*, numbers 1 and 2-3 (the last two are nowadays usually considered as one riddle), the most truly poetic of the collection. Number 1 is a representation of a storm on land; the seventy-two-line riddle (2-3) following describes a series of storm operations: (a) beneath the sea, (b) beneath the land (earthquake), (c) on the surface of the sea, and (d) on land. Segment (c) of this riddle offers a striking picture of a shipwreck:

> Sometimes I stir up the ocean, swooping
> Down, till flint-gray waves fight for
> The shore, whipped into foam, struggling
> High on the cliffs; hills rear up,
> Break, whirling water rising
> And falling, smashing together on the low
> Shore, below the rocks; ships
> Echo with sailors' cries; and towering
> Cliffs, sloping toward the sea, stand
> Unmoved at the edge of wild waves
> Smashing on silent stone. Crowded
> Boats, caught in that savage season,
> Can look for fierce battles, swept
> From their helmsman's hands, lifted and rolled
> On the sea's spiney back, pulled
> And beaten to death. This is one of the horrors
> I bring to men, obediently crashing
> On my rough way. And Who can calm me?
>   [Raffel translation (V, 37), pp. 84–85]

The "Storm" *Riddles* are learned, fusing a knowledge of Graeco-Roman cosmology (Plato, Lucretius, Pliny) and medieval Christian science (Isidore of Seville, Bede).[16] At the other

---

16. See E. von Erhardt-Siebold, "The Storm Riddles," *PMLA*, LXIV (1949), 884–888.

extreme of presentation we find several kinds of riddles. The aphoristic Christian "Chalice" (no. 48) is one example:

> I have heard of a ring   bright without tongue
> intercede for heroes.   Well it spoke
> with strong words   though not loud.
> This treasure for men   silently said:
> "Heal me   helper of souls."
> May men understand   the magic meaning
> of the speech of the red gold.   May the wise entrust
> their salvation to God,   as the ring said.
>
> [Baum trans., see n. 13]

The obscene *double entendre* of the "Ornamented Shirt" *Riddle* (no. 61) is quite a different type:

> Often a goodly damsel,   a lady, locked me
> close in a chest.   Sometimes with her hands
> she took me out   and gave me to her lord,
> a fine chieftain,   as he commanded her.
> Then he thrust his head   well inside me,
> up from below,   into the narrow part.
> If the strength prevailed   of him who received me,
> adorned as I was,   something or other rough
> was due to fill me.   Guess what I mean.
>
> [Baum trans.]

In still a different vein is the paradoxical "Anchor" (no. 16):

> I war oft against wave   and fight against wind,
> do battle with both,   when I reach to the ground,
> covered by the waters.   The land is strange to me.
> I am strong in the strife   if I stay at rest.
> If I fail at that,   they are stronger than I
> and forthwith they wrench me   and put me to rout.
> They would carry away   what I ought to defend.
> I withstand them then   if my tail endures
> And the stones hold me fast.   Ask what my name is.
>
> [Baum trans.]

In form and formula the *Riddles* also vary considerably. Some use runes rather straightforwardly to spell out their objects; others use runes cryptographically.[17] Some use the opening formula "I saw . . ." and conclude with "Say how it is

17. See N. E. Eliason, "Four Old English Cryptographic Riddles," *SP*, XLIX (1952), 553–565.

called"; others begin "I am . . ." and conclude with "Tell
what my name is." One of the finest, "Horn" (no. 14), employs
an anaphoric series of *sometimeses* to characterize the wide-
ranging uses of the instrument:

> I was an armed fighter.   Now a young home-dweller
> covers me proudly   with twisted wires,
> with gold and silver.   Sometimes men kiss me.
> Sometimes with my song   I summon to battle
> happy comrades.   Sometimes a steed carries me
> over the marches.   . . . .
> Sometimes a good weapon,   the warriors bear me,
> riding on horseback,   when treasure laden,
> I must breathe in the breath   of a man's breast.
> . . . .   Sometimes with my voice
> I rescue the booty,   put foe to flight.
>   Ask me my name.
>
>   [Baum trans.]

As a final illustration of the wisdom encapsulated in the *Riddles*,
I should like to cite the following:

> I wear grey, woven over
> With bright and gleaming gems. I bring
> The stupid to folly's paths, fool
> The ignorant with sin, urge all useless
> Roads and ruin the rest. I can't
> Explain their madness, for I push them to error
> And pick their brains, yet they praise me more
> For each seduction. Their dullness will be sorrow,
> When they lead their souls on high, unless
> They learn to walk wisely, and without my help.
>
>   [Raffel trans.]

The solution to this riddle would seem to be "Wine"; *in
aenigmate veritas.*

    Wisdom and truth of greater religio-philosophical depth
are the substance of the two poetical dialogues of *Solomon and
Saturn.* These ninth- or tenth-century poems—presumably based
on an undetermined Latin source—survive in fragmentary form
in two manuscripts: CCCC 422 (MS A), which contains
Poem I, a prose dialogue, and Poem II; and CCCC 41 (MS B),
which has only lines 1–93 of Poem I written in the margins of

three pages of the Old English translation of Bede's *HE*. The dialogues offer a strange combination of Oriental, Germanic, and Christian lore; they employ runes, gnomes, and riddles, and have some of the properties of the charms. A brief discussion of their elements thus makes a fitting conclusion to this chapter on lore and wisdom.[18]

The poetical *Solomon and Saturn* and the prose "continuation" of Poem 1 in MS A should not be confused with the prose piece of the same name mentioned in Chapter III. All the English works, it is true, have the unique Saturn, in the poems represented as a prince of the Chaldeans, as Solomon's opponent in debate, whereas the later Latin and Continental vernacular versions have the name Marcolf; nevertheless, the Old English prose is catechistic in nature and the Old English poems, especially *Solomon and Saturn* II, are more far-reaching in their substance and more directly in the dialogue genre. Saturn is the embodiment of pagan (Oriental and Germanic) wisdom, while Solomon, through his Patristic association with Christ as forerunner and type, is the more knowledgeable exponent of Christian wisdom, though obviously he also preserves some of his Hebraic-Arabic character of magician and subduer of demons; as the latter he likewise resembles Christ. Solomon's magical propensities are more pronounced in Poem 1, in which the king expounds on the virtues of the *Pater noster*: he describes the manner in which each letter of the Lord's Prayer, personified as an angelic warrior, overcomes the devil, *P*, for example, having a long rod with which he scourges the devil (ll. 90–92a), and *T* stabbing at the devil's tongue, twisting his throat, and smashing in his cheeks (ll. 94–95).[19] This unique

18. Edited in *ASPR*, VI, pp. 31–48; this does not contain the prose portion, which is edited in an appendix in the important edition of R. J. Menner, *The Poetical Dialogues of Solomon and Saturn* (New York, 1941). For translation, one must have recourse to Kemble's older edition of the prose and poetry (III, 44).

19. "The poet's text may be represented as follows: Pater nos(ter), qui (es) (in) c(ae)l(is): (sancti)f(icetur) (no)m(en) (tuum). (A)d(veniat) (re)g(num) (tuum). (Fiat voluntas tua, sicut in caelo, et in terra.) (Panem nostrum) (quotidianum) (da) (no)b(is) h(odie).

presentation of the *Pater noster* suggests the pagano-Christian exorcistic rites of the charms; the magical association is reinforced on a more clearly pagan level by the use in the manuscript of the Germanic runic characters for each of the letters of the Lord's Prayer, and on a more Christian level by reference to the *Pater noster* as "palm-twigged," the palm being a traditional medieval symbol for victory over the devil.

As a poem *Solomon and Saturn I* is not very interesting. It does not sustain the dialogue structure with which it opens, Saturn having only three speeches: in 1–20 stating his desire for wisdom, in 36–38 asking who may open heaven's door for him, and in 53–62 asking how the *Pater noster*, the key to the door, is to be used. Solomon's reply occupies the remainder of the 169-line poem: the fictitious listener is forgotten, and the verse becomes the author's didactic instruction of his ignorant contemporaries. Perhaps the most interesting part poetically is the series of *hwilum* 'sometimes' clauses (cf. "Horn" *Riddle*) near the end (ll. 151b ff.), describing the various shapes devils assume in their sudden attacks on man and beast. The poem concludes on the stirring note that when one draws his sword to fight human and spiritual enemies, a singing of the *Pater noster* and a prayer to the palm tree will offset the devil's incantations and lead to success.

Poem II, which follows the separate and distinct, exaggerated and allegorized prose treatment of the contention between the devil and the hypostasized *Pater noster* itself (rather than its letters), is probably the earlier of the two poems and infinitely the superior. Its contestants are truly engaged in dialogue, and Saturn is not only the recipient of instruction but a propounder of difficult riddles in his own right, a worthy if inferior opponent to the great Solomon. The differences in quality between the poems are well summarized by Menner (pp. 49–50):

The letters in parenthesis are those which have already occurred earlier in the prayer and are hence not repeated by the poet; after *hodie* only letters already used are found."—Menner, pp. 36–37. Of the nineteen letters that should appear, only sixteen are found in the MS.

the poem (II) never loses its dialogic character to become merely instructional. . . . Saturn's rôle of pagan prince is maintained throughout. His questions are those natural to a pagan acquainted only with Oriental and Germanic beliefs, and he knows of Christ only by hearsay. In the first part of the poem his questions are sometimes those of a man already aware of the answers, . . . [and] he seems to be testing Solomon's knowledge rather than seeking enlightenment. As the dialogue proceeds, Saturn is apparently convinced of Solomon's wisdom and asks for explanations of matters that he does not truly comprehend and that Christianity may explain.

Poem II . . . is of more serious import, ranging from curious Oriental legends to such favorite themes of Old English poetry as the exile's misery and the passing of life, and from the Christian interpretation of good and evil to universal problems of fate and foreknowledge. Solomon consistently but unobtrusively, for the most part, points out to Saturn how the Christian view of life answers the troubling questions concerning the unequal blessings of earthly life (331–338), the mingling of joy and sorrow (339–343), the wicked man's length of days (350–354), and the heavy hand of Wyrd (416–433).

Finally, the second dialogue . . . rises above [Poem I] in passages that reveal its author as something more than a mere versifier. The poet was capable both of writing in dark, riddling vein and of composing a vivid description of falling snow or a poignant picture of the homeless exile. His gnomic observations and his prophetic warnings sound a solemn and mysterious note that lifts his poem above conventional moralizing.

I cannot here document the many points Menner so cogently makes, but in closing wish to cite two brief passages which will serve as a bridge to the next chapter. At one point Saturn's gnomic speech (ll. 303 ff.) that "Night is the darkest of weathers, need is the hardest of fates,/ Sorrow is the heaviest of burdens, sleep is most like unto death," provokes Solomon into the famous:

> A little while   are the leaves green;
> Afterwards then they fade,   fall to earth,
> And perish,   change into dust.
> Thus then perish   those who formerly long
> Pursue a life of crime,   who dwell in wickedness,
> Hoard rich treasure, ...

In lines 363 and following, beginning with a passage suggestive of *Fortunes,* lines 10–14, Solomon says that a mother cannot control her son's destiny but must weep therefor:

	ðonne he geong færeð,
hafað wilde mod,	werige heortan,
sefan sorgfullne;	slideð geneahhe
werig, wilna leas,	wuldres bedæled.
Hwilum higegeomor	healle weardað,
leofað leodum feor;	locað geneahhe
fram ðam unlædan	ænga hlaford.

	(when he young sets forth,
He has a wild spirit,	a weary heart,
A mind sorrowful;	he errs frequently
Weary, deprived of joys,	parted from glory.
Sometimes sadminded	he guards a hall,
Lives far from his own people;	frequently his only lord
From that wretched man	turns away his favors.)

The motif of the transitory nature of earthly splendor, so vividly depicted in the first passage, and the formulaically expressed theme of exile in the second are but part of the rich pattern of wisdom and knowledge exhibited in the *contentio* of *Solomon and Saturn II;* but they are centrally significant in the elegiac poetry which is the concern of my last chapter, and to which I now turn.

XI

Elegiac Poetry

IN THE COURSE of this history we have had occasion to notice the pervasiveness of the elegiac, as well as of the heroic, mood in Old English poetry: the epic *Beowulf* is in its larger patterning a combination of the heroic and elegiac; Andrew's disciples in the *Andreas* mourn elegiacally when told they may be put ashore without their chieftain, as do Christ's followers on their leader's departure in the *Ascension* (*Christ II*); the devil in *Juliana* and Satan in *Christ and Satan* are exilic lamenters; and poems of wisdom, we have just seen, incorporate passages in the same spirit. We began our survey of the poetry with poems predominantly heroic in character, and we conclude with those which stress the other main mood of our Anglo-Saxon poetic heritage, the elegiac.[1]

The eleven poems to be considered, with the exception of two elegiac passages from *Beowulf*, are all extant in the Exeter Book: the *Ruin*, *Wanderer*, *Seafarer*, *Resignation*, *Riming Poem*, *Wulf and Eadwacer*, *Wife's Lament*, *Husband's Message*, and *Deor*.[2] These are dramatic-lyric pieces, generally

1. See B. J. Timmer, "The Elegiac Mood in Old English Poetry," *ES*, XXIV (1942), 33–44.
2. In addition to inclusion in Exeter Book editions, most of these poems appear in N. Kershaw, *Anglo-Saxon and Norse Poems* (Cambridge, 1922) and in E. Sieper, *Die altenglische Elegie* (Strassburg, 1915). For editions of individual poems or small groups of them, see below. Miss Kershaw provides translations; see also C. W. Kennedy, *Old English Elegies* (Princeton, N.J., 1936), K. Malone, *Ten Old English Poems*

though not unanimously referred to as *elegies* by critics. Their dates and places of origin have been variously assigned from the seventh to the tenth centuries and from Wessex to Northumbria. Although they are to differing degrees secular or Christian in their content and attitudes, they have in common two overlapping concerns: (1) a contrast between past and present conditions, and (2) some awareness of the transitory nature of earthly splendor, joy, and security. Although structured in different ways, they all present as a central feature a pattern of loss and consolation, ranging in emphasis from the hope for a brave new terrestrial world envisaged by the speaker of *The Husband's Message* and for an eternity of bliss in *The Seafarer* to the sense of loss irrecoverable in the *Ruin*.

The *Ruin* is a poem of some forty-nine lines, lines 12–18 and 42 and following having suffered damage from the same destructive agent that has obliterated so much of the Exeter Book *Riddles*.[3] The poet begins with a panoramic view of the ruins of a nameless city, usually taken to be Bath, though it is quite possible the scene is an imaginative amalgam of various locales:

> Fate has smashed these wonderful walls,
> This broken city, has crumbled the work
> Of giants. The roofs are gutted, the towers
> Fallen, the gates ripped off, frost
> In the mortar, everything moulded, gaping,
> Collapsed.

The rulers and builders are long since destroyed, too; but once, the poet continues, it was a bright city filled with bathhouses and the sounds of revelry. Then pestilence came, the people died, tiles parted from the buildings' frames,

(Baltimore, 1941), and B. Raffel (V, 37). Translations in this chapter are taken from Raffel, except where otherwise noted. For critical analyses, in addition to Kershaw, Sieper, and Kennedy, see E. D. Grubl, *Studien zu den angelsächsischen Elegien* (Marburg, 1948), and S. B. Greenfield, "The Old English Elegies," *SOEL*; also articles cited in notes below.

3. R. F. Leslie, ed. *Three Old English Elegies* (Manchester, 1961). For commentary, see C. A. Hotchner, *Wessex and Old English Poetry* (New York, 1939), S. J. Herben, *MLN*, LIV (1939), 37–39, and *MLN*, LIX (1944), 72–74, and G. W. Dunleavy, "A 'De Excidio' Tradition in the Old English Ruin?" *PQ*, XXXVIII (1959), 112–118.

> And the ruined site sank
> To a heap of tumbled stones, where once
> Cheerful, strutting warriors flocked,
> Golden armor gleaming, giddy
> With wine; here was wealth, silver,
> Gems, cattle, land, in the crowning
> City of a far-flung kingdom.

The end of the poem, or what can be deciphered of it, re-creates the scene of the hot baths as they functioned in happier days.

The vanished splendor of the city becomes, in the poet's treatment, a symbol of the impermanence of human endeavor. As such, it has obvious affinity with the ruined halls of Urien and Cyndallan lamented by the Old Welsh poets Llywarch Hên and Heledd, and with the ruined hall in Venantius Fortunatus' sixth-century poem *De Excidio Thoringiae*. The *Ruin's* specific quality, however, inheres in its use of alternation: between the present ruins and past beauty, between the dead builders and kings and the once-breathing and once-strutting warriors in their halls, with the climax narrowing in focus from the "far-flung kingdom" to the pride of the city, its baths. Mr. Raffel's translation, I believe, captures the stylistic variation of the Old English original, the compressed, packed lines describing the decayed present and the more sweeping movement of the verse conveying the reconstitution of the glorious past. The poet of the *Ruin* does not sentimentalize or moralize; he presents his picture detachedly and disinterestedly, perhaps suggesting in his poetic re-creation of the prosperous city the only consolatory answer he knew for fate's destructive embrace.

The Wanderer, a poem of 115 lines, is even more impressive than the *Ruin*. More complex, it incorporates Christian attitudes and values in its use of the exile theme, the ruin theme, and the *ubi sunt* motif.[4] These three *topoi* occupy in succession the major segments of the body of the poem, lines 8–110, the purported speech of a homeless exile or wanderer, a

4. On the derivation and use of the *ubi sunt* motif in OE, see J. E. Cross, "*Ubi sunt* Passages in Old English—Sources and Relationships," *VSL Arsbok* (1956), 25–44.

thane who has lost his lord and kinsmen. The poem opens with a commentary on the fate of and prospects for a sea-driven exile:

> This lonely traveller longs for grace,
> For the mercy of God; grief hangs on
> His heart and follows the frost-cold foam
> He cuts in the sea, sailing endlessly,
> Aimlessly in exile. Fate has opened
> A single port: memory.

It then launches into the *eardstapa*'s monologue:

> "I've drunk too many lonely dawns,
> Grey with mourning. Once there were men
> To whom my heart could hurry, hot
> With open longing. They're long since dead.
> My heart has closed quietly on itself, quietly
> Learning that silence is noble and sorrow
> Nothing that speech can cure. Sadness
> Has never driven sadness off;
> Fate blows hardest on a bleeding heart."

The gnomic mood continues as the speaker recounts his loss of lord and his vain efforts to secure another. In a much-quoted passage, he tells how he dreams of former days when

> ". . . it seems I see my lord,
> Kiss and embrace him, bend my hands
> And head to his knee, kneeling as though
> He still sat enthroned, ruling his thanes."

But even this consolation is ephemeral, for

> ". . . I open my eyes, embracing the air,
> And see the brown sea-billows heave,
> See the sea-birds bathe, spreading
> Their white-feathered wings, watch the frost
> And the hail and the snow."

This exilic and self-centered tale broadens in its scope and in its gnomic wisdom as the speaker places his position in the perspective of the evanescence of all worldly joys, recalling how suddenly warriors have "given up the hall" (i.e., died). Here he utilizes the ruin theme:

"What knowing man knows not the ghostly,
Waste-like end of worldly wealth:
See, already the wreckage is there,
The wind-swept walls stand far and wide,
The storm-beaten blocks besmeared with frost,
The mead-halls crumbled, the monarchs thrown down
And stripped of their pleasures. The proudest of warriors
Now lie by the wall. . . ."

In the third part of the monologue, the sense of destruction leads the speaker to postulate a wise man who, understanding the remorselessness of fate, utters the *ubi sunt* lamentation:

"Where is the war-steed? Where is the warrior? Where is
his war-lord?
Where now the feasting-places? Where now the mead-
hall pleasures?
Alas, bright cup! Alas, brave knight!
Alas, you glorious princes! All gone,
Lost in the night, as you never had lived.
And all that survives you a serpentine wall,
Wondrously high, worked in strange ways.
. . . .
Everything earthly is evilly born,
Firmly clutched by a fickle Fate.
Fortune vanishes, friendship vanishes,
Man is fleeting, woman is fleeting,
And all this earth rolls into emptiness."

The poet himself concludes with a gnomic-homiletic exhortation to find true security in the fastness of God.

The Wanderer and its companion piece *The Seafarer* were, in earlier criticism, disintegrated into pagan and Christian strata; but since Lawrence's seminal article, both poems have been viewed as unified structures and the product of the cloister, though different interpretations thereof have been proposed.[5] *The Wanderer* presents a consolatory Christian

5. W. W. Lawrence, "*The Wanderer* and *The Seafarer*," *JEGP*, IV (1902), 460–480. Of the many recent articles on this poem I cite only a few: B. F. Huppé, "*The Wanderer*: Theme and Structure," *JEGP*, XLII (1943), 516–538, R. M. Lumiansky, "The Dramatic Structure of the Old English *Wanderer*," *Neophil*, XXXIV (1950), 104–112, S. B. Greenfield, "*The Wanderer*: A Reconsideration of Theme and Structure," *JEGP*, L (1951), 451–465, I. L. Gordon, "Traditional Themes in *The Wanderer*

218   HISTORY OF OLD ENGLISH LITERATURE

answer to the misfortunes of individual fate and to the degeneration of the world; whether it was influenced by Boethius'
Consolation of Philosophy is debatable and unprovable, but it
is certainly in the tradition of the Classical and Christian
literary genre of the *consolatio*.⁶ The Christian view is explicit
in the introduction and conclusion of the poem, but mainly
implicit in the wanderer's monologue, the exiled speaker's
awareness developing from a concern with himself alone to a
reflective wisdom embracing all this transitory life, but never
achieving specific Christian knowledge of salvation. That the
exile *topos* of the first part of the speech is to be taken as a
Christian allegory of man's earthly existence as an exile from
Eden, as has been proposed,⁷ is questionable.

The *Wanderer* is very well structured, its themes being developed within parallel units both in the introductory lines and
the concluding ones and in the "I" section and the more generalized reflections which follow.⁸ Matching the architectonic
beauty is a deft handling of imagery: the personal difficulties
of the wanderer are mirrored in his several uses of terms for
"hall," implying the warmth he has found and had hoped again
to find in civilized society, in the *comitatus*, whereas his more
mature observations on earthly transience are symbolized by
the external and forbidding "wall"; his wretched personal circumstances find verbalization in adjectives denoting his un-
happy state of mind, whereas his later observations invoke wisdom and sagaciousness. And a metaphoric thread running

---

and *The Seafarer*," RES, N. S. v (1954), 1–13, J. C. Pope, "Dramatic
Voices in *The Wanderer* and *The Seafarer*," in *Franciplegius*, eds. J. B.
Bessinger, Jr., and R. P. Creed (New York, 1965), pp. 164–193.
6. See J. E. Cross, "On the Genre of *The Wanderer*," *Neophil*, XLV
(1961), 63–75.
7. See G. V. Smithers, "The Meaning of *The Seafarer* and *The
Wanderer*," MÆ, XXVI (1957), 137–153, and MÆ, XXVIII (1959), 1–22,
99–104.
8. In particular on structure, see W. Erzgräber, "*Der Wanderer*: Eine
Interpretation von Aufbau und Gehalt," *Festschrift zum 75. Geburtstag
von Theodor Spira* (Heidelberg, 1961), pp. 57–85. For a view that there
is not *one* speaker but *two* (ll. 1–5 and 8–57 for the first, ll. 58–110 for
the second), see Pope (n. 5), pp. 164–173.

throughout the poem, suggesting the monologuist's isolation, is the wintry scene, the several images culminating in an extended passage near the end of the "wise man's" speech:

> "These rocky slopes are beaten by storms,
> This earth pinned down by driving snow,
> By the horror of winter, smothering warmth
> In the shadows of night. And the north angrily
> Hurls hailstorms at our helpless heads."

This Old English elegy is, in short, a poem that strikes a very responsive chord to our modern ears, without the help of Patristic exegetical commentary.

But though allegory has not been viewed by most critics as a needful component of *The Wanderer's* esthetic, it has found a more welcome reception in interpretations of the 124-line *The Seafarer*,[9] a more difficult poem, on the surface, in which to find the unity, coherence, and emphasis demanded by our modern critical sensibilities. For *The Seafarer* appears to divide into two distinct segments. The first vividly and graphically presents the personal experiences of the narrator of the poem with the sea:

> This tale is true, and mine. It tells
> How the sea took me, swept me back
> And forth in sorrow and fear and pain,
> Showed me suffering in a hundred ships,
> In a thousand ports, and in me. It tells
> Of smashing surf when I sweated in the cold
> Of an anxious watch, perched in the bow
> As it dashed under cliffs. My feet were cast
> In icy bands, bound with frost,
> With frozen chains, and hardship groaned
> Around my heart. . . .
> . . . drifting through winter
> On an ice-cold sea, whirled in sorrow,
> Alone in a world blown clear of love,
> Hung with icicles. The hailstorms flew.

Here the wintry scene emerges in more detail than in *The Wanderer*, the desolation and isolation of the *persona* rein-

9. I. L. Gordon, ed. *The Seafarer* (London, 1960).

forced even more strongly by references to the sea birds as his only companions (ll. 19b–26). And yet, says the speaker, his spirit urges him to further travel, to seek the home of foreigners/exiles,[10] though he has trepidations about the outcome of such a journey. But the blossoming world spurs on those who, like him, lay their exile tracks the widest, for

> . . . the joys of God
> Are fervent with life, where life itself
> Fades quickly into the earth.

It is thus that the first or seafaring portion of the poem passes over into the second or homiletic section. (Raffel's translation follows the older tradition of separating the two parts with a period, but recent commentary agrees on the pivotal unity I have indicated.) What follows is essentially eschatological in nature: an acknowledgment of the inevitability of death, a comment on the decline of earthly splendor, a reminder of the real and terrible power of God, and a stress on the necessity of recognizing our true home in heaven and striving to reach it.

Like the speaker in *The Wanderer*, the *persona* of *The Seafarer* develops in outlook as the poem progresses: from an attitude of despair and suffering as he relives his former seafaring existence, he passes to a state in which he desires further travel, but of a different kind, to an unknown shore far hence; still, he has fears about such a journey, but when he thinks about the joys of God, all doubts and hesitations vanish, for in the mirror of eternity he recognizes the mutability of all earthly happiness. The poem begs for some kind of rapprochement revolving around this momentous "sea change." Either we can take the proposed sea journey literally, seeing in it an ascetic resolution to forsake the things of this world for a *peregrinatio pro amore Dei*, or we can take it as an allegory of man's passage to the land from whence he was exiled in the Fall of Adam, the

10. A central crux, *elþeodigra eard:* does it mean simply a literal journey to foreign shores, or is it a reference to heaven, the true home of fallen man, an exile in this world? See n. 11.

heavenly *patria*, his earlier voyaging being an allegory for his life on earth, as in the sea-voyage simile at the end of *Christ II*.[11]

The Seafarer bristles with interpretative cruxes, partially because of its deliberate ambiguity. But in that ambiguity lies much of its poetic fascination. The same words in different contexts, for example, point up the contrast between the joys and comradeship of this world and of heaven (ll. 78–90), and between a man's earthly lord and the Lord (ll. 39–43):

> For there is no man   so proud on this earth,
> Nor in his gifts so favored,   nor in his youth so brave,
> Nor in his deeds so daring,   nor his *lord* so gracious to him,
> That he will not ever have a care   about his sea voyage
> As to what the *Lord*   will ordain for him.
>   [My trans.]

Or double meanings reside in the single use of word or phrase, as possibly in the "home of foreigners/exiles" mentioned above, or as in the lovely

> The groves take blossoms,   the cities beautify,
> The plains brighten,   the world hastens;
> All these admonish   the ready spirit
> To take leave   . . .
>   [ll. 48–51b, my trans.]

where the "hastening" of the world looks two ways, to the cyclical movement into springtime that is a call to travel, and to the movement of the world degeneratively toward its rendezvous with the millennium that is added reason for the "seafarer's" embarkation on his literal-allegorical journey to the only lasting security in heaven.[12]

The literal-allegorical possibilities of the sea-voyage image

11. For literal interpretations, see D. Whitelock, "The Interpretation of *The Seafarer*," *Early Cultures of North-West Europe* (Cambridge, 1950), pp. 261–272, and S. B. Greenfield, "Attitudes and Values in *The Seafarer*," *SP*, LI (1954), 15–20; for allegorical, see O. S. Anderson, "The Seafarer: An Interpretation," *KHVL Arsberättelse* 1 (1937–38), pp. 1–50, and Smithers, n. 7. See Pope (n. 5), pp. 173–188, for the suggestion of two speakers or dramatic voices (ll. 1–33a the first, ll. 33b–102 the second) and an epilogue by the poet (ll. 103–124).

12. See Mrs. Gordon's Introduction to her edition for a judicious evaluation of homiletic and Patristic learning in the poem, and for the relation of the poem to Old Welsh elegiac verse.

are also present in *Resignation* (or *The Exile's Prayer*). This 118-line poem might well have been considered with *A Prayer* in the chapter on miscellaneous religious verse, since the first eighty or so lines are a plaintive prayer for mercy and grace from God so that devils may not harm the sinful speaker's soul. But in the last part of the poem, the supplicant tells about his enforced exile, wretched and friendless and dependent on alms, sad and sick at heart. He would fain take ship, but cannot afford to purchase a boat. "The forest may grow, await its destiny,/ Put forth twigs," but the "I" cannot love anyone. His only hope for amelioration lies in God; with stoic resignation he must meanwhile bear the fate he cannot change.

As in *The Seafarer*, we are confronted with a dual exile: enforced and desired. The context of *Resignation* suggests that the present imposed exile is a symbol of man's sinful life on earth; it is as ambiguous as *The Seafarer's*, however, as to whether the longed-for sea journey of the penitent is to be interpreted as a literal *peregrinatio pro amore Dei* or as the ecclesiastical metaphor for a longing to seek the heavenly *patria*. But though *Resignation* may utilize the same motifs as *The Seafarer*, it does not fuse them well with the *planctus* genre, it is narrow in its focus upon the penitent alone, and it has nothing of the dictional reinforcements of themes we find in the more justly famous elegy.[13]

The Wanderer, The Seafarer, and *Resignation* all begin with a presentation of the speaker in his present condition—exiled, weary, sinful—and then proceed to contrast this state with a golden age of the past and the potentialities of the future. The *Riming Poem*, a *tour de force* of eighty-seven lines, in which the first verse, or half-line, not only rhymes with the second but also preserves the customary alliterative pattern of Old English meter, operates differently, beginning with a testimony to past wealth and honors and moving to the present state of wretchedness of the *persona*. Five main stages of development may be observed: (1) to line 42, the former pleasures

13. See E. G. Stanley, "Old English Poetic Diction . . ." (IV, 9).

of the speaker, one born to rank and riches are detailed: feasts, horses, ships, company, music, and ultimately power as lord and protector of the people, as distributor of treasure; (2) but the very largess of the lord in his dispensing of gold seems to have led to unspecified trouble, and in lines 43–54, the speaker suggests his vexations of mind as he contemplates men's loss of courage, joys, and desires under the distresses inflicted by life; (3) in lines 55–69, the *persona* contemplates the slackness of the world in more general terms; (4) in lines 71–79, returning to a first-person account, he recognizes the inevitability of the grave he must inhabit and the fate of his body; (5) in lines 80–87 he stresses the good man's awareness of the path he must follow to righteousness, and exhorts his audience to hasten along that path to eternal bliss.[14] Though individual lines are often hard to decipher because of the compression and distortion of thought enjoined by the exigencies of rhyme, the *Riming Poem* has a better sense of structure than *Resignation* and, in its parallel between the microcosm of man in his decline from the joys of high estate and the macrocosm of the world in its degeneracy,[15] the poet achieves an esthetic density and complexity commensurate with that of the verse form he attempted.

The elegies so far considered treat of man's misfortunes as an aspect of his temporal existence; the next three poems deal instead with patterns of concord and discord in the relations between men and women. Of these elegies the most obscure yet somehow the most haunting is the very brief *Wulf and Eadwacer*, by early critics mis-taken as "The First Riddle" because of its enigmatic quality and because it immediately precedes the first group of *Riddles*. I quote in full Raffel's translation, emphasizing that it is only one of several interpretations:[16]

14. Cf. Smithers, n. 7 (1959 article), pp. 8 ff.
15. See J. E. Cross, "Aspects of Microcosm and Macrocosm in Old English Literature," *AGB*, pp. 11–15.
16. For other interpretations and analogues, see J. C. Adams, " 'Wulf. and Eadwacer': An Interpretation," *MLN*, LXXIII (1958), 1–5, K. Malone, "Two English *Frauenlieder*," *AGB*, pp. 106–117, P. J. Frankis, "*Deor*

My people may have been given a warning:
Will they receive him, if he comes with force?
    It is different for us.
Wulf is on an island, I on another.
An island of forts, surrounded by swamp.
That island belongs to bloody barbarians:
Will they receive him, if he comes with force?
    It is different for us.
Hope has wandered in exile, with Wulf.
When the rain was cold and my eyes ran red
With tears, when heavy arms reached out and took me
And I suffered pleasure and pain. Wulf,
Oh my Wulf, it was hoping and longing for you
That sickened me, starved for the sight of you,
Bent with a despair deeper than hunger.
Listen, Eadwacer! The wolf will carry
Our wretched suckling to the shade of the wood.
It's easy to smash what never existed,
You and I together.

The speaker is obviously a woman, her lover Wulf an out-
law. Eadwacer is probably her husband, whom she detests and
whose child she will bear and deliver to Wulf. The situation
seems so specific that many attempts have been made to base
the poem on Germanic story, the Signy-Sigmund lay and the
Wolfdietrich B saga being the leading candidates; but all
proposals fall short in some way of matching the details of the
Old English elegy. Whatever the background, *Wulf and
Eadwacer* is an impassioned example of the *Frauenlied*, a type
of medieval lyric placing in the mouth of a woman a lament of
love. Notable features of our Anglo-Saxon poem are the refrain
"It is different for us," the islands symbolic perhaps of the
separation of the lovers, and the pathetic fallacy whereby the
external rain falls as counterpart to the speaker's tears. The
consolation of the *persona* for the denial of relations with her
lover seems to lie in her thoughts of revenge upon her husband
through their child.

    Separation from the beloved is also the dramatic situation

and *Wulf and Eadwacer*: Some Conjectures," *MÆ*, xxxi (1962), 161–
175, and A. Renoir, "*Wulf and Eadwacer*: A Noninterpretation," in
Franciplegius (n. 5), pp. 147–163.

in both *The Wife's Lament* and *The Husband's Message*.[17] In
the former poem the *persona* is again a woman, in the latter a
man. Although these two elegies have been felt by some to be
part of the same story cycle, most critics nowadays view them
as individual entities. Of the two, the *Frauenlied* is the more
difficult, despite its wealth of detail and its suggestiveness of a
well-known tale. Among the candidates advanced as plot source
have been the Constance saga (later in English literature to
appear in both Gower and Chaucer), the Crescentia tale, and
the Old Irish *Liadain and Curithir;* as with *Wulf and Eadwacer,*
none of them will quite do. But absence of such source knowledge does not diminish our awareness of the elegy's emotional
power.

The wife, like other exiles, will tell a true tale about her
sufferings, "never more than now." Her husband-lord departed
over the seas, his kinsmen schemed against her in her friendless-
ness, and convinced her lord to exile her in an oakgrove; perhaps they accused her of infidelity—the text does not elucidate.
She recalls in this briar-thatched dwelling how well she and her
husband were matched, the oaths they'd sworn never to part;

> now only the words are left
> And our friendship's a fable that time has forgotten
> And never tells. For my well-belovèd
> I've been forced to suffer, far and near.

In her oak grove she writhes with longing:

> The valleys seem leaden, the hills reared aloft,
> And the bitter towns all bramble patches
> Of empty pleasure. The memory of parting
> Rips my heart. My friends are out there,
> Savouring their lives, secure in their beds,
> While at dawn, alone, I crawl miserably down
> Under the oak growing out of my cave.
> There I must squat the summer-long day,
> There I can water the earth with weeping
> For exile and sorrow, for sadness that can never
> Find rest from grief nor from the famished
> Desires that leap at unquenched life.

17. See Leslie edition, n. 3.

The last section of the poem, lines 42–53, offers a knotty problem of interpretation. It may well present consolatory thoughts
of revenge, as in *Wulf and Eadwacer*, though whether upon
husband, kinsmen, or a third party is not clear. Most likely,
the wife is here expressing her thoughts about the concomitant
fate of her husband: if outwardly fortunate, nevertheless bearing within a sorrowing spirit by virtue of his nature; if outwardly
unfortunate, say in a desolate, sea-surrounded hall, he will remember a happier dwelling, even as *she* does in her abode of
sorrow.[18] The poem concludes gnomically:

> There are few things more bitter
> Than awaiting a love who is lost to hope.

The emphasis in *The Wife's Lament* is upon the miserable
state of mind of the speaker, the contrast between happiness in
love and the frustration of separation. The poem abounds in
words for misery, sorrow, enduring, longing, trials, and tribula-
tions. And parallels of phrasing aid in the pathetic futility of
mood, as when the wife says, in line 12b, that her lord's kinsmen
succeeded in forcing them apart (*þæt hy todælden unc*) and
later, in line 22, that she and her husband had vowed that nothing save death would ever part them (*þæt unc ne gedælde
nemne deað ana*). Of all the Exeter Book elegies, *The Wife's
Lament* is the most devoid of consolatory hope: there is no
Christian God whose ultimate mercy the speaker feels she can
rely on, nor any pleasure in the remembrance of happier days
(as in the *Ruin*); only a stoic fortitude can cope with intense
personal anguish.

 The Husband's Message, on the contrary, is the least
elegiac of the elegies, and perhaps cannot properly be so classi-

18. See Greenfield, "Old English Elegies," n. 2; for further analyses
see among others Leslie and Kershaw editions, Malone (n. 16), S. B.
Greenfield, "*The Wife's Lament* Reconsidered," *PMLA*, LXVIII (1953),
907–912, R. D. Stevick, "Formal Aspects of *The Wife's Lament*," *JEGP*,
LIX (1960), 21–25, J. A. Ward, "*The Wife's Lament*: An Interpretation,"
JEGP, LIX (1960), 26–33, and R. C. Bambas, "Another View of the Old
English *Wife's Lament*," *JEGP*, LXII (1963), 303–309. The last-men-
tioned article returns to an older, discarded theory that the speaker is a
man, not a woman.

fied. Yet it does furnish a similar pattern of contrast between past and present, only in this case it is the present which is the better, and it does include the exile theme. In the poem, a messenger delivers a husband's call to his wife to join him over the sea, in exile to be sure, but an exile whose miseries have so far been overcome that the husband can promise his wife, a prince's daughter, that they will once more be able to distribute treasure from the high seat. For, says the messenger,

> though his home
> Is with strangers, he lives in a lovely land
> And is rich: shining gold surrounds him.
> And though my master was driven from here,
> Rushing madly down to his ship
> And onto the sea, alone, only
> Alive because he fled, and glad
> To escape, yet now he is served and followed,
> Loved and obeyed by many. He has beaten
> Misery: there's nothing more he wants,
> Oh prince's daughter, no precious gems,
> No stallions, no mead-hall pleasure, no treasure
> On earth, but you . . . .

Some difficulties inhere in the text of this fifty-four-line poem. In the first place, it follows in the manuscript a poem generally taken to be *Riddle* 60 ("Reed-pen"); but some have preferred to view the riddle as a prologue to *The Husband's Message*, in which a piece of wood speaks of its origins before it itself, as messenger, delivers the husband's summons. The end of the poem, in the second place, incorporates runes which are involved in an oath; and there is disagreement about the reading of the runes.[19] Further, the holes in the manuscript have effectively destroyed some of the lines. However we wish to take the cruxes, there can be no doubt about the note of cautious optimism that runs through the dramatic lyric, as the messenger tries to convince the lady—and evidently, for some unspecified reason, she needs convincing—that her husband is indeed true and will perform according to ancient vows they

19. See Leslie and R. W. V. Elliott, "The Runes in *The Husband's Message*," *JEGP*, LIV (1955), 1–8.

swore together, and according to new vows embodied in the runic ending.

It is with a return to the combination of heroic and elegiac that I bring this history to an end, first in the poem *Deor* and then in two passages from *Beowulf*. *Deor*,[20] like *Wulf and Eadwacer*, has a refrain: *þæs ofereode, þisses swa mæg* 'That [misfortune] passed away, so will this.' The passing away of the specific misfortunes alluded to in the irregular stanzas of the forty-two-line poem may mean that improvement occurred and will occur, akin to the upturn of Fortune's wheel, or it may mean that the sorrows (and joys) of this world are transitory because they *are* of this world. Of the seven stanzas into which the poem is divided—some see only six, with no break after the sixth, which lacks a refrain—the first five allude to specific characters and/or stories from the realm of Germanic legend: Weland's captivity by Nithhad; his revenge upon the king's sons and daughter, Beadohild;[21] the love of Mæthhild and Geat; Theodric's exile; and Eormanric's tyranny. The sixth is a gnomic reflection on the "gifts of men," on the wise Lord's dealing of mercy to some men and of a portion of woe to others. The last stanza provides the fictitious elegiac framework for the whole poem:

> Of myself I will say that once I sang
> For the Héodénings, and held a place

20. K. Malone, ed. *Deor*, 3rd ed. (London, 1961). For other commentaries, see works mentioned in n. 2 and Frankis, n. 16. For a view of *Deor* as a kind of charm, see M. Bloomfield, "The Form of *Deor*," *PMLA*, LXXIX (1964), 534–541.

21. Of interest in connection with the Weland story is the scene carved on the left front panel of the whalebone casket of early eighth-century Northumbrian provenience presented to the British Museum in 1867 by Sir Augustus W. Franks. This scene on the Franks casket depicts Weland standing before the decapitated body of one of Nithhad's sons, holding a cup made of his skull; in the middle of the scene is Beadohild with an attendant, and next to them is Egill, Weland's brother, strangling birds from whose wings he fashioned the means of Weland's escape from Nithhad's captivity—see Elliott, *Runes* (X, 1), p. 98. The casket contains several other scenes and two sets of runic alliterative verse inscriptions—ed. in *ASPR*, VI, p. 116; see also Elliott, pp. 99 ff., for interpretations and bibliography. See frontispiece.

In my master's heart. My name was Deor.
I sang in my good lord's service through many
Winters, until Héorrend won
My honors away, struck his harp
And stole my place with a poet's skill.
    That passed, and so may this.

The first of the two *Beowulf* elegiac passages, "The Lament of the Last Survivor," utilizes the motif of useless treasure implicit in the *ubi sunt* lamentation of *The Wanderer* and in the desolation of the *Ruin,* and explicit in the homiletic portion of *The Seafarer.* It contrasts former days of earthly wealth and glory with the present decline of the speaker's nation, he only surviving to bury the hoard that was once the joy of his people —the hoard the dragon finds and which becomes the source of Beowulf's tragedy. I quote from Raffel's translation of *Beowulf,* lines 2247–66:

"Take these treasures, earth, now that no one
Living can enjoy them. They were yours, in the beginning;
Allow them to return. War and terror
Have swept away my people, shut
Their eyes to delight and to living, closed
The door to all gladness. No one is left
To lift these swords, polish these jeweled
Cups: no one leads, no one follows. These hammered
Helmets, worked with gold, will tarnish
And crack; the hands that should clean and polish them
Are still forever. And these mail shirts, worn
In battle, once, while swords crashed
And blades bit into shields and men,
Will rust away like the warriors who owned them.
None of these treasures will travel to distant
Lands, following their lords. The harp's
Bright song, the hawk crossing through the hall
On its swift wings, the stallion tramping
In the courtyard—all gone, creatures of every
Kind, and their masters, hurled to the grave!"

The other passage occurs in the midst of Beowulf's account of Geatish history as he prepares to face the dragon (ll. 2435 ff.). He tells of King Hrethel's inability to take revenge upon his son Hæthcyn for his accidental killing of his eldest son, comparing the old king's plight to that of a father who mourns for his son on the gallows, a similarly unavengeable fate. Rather oddly for the context, he pictures the father viewing the desolate ruins of his son's erstwhile establishment, where

> "riders and ridden
> Sleep in the ground; pleasure is gone,
> The harp is silent, and hope is forgotten."

The ruin *topos* which here makes its appearance evidently had a metaphoric quality that made it applicable not only in poems like the *Ruin* and *The Wanderer* but in elegiac verse in which it was literally uncalled for. This *Beowulf* passage is a fine illustration of the *mana* residing in the conventional Old English formulas and themes that rendered them adaptable to different poetic situations and which made them ever fresh, however old, in the hands and on the tongues of those to whom God, in his distribution of gifts, had granted the power of poetic song among the Anglo-Saxons.

This critical history has, I hope, presented convincing evidence of the stature of our earliest English literary heritage and of its continuity with the literature following the Norman Conquest. In its special fusion of Christian and pagan materials and attitudes, it nevertheless reveals its peculiar individuality as a body of literature within the larger continuum; it also, in that fusion, abides Alcuin's question, with which I began. But as individual pieces of prose and poetry, a goodly portion of Old English literature, as I have tried to show, still out-tops knowledge, serene in its immutable and imperishable beauty.

THIS INDEX is designed to cover fully Anglo-Latin and Old English authors and works mentioned in the text and footnotes. In other respects, it is highly selective; it contains no references to modern scholars mentioned either in text or footnotes.

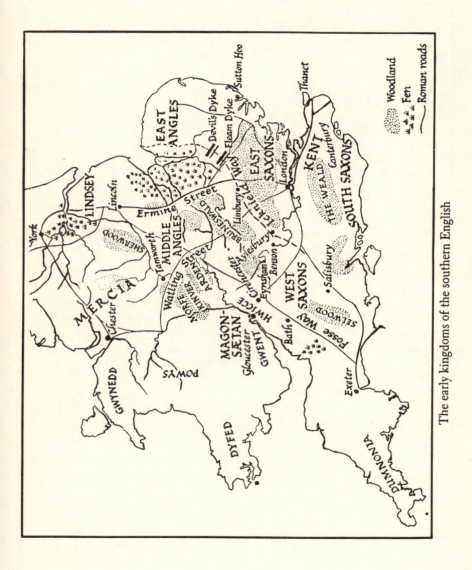

The early kingdoms of the southern English

Within the map:

GWYNEDD

POWYS

DYFED

MERCIA

LINDSEY

York · · Lincoln ·

SHERWOOD

Ermine Street

MIDDLE ANGLES

Tamworth ·

Watling Street

ARDEN

KINVER

MORFE

Chester ·

MAGON-SÆTAN

GWENT

Gloucester ·

Cirencester ·

HWICCE

Bath ·

Fosse Way

WEST SAXONS

SELWOOD

Salisbury ·

Exeter ·

DUMNONIA

Devil's Dyke

Fleam Dyke

Sutton Hoo

EAST ANGLES

BRUNESWALD

Link·· Limbury ·

Wye

London ·

Icknield

Aylesbury ·

Benson ·

Eynsham ·

EAST SAXONS

KENT

Canterbury ·

Thanet

THE WEALD

SOUTH SAXONS

Woodland

Fen

Roman roads

England in the Tenth Century

Norse settlements
Danish settlements
Boundary of Guthrum's Kingdom
Woodland